Picture Yourself Building a Website with Joomla!® 1.6:

Step-by-Step Instruction for Creating a High-Quality, Professional-Looking Site with Ease

Robin D. Turner and Herb Boeckenhaupt

Course Technology PTR

A part of Cengage Learning

COURSE TECHNOLOGY
CENGAGE Learning™

Australia, Brazil, Japan, Korea, Mexico, Singapore, Spain, United Kingdom, United States

COURSE TECHNOLOGY
CENGAGE Learning™

Picture Yourself Building a Website with Joomla!® 1.6
Robin D. Turner and Herb Boeckenhaupt

Publisher and General Manager, Course Technology PTR:
Stacy L. Hiquet

Associate Director of Marketing:
Sarah Panella

Manager of Editorial Services:
Heather Talbot

Marketing Manager:
Jordan Castellani

Acquisitions Editor:
Megan Belanger

Project Editor:
Karen A. Gill

Technical Reviewer:
Ryan Fidler

Copy Editors:
Mike Beady, Karen A. Gill

Interior Layout:
Shawn Morningstar

Cover Designer:
Mike Tanamachi

Indexer:
Sharon Shock

Proofreader:
Melba Hopper

Printed in the United States of America
1 2 3 4 5 6 7 13 12 11

© 2012 Course Technology, a part of Cengage Learning.

ALL RIGHTS RESERVED. No part of this work covered by the copyright herein may be reproduced, transmitted, stored, or used in any form or by any means graphic, electronic, or mechanical, including but not limited to photocopying, recording, scanning, digitizing, taping, Web distribution, information networks, or information storage and retrieval systems, except as permitted under Section 107 or 108 of the 1976 United States Copyright Act, without the prior written permission of the publisher.

For product information and technology assistance, contact us at

Cengage Learning Customer and Sales Support, 1-800-354-9706

For permission to use material from this text or product, submit all requests online at
cengage.com/permissions

Further permissions questions can be e-mailed to
permissionrequest@cengage.com

Joomla!® is a registered trademark of Open Source Matters, Inc. in the United States and other countries. All other trademarks are the property of their respective owners. All images © Cengage Learning unless otherwise noted.

Library of Congress Control Number: 2008932480
ISBN-13: 978-1-59863-814-1
ISBN-10: 1-59863-814-9

Course Technology, a part of Cengage Learning
20 Channel Center Street
Boston, MA 02210
USA

Cengage Learning is a leading provider of customized learning solutions with office locations around the globe, including Singapore, the United Kingdom, Australia, Mexico, Brazil, and Japan. Locate your local office at **international.cengage.com/region**.

Cengage Learning products are represented in Canada by Nelson Education, Ltd.

For your lifelong learning solutions, visit **courseptr.com**.
Visit our corporate Website at **cengage.com**.

ISLAND PARK PUBLIC LIBRARY

006.786
TUR

We dedicate this book to Smokey, one of our cats, who went "Angelical" during the writing of this book.

He was a beautiful, loving, affectionate, and special cat. He will never know how much he will be missed and how much his loss, and the manner in which he died, has affected our lives.

Smokey, this book is in your memory.

Acknowledgments

WHEN ONE SETS OUT TO WRITE A BOOK, writer's block immediately enters the picture. Our process for overcoming writer's block was to go to the golf practice range. While we were hitting golf balls, the topics to include and how to include them became much clearer. So first, we would like to thank Mike, Bob, and Maryanne at Carolina's Golf Mart for the hours they put up with us and enabled us to overcome writer's block one bucket of golf balls at a time.

Next, we would like to thank Jennifer Blaney, who first gave us the opportunity to write this book. We also thank Megan Belanger for being patient with us as the software release date was postponed months at a time. Megan, we are finally finished, a year later! We hope your new massage therapy career is lucrative.

We also sincerely thank Ryan Fidler, our technical editor, who read through every draft, following each exercise step by step to make sure the language was clear, correct, and understandable. He is a great programmer and has acquired a high level of Joomla! skills. He had "our back" on every page of the manuscript. Thank you, Ryan.

We also thank the many behind-the-scenes people at Cengage Learning, who proofread, prepared the layout, and helped bring this book to fruition. Karen Gill was a rock as we plowed forward. We also thank Mike Beady, who provided editing support in the final stages.

Finally, we want to thank our cats for their patience as they walked across our keyboards, laid in our laps, snuggled up next to our keyboards as we typed, and entertained us with their "chase me, chase you" antics, which kept us laughing and provided us with the mental breaks we needed.

We humbly and thankfully acknowledge all of you.

About the Authors

ROBIN TURNER is a program head and instructor of accounting and economics at Rowan-Cabarrus Community College. She has 25 years of teaching experience at both the university and community college levels of higher education. She has authored print and digital educational support materials for more than 25 college accounting texts and has been a reviewer of an unknown number of business and economic college-level texts.

Robin has received several teaching excellence awards, was a nominee for the R. J. Reynolds North Carolina Excellence in Teaching Award, is a five-time winner of Who's Who Among American Teachers, and has distinguished herself and provided training in 21st Century Learning: Hybrid & Blended Courses—Bringing Web 2.0 to your classroom, blended or hybrid courses.

Robin received a 2009 Distinguished eLearning Educator Award, appointed by the Instructional Technology Council (ITC), among others. She has received awards for Phi Theta Kappa Outstanding Advisor, Phi Theta Kappa Horizon Advisor, State Council of Higher Education of Virginia Outstanding Faculty Award nominee, and Outstanding Faculty Among Students.

In her spare time, she cooks, makes candy to die for, reads mystery novels, gardens, and golfs with her spouse.

HERB BOECKENHAUPT had a background in the printing and graphics business for some 35 years in Maryland, serving clients in the Washington, DC, area. He retired from that business in the late 1990s just as the Internet was emerging. Following the sale of his business, he became a full-time Website designer and developer and has helped hundreds of clients over the past 12 years.

Herb's Joomla! involvement began soon after Joomla! was "invented" from the Mambo platform. Shortly after that, he narrowed his focus and built Websites only on the Joomla! platform. His expert knowledge of Joomla! 1.0, and then Joomla! 1.5, was channeled into the Joomla! 1.6 version as soon as it was released in early beta form.

In 2010, Herb brought this expertise to the North Carolina Phi Beta Lambda organization and developed a Website for the chapter at Rowan Cabarrus-Community College and the State organization's Professional Division. He was recognized as the North Carolina Businessman of the Year by the organization. He also built the Joomla!-based Website for the local battered women's support organization as a pro bono volunteer.

Herb volunteers as a member of the Information Technologies and Web Technologies Advisory Committees at Rowan-Cabarrus Community College. He also builds Moodle courses and recently completed courses for Emergency Action Planning for 60 high-rise buildings in New York City.

Robin and Herb operate the 200mph Media Group, LLC, and their Website is located at www.200mphmedia.net.

Table of Contents

Chapter 2
Fast Track Start 17

Chapter 3
Default Joomla! Installation 33

Introduction

JOOMLA! HAS NOT BEEN AROUND THAT LONG COMPARED to some of the other open source Content Management Systems (CMSs). But in the relatively short time that Joomla! has been available, it has made a huge impact in the world of CMS Websites. There are thousands of Joomla!-based Websites on the Internet today, and the number is growing by leaps and bounds as word about Joomla! circulates.

What's a CMS?

CMS is the commonly used term for Content Management System. It describes a Website configured so that content can be added, changed, or separated from its design, layout, and interactivity.

A CMS separates the Website designer or programmer from the person creating or managing content. Once the site is designed and is online, the editor or manager takes over and adds content, which then appears according to the preconfigured site design and layout.

This means that content editors who have little or no experience in Website layout and design can edit or add content via a user interface or administrator back-end, and the result visually conforms to the design and layout of the site.

Within that context, Joomla! 1.6 is a true CMS.

Joomla! was not created from the ground up as someone's bright idea. It was derived from another program called Mambo. Joomla! actually started as Mambo, which was created by an Australian group in 2002.

As happens with many projects (the Mambo/Joomla! evolution not being the exception), there was a separation of thoughts on project direction among the participants. The result of this separation of minds was that Joomla!, which was a near-mirror image of Mambo, found its first release as Joomla! 1.0 not long afterward.

How Joomla! 1.6 Arrived

The transition from Mambo to Joomla! was rather seamless. The Mambo license permitted others to take the code and start their own projects. In "open source" parlance, Joomla! is a "fork" of Mambo that now runs as a completely separate project with an increasing number of code differences in the program's core platform.

As a result of this "forking" by Joomla! from Mambo in 2005, the headquarters of Joomla! shifted from Australia to Europe, resulting in a major ground swell of interest in Joomla! across Europe as a Website platform that was available at no cost. Many thousands of Websites are built on the Joomla! 1.0 platform, mostly for Websites outside of the United States where Joomla! has been a little slow in catching on as a Website development tool. More information is available on the Joomla! wiki at http://en.wikipedia.org/wiki/Joomla.

Joomla! 1.0 has progressed through code improvements up to version 1.0.15. At that point, the Joomla! team discontinued support and shifted emphasis to a completely reworked package for Joomla! and introduced version 1.5 in early 2008. The changes and enhancements were plentiful and resulted in a greatly improved CMS product.

Joomla! 1.5 jumped the Atlantic Ocean and became more popular on this side of the pond. Joomla! now has a huge following in Europe, the United States, and other countries across the world.

Improvement Was Needed

Shortly after the Joomla! 1.5 release, it became obvious to the Joomla! core team that some major improvements were needed to bring 1.5 to a higher level. After examining all the options, the team members determined that a complete rework was necessary and proceeded to develop version 1.6, the current release. They determined that streamlining of the software was necessary for today's Websites and, rather than patching up 1.5, decided to create a new version.

Extending Joomla! Beyond the Core Level

Joomla! in its basic form, out of the box so to speak, has certain core functionalities built in. The software operates in a certain way and is somewhat limited in what it can do, given the method the developers initially chose to set it up for operation. This is only natural because the whole idea is to provide a platform with core features upon which other developers in the open source community can build. And they do, as evidenced by the thousands of extensions that are available for the 1.5.x version and that are now becoming readily available for the 1.6 version.

What makes Joomla! such a great CMS is the manner in which you can enlarge and extend its functionality. This is accomplished through Joomla!-compatible extensions, which fall into a few basic categories:

- ▶ Components
- ▶ Modules
- ▶ Plugins
- ▶ Libraries
- ▶ Templates
- ▶ Languages

Each of these is explained in greater detail in later chapters of this book, so don't worry about what they are or what they do at this point.

Suffice it to say that after reading this book, following the tips, and doing the exercises, you'll have not only a fundamental mastery of Joomla!, but a working knowledge of the ways to enlarge its capabilities via extensions.

Improvements in Joomla! Version 1.6

Joomla! 1.6 has made a number of distinct improvements over version 1.5.x. Probably the most significant areas are in content and user management. These changes were implemented after the Joomla! open source community at-large submitted a long wish list of improvements. The Joomla! core team selected those elements it determined to be the best ones for the next release version.

Joomla! 1.6 also has an abundance of improvements that only developers and computer code geeks understand. This is technical stuff, and you don't need to know it to install and run an efficient Joomla!-based Website, so let's not delve into it. You need to know that Joomla! 1.6 is better than 1.5. Let's just leave it at that for the time being.

There are a host of other leap-forward improvements in Joomla! 1.6, but rather than reviewing them here as a comparison to Joomla! version 1.5, our focus will be on the whats and hows of version 1.6 and how to install, administer, and use Joomla! to build your Website project and start adding extensions.

Types of Websites You Can Build

One of the major features of the Joomla! 1.6 CMS is its function as a solid platform upon which any number of Website formats can be constructed. This is accomplished through the implementation of templates and extensions. You can use templates to change the Website's look. In fact, you can assign different templates to different parts of the Website to give each a distinct appearance. This neat trick is discussed in Chapter 10, "Template Basics."

Although the terms may not be exactly clear to you right now, templates are typically spoken about as different elements of a Website, other than those features added through regular extensions. Templates are actually extensions tried and true, but when discussed in this book, they may appear to be separate Website elements. Keep that in mind when you run across what appears to be conflicting statements. Templates are extensions, but due to their special use, they are sometimes discussed without associating them with general extensions.

Building Your Site with Extensions

By using extensions, you can change the entire site's purpose. Let's say you install Joomla! as a general content site, but you want to use it for blogging. You do this by adding an extension to the basic install. Extensions come in many forms, both free and commercial. Some you don't pay for, and others you do. Either way, the core Joomla! install instantly becomes a blogging site as soon as you install and activate the blogging extension. Or you can make it a combination general content site with a blogging feature page.

The possibilities are endless on the combinations of extensions you can add that can change the entire operation and makeup of the Joomla! site.

One thing to keep in mind when looking for extensions is that several extensions can do the same thing or something similar. Find out which one works best for you, but don't expect the developers to tell you. These guys (and gals) are programmers and usually are not good at product support or help questions. After a while, you'll find out which companies or developers have the best extensions for Joomla!, and you'll be looking at their products on a regular basis. Visiting the Joomla! Extension Directory (JED) daily can keep you abreast of the latest releases.

The topic of extensions and Joomla! 1.6 compatibility is covered in Chapter 6, "Extension Basics."

The Basics:

Installing Joomla!

PICTURE YOURSELF SECURING A DOMAIN NAME for your Website and performing the steps necessary to install Joomla! 1.6, planning the content, adding articles, and allowing visitors to view the Website.

Although you might not have pictured yourself working on a Website server when you decided to create a Website, it's essential to establishing a Joomla!-based Web presence. It really isn't all that difficult, but let's assume you have no experience in working with a Website installation on a hosted or shared server, and we'll go from there—taking you step-by-step through the process of installing Joomla! 1.6 properly and putting your Website online.

Webservers come in different types. Windows and Linux are the most popular server platforms, but some others that are Linux-like do the same thing. The one great thing about Joomla! is that you can install it on almost any server, and most Website hosting companies have servers that will host a Joomla! Website installation. In fact, many of the larger Internet service providers (ISPs) and hosting companies have a simple one-click feature for installing Joomla!, which is discussed near the end of this chapter.

You should know how to install Joomla! 1.6 conventionally on whichever type of server space you are renting or leasing from a service provider.

Downloading the Latest Release

BEFORE YOU START THE INSTALLATION PROCESS, it's a good idea to create a separate folder in the Documents and Settings area of your computer called My Joomla, and inside it, additional folders for Joomla Downloads, Joomla Extensions, and Joomla Templates, shown in Figure 1-1. This is especially important if you will be downloading extensions and templates in the future, which we'll cover in Chapter 10, "Template Basics."

After you have completed this task, the next step is to download the Joomla! 1.6 program.

You can always obtain the latest version of Joomla! from the Joomla! Website (www.joomla.org/). See Figure 1-2 to view the Download button on Joomla!'s front page.

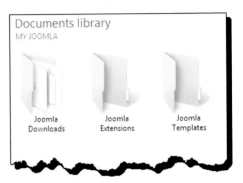

Figure 1-1
Create folders to store Joomla! downloaded files.

Figure 1-2
Joomla! Download button.

Don't Sweat the Installation

Installing Joomla! is the most awkward part of building your Website. The text covers a lot of eventualities of installation scenarios, some of which might not apply to your server configuration. Still, there are topics that need to be covered so everyone can install the program. Be patient when going through the steps. Installation is really easy once you understand the process.

Click on the Download graphic and select Joomla! Version 1.6 Full Package. It may be identified by another number, such as 1.6.2 or something similar. If that's the case, download the highest numbered version. The download is a compressed ZIP file. You need to save that file to the Joomla Downloads folder you created earlier.

Look for the file ending in .zip identified as the Full Package, and select that one (see Figure 1-3).

Figure 1-3
Select the Full Package ZIP file to download.

What You Don't Need to Do

Notice that during the download process, there is no need to identify the Website domain name onto which Joomla! 1.6 will be installed, nor do you need to go through any sort of licensing or software registration procedure. Also, it's not necessary to obtain an activation code or serial number to use Joomla!. Joomla! is open source, which nearly eliminates the need for any kind of registration-to-use process.

Contribution to Joomla! Development

Be generous and make a contribution to Joomla! If, after you install Joomla! and get it working, you appreciate the work and effort that was put into the program by the volunteer developers, why not make a donation to the Joomla! organization? Your Joomla! 1.6 program is worth a lot of money on the commercial market, so give a little back to Joomla!. Look for a link in the upper corner of the Joomla.org Website to donate if you are inclined to do so.

Unpacking of the Download

Assuming you have a computer that operates under Windows XP, Windows Vista, or Windows 7, the ZIP file that was downloaded needs to be uncompressed or unpacked. You need to expand the file so that all the folders, subfolders, and files are visible in a standard directory tree. It's not difficult to do.

Go to the folder where the ZIP file was downloaded (Joomla Downloads, which you created earlier), and right-click on the filename. The expanded menu should look like Figure 1-4.

Right-click on the zipped folder icon, mouse over WinZip, and select the Extract to Here option shown as highlighted lines in Figure 1-4. The unzipping process starts automatically, and the files are stored in the same folder. Your system may not have WinZip installed, so look for a functional item on the list that indicates Extract or Extract Here as the option to select to unzip files.

In Windows 7, use the Extract All link when you right-click, and then select the Joomla Downloads folder created in the My Joomla folder of the Documents Library, or My Documents if using Windows XP.

Different operating systems have different ways of extracting files, or accessing the feature to do so. Check your system help area if the link isn't immediately obvious when right-clicking on a zipped file.

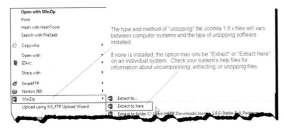

Figure 1-4

You should see something like this when you expand the folders shown. Your computer may not have the same unzipping program, or it may just have an option that says Extract Here, which is the same type of unzipping process.

The contents of the My Joomla folder will be FTPd (File Transfer Protocol) to your Website's location. Transfer the folders and files within that folder only, as illustrated in Figure 1-5.

Don't FTP the Zipped File

When FTPing the folders/files to the server, *do not* copy the source zipped file from which Joomla! was extracted. You don't need it on the server. However, do leave it on your system in case you need to unzip the folder again should a file be corrupted during FTP transfer. That does happen occasionally!

Figure 1-5

List of folders you should see on the server after you unzip or extract the files.

A Better Way to Unzip Files

Some servers allow uploading of zipped files to the host destination so you can unzip them via the control panel for your domain. Check to see if you can do that before uploading folders and files as described earlier via FTP—which does take a while depending on the speed of your Internet connection. Moving ZIP files takes less time, so explore the opportunity to unzip them via the hosting control panel on your server after transfer.

If your server/control panel has the extract capabilities, go ahead and upload the zipped file you downloaded from the Joomla.org Website.

With the control panel for your Website open, look in the top menu bars for a link that says Extract. Once you find that, drill down via the File Manager, select the Joomla! 1.6 ZIP file, and execute the Extract command. Make sure that you are not installing the files into the subdirectory of the ZIP file extraction, but one level up into the httpdocs or public_html folder directly, which is generally known as the *root* folder for your site.

If you're unsure about doing this via the server control panel, just FTP the files in the folder to the root or httpdocs or htpdocs folder on your server. The root folder may also be named public_html on some servers. It may take a while for all the files to upload depending on FTP connection speed. Be patient. The files will upload eventually.

If you accidentally installed the Joomla! files within a /Joomla/ subdirectory, no problem. Just open that folder, select all the files, and copy or move them up one level. The control panels are usually intuitive about that stuff, so just spend a minute and look around before you do it.

Be Aware of File Locations

Your FTP connection to your server should take you to the server root level, where you will find folders that may be called htpdocs, htdocs, httpdocs, or public_html. It is into those folders (whichever applies to your server) that you should FTP the Joomla! files, or ZIP file as the case may apply.

Requirements for Installation

THERE ARE SOME prerequisites to installing a Joomla! Website on a server, as explained next. You must purchase a domain name and select a hosting company. You probably already have a domain name in mind, so purchasing that is a first step. Domain names, beyond their initial cost, have a small annual fee you must pay to keep the domain active. It's not much, but many people have ignored the renewal fee and lost their site. In some cases, someone else has purchased the orphan domain, so be sure to renew annually.

Domain Name

To put a Website online, you must own a unique domain name. Domain names are available from many sources, such as Go Daddy (www.godaddy.com/default.aspx). Search Google for domain name services, and pick one. They all are pretty much the same, so there are no special criteria to look for when selecting one. All domain name services have a search feature that checks to see if your domain name is available as .com, .net, or .org, along with other suffixes. Remember, the domain name must be unique, and once you buy it, you own it as long as you pay the annual renewal fees, which are modest.

If you have a special domain name and you want to protect all variations of it, you should buy all domain name extensions: .com, .net, .org, .biz, and .info. (There are others beyond these, but they're not popularly used.)

This will prevent anyone else from purchasing the same name with a different suffix and running a Website that conflicts with yours. You only need to connect one domain name extension (perhaps .com) to your site; the others can remain unconnected or can be configured to forward visitors to the .com site, if that is what you choose for your domain identity.

Hosting Service

The next thing you need to deploy a Joomla! 1.6 Website is a hosting service. There are hundreds, if not thousands, of Website hosting services. Google can help you find one for hosting a simple or complex Website. Keep in mind that cheap hosting services often offer limited hosting services, so be diligent and select a hosting provider within your monthly budget *and* that offers the fullest range of features and services, such as a full control panel, the correct version of MySQL, and PHP. The cheaper hosting services may not have the correct versions, so inquire about which versions are available on the server before you enter into a hosting agreement. Also, if you plan to have a lot of visitors to your site, inexpensive hosting companies limit the bandwidth (amount of traffic on a site), so make sure you don't underbuy your hosting package by being "on the cheap" if you expect a lot of hits on your site.

The DNS for Your Domain Name

This is sometimes the tricky part of getting your domain to be visible on the Internet, especially if you purchased your domain from one source and host the site with another provider.

DNS is short for domain name server. It is a set of Internet Protocol (IP) addresses assigned to your domain so that Internet browsers, when your domain name is in the location bar, know where to go to find your Website. Usually, there are two—NS1 and NS2—and each has a different set of numbers to identify your Website. Sometimes the numbers are sequential, but other times they are very different. It doesn't matter. Once those numbers are assigned to your Website domain name, that's it. Everyone on the Internet accesses your site the same way, being pointed there by the DNS. Each ISP hosting company has name server numbers for its hosting servers. You need those to identify the exact physical location of your Joomla! Website by the IP address.

Check Your Server

Do *not* attempt to host a Joomla! 1.6 Website on a server without the proper versions of PHP and MySQL, which are MySQL 5.0.4 or higher and PHP 5.2.x or higher. If your server does not have at least those versions, your ISP isn't likely to be upgrading it anytime soon, so select a hosting environment that is properly configured for Joomla! 1.6 installation.

Don't be alarmed if several Websites on the server have the same DNS. Servers are often set up to share DNS addresses and then split them apart automatically. It is not an area of concern, so just accept it as part of being on a low-cost, shared server. Sharing addresses has no effect on your Website and the way it displays for site visitors.

Your Own Server

You can also host your site on a virtual dedicated server, or a dedicated server, which you can lease on a monthly basis from a service provider. These types of hosting configurations are more expensive but well worth it if you are going to have a Website with a lot of content and a high number of visitors to the site, or if you are going to operate a business Website. If you are using Joomla! 1.6 for a personal site, a simple hosting arrangement is all you need from an ISP. However, if you are hosting a larger site, or one for a small- to medium-size business, consider a virtual dedicated or a dedicated service. Again, these are available from the service provider at varying levels of monthly costs depending on the exact configuration. You may also want a virtual dedicated server if you are hosting a number of Websites and want to keep the control of them centralized. Basic virtual servers usually allow 10–30 different Websites to be hosted at the same time under your control.

MySQL Database

Regardless of which way your site is hosted, one thing that is essential for a Joomla! 1.6 Website is a MySQL (*my-see-quill*) database. Joomla! is written in a programming language called PHP, and it requires a MySQL database to hold the information and site configuration data. Most service providers have MySQL databases available for simple hosting; virtual and dedicated services have MySQL and PHP services included.

Sometimes ISPs offer only one MySQL database per site; some offer several or "up to" a certain number, and others offer unlimited databases. You need one database for each Joomla! 1.6 installation.

Once you have opened the MySQL administration area, you give your database a name (write it down somewhere) and establish it as being part of your Website hosting, which is usually an automatic connection.

Is Your Server Joomla!-Installation Ready?

Joomla! 1.6 requires that all installations be performed only on Website servers that operate using PHP Level 5.2.x, so before leasing server space, ensure that the ISP is providing the correct version of PHP and MYSQL to allow a proper install to be performed. They should be PHP 5.2.x and MySQL 5.0.4.

Username and Password for Database

After you have created the database, you must assign a username and password (U/P) that are unique to that database. Joomla! needs this information to install itself on your server. Once it's installed, you are not likely to ever need to access the database or do anything else to it. Sometimes the ISP assigns the username/ password when you open your account; it may be the same one used for the database username/ password. If not, create your own. Keep a record of the name of the database, your username, and your password. Of course, if you want to move your site to another server, that's a different set of circumstances that is covered in Chapter 17, "Advanced Topics."

Before You Install Joomla! 1.6

THERE ARE SOME THINGS THAT you must do before you actually install the Joomla! 1.6 program. The tasks are not complicated, but if you have never done them, they may seem a bit daunting. If you are having trouble, search Google for help on FTP programs or on creating MySQL databases.

FTPing Files to Your Hosting Location

FTP is short for File Transfer Protocol. It's the way files are moved from your local computer (to which you downloaded the Joomla! ZIP file and unzipped it) and the location of your new Website on your hosting provider's server, or server farm. You need to transfer all the Joomla! 1.6 unzipped files (from inside the folder) to the server. Don't transfer the folder itself, just the contents that start a list of folders and files with a folder called `administrator`.

There are a number of free open source FTP programs available that you can install on your computer, or you can spend a few dollars to buy a good commercial one. It doesn't make any difference if you buy a program or get one free. Both types do the same thing: they move files from one computer to another.

Creating a MySQL Database

As mentioned earlier, you must create a MySQL database on your server or hosting location to install a Joomla! 1.6 Website. Naming a database isn't difficult. Pick a name that relates to your domain, or a simple name. It's not important that the name follows any conventions, but the database needs a unique name for identification. When the system accepts the name, write it down for future reference.

Your ISP hosting provider may use a control panel for Website management specific to the type of server you are using. This whole book could be consumed with identifying them and how they operate. This is a Joomla! book, so no additional page space will be devoted to describing the variety of server control panels.

Assigning a User to the Database

Every database must have a user assigned to it or authorized to use it. After you create a database, you must associate a user with a username and password with the database. Joomla! asks you for that information during the installation process so, again, write it down.

Remember that the ISP may assign a username/password that you must use to connect to the database. If it doesn't, you create the username and password. It is suggested that you make the password a character mix of 8–12 characters, varying the casing and using numbers in addition to letters.

Two Ways to Install Joomla! 1.6

ONE NICE THING ABOUT JOOMLA! 1.6 is that you can install it anywhere on a server. Generally, it is installed at the root level, or the top level of access. You can also install it in sub-directories, which are below the root level. It all depends on personal preferences. Both methods are described next.

Method 1: Install in the Root Directory

Once you own a domain name, have assigned the DNS servers, and have information that is propagated across all the name server directories on the Internet, for all practical purposes, your site is live. Anyone can view it, regardless of whether it contains data. ISPs usually put a default page into place that appears when you attempt to access the domain to verify that the connect works and the site is live.

Without getting too technical, let's talk about filenames that Websites use. Joomla! uses a page called index.php, whereas normal Websites typically use index.html or index.htm (could also be default.htm or default.html). The default page that an ISP puts on the site is the first to be accessed when the site is visited. The default page is likely to be index.htm or index.html. So, based on this bit of technical knowledge, you can install the Joomla! files at the server root level, and the site won't be publically accessible until you remove the index or default files that show the temporary home page for the site.

When those files are disabled or deleted, the index.php file that Joomla! uses is the first to be accessed, and your Joomla! Website will display.

Method 2: Install in a Subdirectory

Another way to install Joomla! 1.6 is to place all its files into a subdirectory below the httpdocs or public_html folder level on the server. You can name it anything you like. The domain name plus the folder name is the full path to access the site and administrator sections. The installation works the same way as the method described earlier, except there is an intervening subdirectory to identify.

Typical URL Paths to Joomla! Installations

The site www.domainname.com navigates to the root level.

The site www.domainname.com/subdirectory/ is located in a subdirectory on the server, directly under the root level.

Using this method, after you are ready to deploy the Website, you must delete the files at the server root level and replace them with the Joomla! 1.6 files moved from the subdirectory to the root level. You can bypass these steps if you begin with the first method.

Now that you know that bit of information, put it out of your mind for a while and continue. I'll discuss it again later in this book when your site is ready to go live and be publically accessible.

During installation, one of the first screens, you will encounter is the License Agreement, which covers the conditions for using the software. (Who reads those, anyway?) Once you click past that page, you are off and running and can continue your installation procedures. However, if you do not agree with the terms and use conditions, that will stop the process and you will not be able to install the program.

Seven Easy Steps to a Successful Install

TO START THE INSTALLATION PROCESS, open any Web browser and type your Website address (include the subdirectory if you chose to locate the files there) into the location bar.

Here are the steps you need to perform to install Joomla! 1.6 on a server:

1. Select a language for the site.

2. Let the program perform the preinstall.

3. Review the license agreement.

4. Configure the database.

5. Configure FTP.

6. Configure the main area.

7. Delete the Installation folder.

When you start, if you typed the path correctly, your browser automatically connects to the opening page of the install process.

At the conclusion of each step, click the Next button in the upper-right corner of the screen, as shown in Figure 1-6, to complete that step and move forward. This Next button is standard on Joomla! admin screens, as are other navigation icons that will be discussed as we progress through Joomla! Website administration.

Figure 1-6
Typical Next button on the Joomla!
administrator screens.

In the Joomla! 1.6 back-end, or administration side of things, most of the control and action buttons are located to the upper right of the screen. When you are in a specific section, the section-level control buttons are located to the top-right part of the screen. All the other buttons found in the menu bar or control area are thoroughly explained and discussed as we progress through each section of the Joomla! back-end.

As you begin the install, you will progress through several screens. The first three require no action on your part other than to go to the next screen.

Step 1: Select a Language for the Site

The install automatically defaults using English as the site language. If you want to install and develop your Website in another language, make the appropriate selection. Joomla! accommodates a large number of international languages, and you can elect to invoke them after install and run your site in multiple languages that the users may select as their preference.

Install English Language Version First

If there is no selector for the language you want for your site, install it using English anyway. You can add different languages to the site at any time. Because Joomla! 1.6 is new, it may take some time for other language extensions to be available for Joomla! version 1.6.

Step 2: Let the Program Perform the Preinstall

This page shows the results of some checking the installer program performs on your server and alerts you to any problems or issues that may be present. Usually you can ignore those that are flagged, unless they're serious ones that will not allow continuation of the install until they're corrected. If you do encounter that, contact tech support at your ISP for a resolution of the issue. But in most cases, you will not run into difficulty or problems serious enough to botch the install process.

Step 3: Review the License Agreement

People don't normally read the End User License Agreements (EULAs) that come with software and simply agree with whatever is written. The User Agreement is written to the total advantage and protection of the software author and has nothing in it advantageous to the user. Joomla!'s EULA is no different. If you don't click Agree, you can't proceed, so just click it and carry on. But, be aware that, as a general rule, unauthorized or illegal use of software can have consequences, so the straight-and-narrow is the approach you should follow when using software because that is what you agreed to do when you moved to the next installation screen.

Step 4: Configure the Database

Here's where you need the information collected when you created your MySQL database and created a username/password associated with it.

When installing, make sure that MySQL is selected, not MySQLi. The hostname is usually localhost, or you may need to put something else into that box. Check your hosting control panel for instructions on connecting to the MySQL database, because some Linux servers host the databases on a computer other than the one on which your site is located. The user, password, and database name go into the remaining three boxes. You can ignore the Advanced Settings for a first-install operation.

Figure 1-7
Enter the information you need to connect to the Joomla! database.

Select the Correct Database Type

This is important! Make sure you select MySQL as the database type to use for the installation. Do Not use MySQLi. Use MySQL for the database type.

When you click the Next button, there may be a slight delay while Joomla! creates and writes data into the MySQL tables in the database. When that process is successful, the next screen appears automatically. If the connection to the database was not successful, a message indicates an error, and you are required to return to the previous screen and correct any errors in the container boxes. Errors usually are associated with the username and password or the name of the database, so make sure you have the correct ones and that you've typed them into the boxes correctly. Then try again. When you create the database in your ISP control panel, it usually displays all the information you need, so write it down. Figure 1-7 shows the screen for connecting to the database.

Step 5: Configure FTP

If all has gone well, after the connection to the database, the next screen asks for FTP information. You can bypass this. It is only relevant for use with certain types of Website servers, so you can ignore this step and proceed to the final step. It isn't likely that your server will need this information, so skip this step and execute the Next button.

Step 6: Configure the Main Area

The next screen appears and asks you to name your site and provide the Super User password and an e-mail address, as shown in Figure 1-8. When you want to access the back-end or administration section of your site, you will do so using this password with the username you entered as the default. You can create additional users once you access the back-end, along with changing your username or password whenever you want. In fact, you can (and should!) choose a name for the Super User that is something other than admin, so do so at this time.

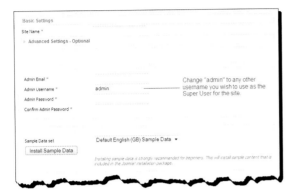

Figure 1-8
Enter information about the administrator and password for access. Click the Install Sample Data button before clicking Save.

Be Aware of Default Usernames

Hackers search the Internet for Joomla! Websites that have `admin` as the Super User. To prevent a possible intrusion, change the default username `admin` to something else that is unique, in the format `MyUniqueAdminName`.

Install the Sample Data

Joomla! 1.6 has a feature that installs sample data into your installation. You should do this so you have the different features available to look and experiment with as you learn how to use Joomla!. The tasks and instructional steps in this book require that the sample data is installed, so make sure you do that in step 6 of the installation process.

After you click the Install Sample Data button, a message displays letting you know the sample data was installed successfully. This is a separate step, so do that first, and then complete the form information on the screen and execute Next.

Step 7: Delete the Installation Folder

If you do not perform this step, Joomla! does not allow you to open your site or access the administration area. If you were to leave the Installation folder as is, anyone could open it and access your site and otherwise create mischief. There's enough of that going around the Internet already, so there's no sense in inviting trouble on your site.

Joomla!'s installation process alerts you to this. To delete the installation directory on the server, click on the Remove Installation Folder button. This automatically deletes the folder on the server.

If you want to delete the Installation folder manually, go to your FTP program (or Control Panel), connect to the server location, and delete or rename the Installation folder. When you have completed that step, you can access your new Website's front-end and back-end.

ISP-Hosted Preconfigured Installation

BECAUSE JOOMLA! IS A FREE, open source software product, many ISPs now offer a range of similar products to help attract people to host their sites with them. It's a convenience that saves much time and trouble. If your ISP has a one-click install feature in its control panel, you can install Joomla! 1.6 that way. If not, you need the longer process to create the database and move the files to their proper location.

Is It the Right Joomla! 1.6 Version?

There is one issue to note with one-click installs using ISP-based files: the Joomla! program to be installed may not be the latest release. This may happen, for example, if the current release is Joomla! version 1.6.3, and the ISP has version 1.6.0 installed as its one-click. Should this be the case, you can use the long installation process to ensure you have the most recent version on your site. Otherwise, after a one-click install, you need to go through an upgrade/update process to get your Joomla! install to the most recent version.

Summary

In this chapter, you learned the following:

▶ Installing Joomla! 1.6 requires a series of steps on a Webserver.

▶ A MySQL database with a username, password, and database name is required.

▶ The database is created via the Website control panel on the server.

▶ You need to transfer the Joomla! 1.6 files to the server root location via FTP.

▶ The most important task is to get the site connected to the database.

▶ There are several methods you can use to install Joomla! 1.6 on your Website location.

▶ You should install the sample data so you have something to reference while you are learning how to use Joomla!.

▶ You must delete or rename the /installation/ directory before your site can display.

▶ After the installation, an administrator username/password is needed to access the Joomla! back-end.

Fast Track Start

JOOMLA! 1.6 CAN BE DAUNTING AT FIRST to get a grasp of the whats and hows of managing a Joomla! 1.6 Website. This chapter leads you through content creation on a fast track, step-by-step process. After you create a category, add an article, and then a menu link item, you will quickly understand how those three work together. After that, the rest of Joomla! will make a lot more sense. Everything works the same way, and the rest of this book will guide you through each of those areas in much greater detail and provide expanded information on the entire Joomla! 1.6 platform. When you are done, there won't be much about Joomla! 1.6 that you don't understand or that you won't be able to do. Got the picture?

Start Right Now

FOR THE PURPOSES OF THIS FAST TRACK set of instructions, the assumption is that you are the site's Super User and the only one permitted to edit content. The objective of this chapter is to illustrate how to create categories, articles, and menu link items, which are the three major parts of the Content Manager, along with components and modules, which are specialized Joomla! extensions.

Here's what you need to do to access the Joomla! 1.6 back-end, or administrator side of the Website.

In your browser's location bar, type in the following, replacing *your domain* with the actual domain name for your Website.

http://*yourdomain*.com/administrator/

Figure 2-1 shows the browser window that should open if you have typed in the domain name properly.

Figure 2-1
Joomla! Administration Login page.

With the screen open, log into the administrator back-end.

1. Log in using the username and password that you assigned to the Super User when you installed the Joomla! 1.6 program.

2. If the username/password entry was proper, you should next see the Admin control panel, as shown in Figure 2-2.

The Admin control panel is the central location for most of the administration you will be performing in the Joomla! 1.6 back-end. Every time you log into the admin back-end, you will view this page and proceed from there to do what you need. Only the left side of the screen is being shown in Figure 2-2.

Figure 2-2
Joomla! 1.6 Admin control panel. Each icon opens to a dedicated administration area of the back-end.

Alternate Administrator Access

You can access additional areas of the administrator back-end using the top/left horizontal menu, which gives you direct access to more areas, such as components, modules, and menus. Access those areas with the menu rather than returning to the Admin control panel each time.

At this point, we are going to discuss only the high points of the Admin control panel functions and give you directions on how to fill your Website with content.

While working with these instructions, remember that there is already some content in place on your site from the Install Sample Data step you performed during installation. You will see those categories, articles, menu link items, and more, so pay close attention to the instructions presented because you will be working with your content created during the learning process, which will be mixed in among the sample content. The "canned content" will be used throughout this book to illustrate certain parts of Joomla! 1.6.

In this chapter, while progressing through the various process steps, your attention will be directed only to what's needed to complete the tasks. On the admin pages, you will see many other parameters, such as controls, options, buttons, fill-in boxes, and various parameters. For this exercise, we will be ignoring them so we can illustrate the basics of creating content in the form of an article assigned to a category that is accessible via a menu link item.

How Content Is Organized

Joomla! 1.6 organizes content in a rather simple manner. Content is primarily comprised of articles that can be classified (stored) in categories as a means of cataloging them. On smaller, personal Websites, article classification isn't very important, but on larger sites with many authors and many areas of content, using categories is vital to keeping things organized.

Once an article has been created and stored in a category, it's important to provide a way to make it display upon a viewer's request. This is performed through a menu link item that, when clicked, opens the article for display on the screen.

The sequence for creating and displaying content goes like this:

1. Create a category in the Category Manager.

2. Create an article and assign it to the category in the Article Manager.

3. Create a menu link item to the article in a menu.

You can generate content on a Joomla! 1.6 Website by the action of components, or you can display it using modules. Those specialized content extensions are discussed in Chapter 7, "Component Basics." For now, let's focus on the fast track and create some content for display so you get the hang of things before going into other subjects in greater detail and the associated exercises.

Joomla! has a timer on it that controls various functions regarding access. One of them manages the amount of time you can be logged into the administrator back-end before it expires and requires you to log in again.

Studying the text in this book and going back and forth to the screen may cause timeouts to occur, so let's set the timer to avoid that eventuality.

Perform the following steps on the Admin control panel screen:

1. Click on the Global Configuration icon in the Admin control panel, and open it.

2. Select the System tab at the top left.

3. At the bottom right, change the Session Lifetime value to 120 (minutes). The default value is 15. Do not change the other default values on the screen.

4. Click Save & Close. The Admin control panel should appear again.

5. That's it. The login session will now stay active for two hours before timing out.

Ready to fast track your Joomla! 1.6 experience? Let's do it!

Creating a Category

Categories are similar to file folders found on all computers. You can have as many of them as you want and may add subcategories as needed to further catalog your information (articles) that comprises the content of the Website. When a subcategory is created, it is called a "nested" category and may have subcategories included in additional levels within it. A category in Joomla! 1.6 functions identically to a folder on your computer system; it's a place to store content. So, knowing that, let's create one now:

EXERCISE 1: CREATING A NEW CATEGORY

In the Admin control panel, open the Category Manager by clicking on the icon shown in Figure 2-3.

Figure 2-3
Clicking the Category Manager opens a manager that includes Articles, Categories, and Featured Articles tabs. The page opens automatically to the Categories tab.

Figure 2-4 shows the Category Manager: Articles view. This is where all categories are listed after you create them.

Before going any further, let's explain the control button icons for the Category Manager that appear in the upper-right area of the screen, as shown in Figure 2-5.

Figure 2-5
This menu array only appears for the Category Manager when you're in the Categories view mode. Different icons appear when you change the view to Articles or Featured Articles admin areas.

Let's do a quick run-through of the Categories menu items, working from left to right.

▶ **New.** This link opens the category creation page.

▶ **Edit.** Used in conjunction with the tick boxes to the left of the Title column. Use this to open a category for editing. You can also click on the category name to open the management screen for editing.

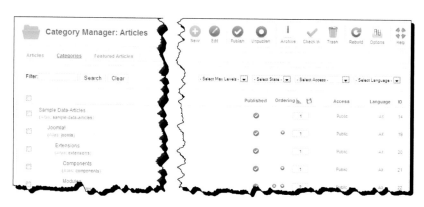

Figure 2-4
This is the category list showing the default installed categories and control icons.

▶ **Publish.** Changes the visibility state of a category from Unpublished to make it and all the articles assigned to it visible.

▶ **Unpublish.** Changes the visibility of the category and all the assigned articles in it until it is published again. This shuts off the selected item. If a category is Unpublished, all articles therein do not display.

▶ **Archive.** Moves the category from this list to an archive library for later retrieval. Can be used as an alternative to Trash or Unpublish if you're uncertain whether you'll want to display the content again at a later time.

▶ **Check In.** If a user has opened articles and not closed them properly, Check In allows you to make the content available for editing, which you could not do while someone else had it checked out. Two administrators cannot edit the same content simultaneously.

▶ **Trash.** Removes the item and places it in the Trash. Select a category, or several, and click Trash, which effectively deletes the categories. There is no warning or confirmation, so once you click Trash, the category is gone. If a category has articles assigned to it, you cannot delete the category before deleting the articles it contains. It's a failsafe to prevent accidental trashing of content. You can trash articles in the same manner. Trash is terminal, so make sure you want to get rid of the content. If not, just choose Unpublish to change the content's visibility on the site until you need it to display again.

▶ **Rebuild.** This rebuilds the list of categories after you have added new ones, arranging them in the proper hierarchal order. It is similar to a screen refresh but works so your screen doesn't change, just the list of categories. Clicking on the column head name Title in the main page area can do the same thing by sorting the categories in order A–Z or Z–A.

▶ **Options.** Allows creation of default settings for all types of content. For example, if you want every new category to be a blog layout, you can set that feature in Options to save additional steps in the future. Or, if you do not want the Date Created or Date Edited lines to appear on articles, you can disable that feature globally in the Options menu. You can override option items at the individual article level, regardless of the global settings.

▶ **Help.** Contains the Joomla! help/ information files that relate to the content of the open page, such as Categories Manager: Articles in this instance.

The control icons in Figure 2-5 are present only in the Category List view. When an individual category is open for editing, the icon array changes to category-specific controls as shown in Figure 2-6.

Figure 2-6
When a category is open for editing, the top right icon array changes to only those actions that can be applied while in that viewing mode.

The buttons in Figure 2-6 do the following, working left to right.

▶ **Save.** Any changes you made are saved, and the window remains open to the same category for further editing. This is useful when you're experimenting with content. It applies on all other editing screens, including articles, menus, and other content.

▶ **Save & Close.** This button saves and closes the edited window and shows the Category Manager: Articles page.

▶ **Save & New.** This saves the current edits and immediately opens a new window to create another category. This method comes in handy when you're performing repeated steps such as adding many categories in succession.

▶ **Save as Copy.** This duplicates the category being edited and puts a Copy of *(name of copied category)* entry into the category list, using the same parameters. After making a copy, you can open the copied category and edit the name.

▶ **Close.** This terminates whatever you are doing and permanently deletes any entry information. It simply shuts down the admin editor and returns the view to the category listings without making changes, even if you typed something on the page.

▶ **Help.** This contains the Joomla! help/information files that relate to the content of the open page, such as Categories Manager: Edit an Articles Category in this instance.

You can control the way a category list is displayed by using the filters, as shown in Figure 2-7. By filtering, you can narrow the list display and make categories easier to locate.

Figure 2-7
The filtering options upon which the category list may be sorted. Filters make it easier to find categories.

Following are the filter variables for sorting the category list. Pull down each and view what options are available. The Select Access options will change based on how the User Access Control is configured, which will be covered in Chapter 13, "User Management and Access Control."

▶ **Select Max Levels.** Refers to limiting the category levels viewed. If you're seeking only top-level categories, set it to 1. If you're seeking top-level and a subcategory, set it to 2, and so on.

▶ **Select State.** Categories have several states, including Published, Unpublished, Archived, and Trashed. Filter by state to find a category as may apply.

▶ **Select Access.** Shows which type of site viewer will have access to view the content within any category. Most are public. But, there may be categories that are limited to registered user viewing only. In that case, filter the list by Registered, and you'll see only those viewers that are designated as such.

▶ **Select Language.** If multiple languages are used on a site, you can filter the list by language.

Buttons Are Buttons!

Throughout Joomla! 1.6, the menu buttons as explained in the preceding list typically function in the same manner but within the administrative areas in which you are working. When future menus or admin areas are explained, only the new buttons are defined and their functions described. This saves you time so you aren't rereading the same information. The information is repeated only if it is unique or special in its application.

When a category is opened, the individual Category Manager: Edit an Articles Category opens as shown in Figure 2-8, which is the screen used every time a new category is to be created. If a category already exists, the same screen opens for a category with the information included. You can edit the information on that screen.

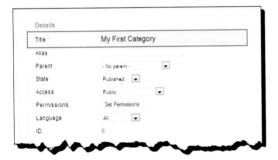

Figure 2-8
Every category function, Create New or Edit Existing, opens to this editing window.

There are no "types" of categories. A category is a single content collector by itself, and it can contain only articles. Categories may have subcategories, and those may contain sub-subcategories.

Consider the simplest category hierarchy for your content, and don't overdo the use of subcategories by building a labyrinth of places to save articles.

Three Clicks to Get There

A good Website practice is to allow the visitor to reach the target information in three clicks or fewer. Use caution when creating subcategories within subcategories. Requiring more than three clicks to access content can frustrate viewers, so let them access content quickly.

Referring to Figure 2-5, a category is created by clicking on the New icon and opening the category administration screen. You can select a number of attributes. Most of them are the default conditions, so only the essential ones are described here.

Here's how to create a category:

1. Enter My First Category in the space provided.

2. Check to make sure No Parent is selected in the Parent field.

3. Check to make sure Published is selected.

4. Check to make sure Public is selected.

5. Click Save & Close. Following Save & Close, the Category List should appear and My First Category should be visible in the list.

6. You may need to scroll down the screen to see the category you created, as in Figure 2-9.

Viewing Full Lists

Sometimes when you look at lists, the file you are looking for isn't there. This is because the list display number is too low. At the bottom of the screen is a drop-down that allows you to display more than a certain number of items at a time. This is a temporary setting. Increase the value as needed. This parameter can be globally changed in the Global Configuration > Site Tab > Default List Limit. Set the option as appropriate, and then click Save & Close.

After completing the steps above, check Figure 2-9 for what you should see when you scroll down to view the categories.

Figure 2-9
If you do not see this, click twice on the column head Title (blue color), which sorts the list alphabetically, or use the Rebuild icon in the top-right menu to refresh the screen.

Number of Items Displayed

If you are not seeing enough items in the display list, go to the bottom of the page and increase the value in the Display drop-down. You may also change that value throughout all of the back-end by going to the Global Configuration > Site and changing the value in the Display List Limit drop-down. Remember to click Save & Close after making the change.

That's all there is to creating a category into which you can assign articles. There are other options and parameters that you can implement, but for this fast track exercise, we'll just leave the rest of them as is and make no changes. The other attributes that you can apply to categories will be covered in later chapters.

Articles in Categories

Articles require placement in a specified category or subcategory. For Websites that do not have much content, the articles can simply remain Uncategorised, which is a preset category during install. Uncategorized is akin to laying documents on top of the file cabinet instead of putting them in folders. That's good for a little bit of content, but it can easily get out of control when you have many articles or pieces of content. You can use categories and subcategories to keep the content tidy and organized. When in doubt, use Uncategorised as the temporary holder of the article. You can always reassign articles to another category, but to only one category, not several.

Creating an Article

Now that you've created a category into which you can assign an article, let's create an article.

Go back to the Admin control panel (top-left menu, Site > Control Panel) and select Article Manager, as shown in Figure 2-10.

Figure 2-10
Article Manager button in the Admin control panel. You can also create articles directly by using the Add New Article icon.

Before going any further, let's take a quick look at the control icons for the Article Manager creation area that appears in the upper-right area of the screen. Notice that these are not much different than the category control icons and function in a similar manner.

In Figure 2-11, the icons serve the same functions as in the Category Manager. For both categories and articles, the Options icon opens a pop-up window that has tabs, as shown in Figure 2-12. The controls under the tabs are discussed later in the book.

Figure 2-11
Controls for articles are similar to those for categories.

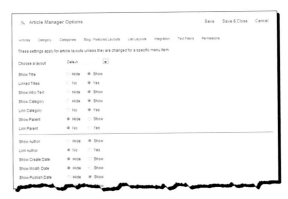

Figure 2-12
When the Options box is open, note the X in the upper-right corner. Click the X to close the window. This applies throughout Joomla! 1.6 with pop-up screens.

Article Category Assignment Limitations

You cannot assign articles to multiple categories. Also, you can assign an article to only one category at a time. If the article is to be assigned to two or more categories simultaneously, you must create duplicate articles with separate category assignments.

As is the case with categories, when you open the Article Manager: Articles, an article list view is shown for all the articles on the site, with references to their respective categories (see Figure 2-13).

Articles also have an editor screen, as did the categories explained earlier. This screen, shown in Figure 2-14, is accessed in three ways:

▶ From the Admin control panel, by clicking the Add Article icon

▶ In the Content > Article Manager drop-down > Add New Article

▶ With the Article Manager open, clicking the New icon

Using any of these three methods opens an Article Manager/Editor screen.

EXERCISE 2: CREATING A NEW ARTICLE

Follow these steps to create a new article:

1. Enter My First Article as the title.

2. Select My First Category in the Category pull-down. You may need to open the list and scroll down to find it.

3. Check to make sure Published is selected.

4. Type some relevant text into the Article Text window of the Article Editor. If you want to paste some text from Word, make sure to click the W icon in the editor top menu bar so that code is not inserted as text.

5. Click Save & Close.

6. The Article List should appear, and My First Article should be visible in the list, as shown in Figure 2-15.

Figure 2-13
The article list has a similar appearance to the category list, but it displays only information that's relative to articles.

Figure 2-14
Only the top part of the screen is shown for this exercise.

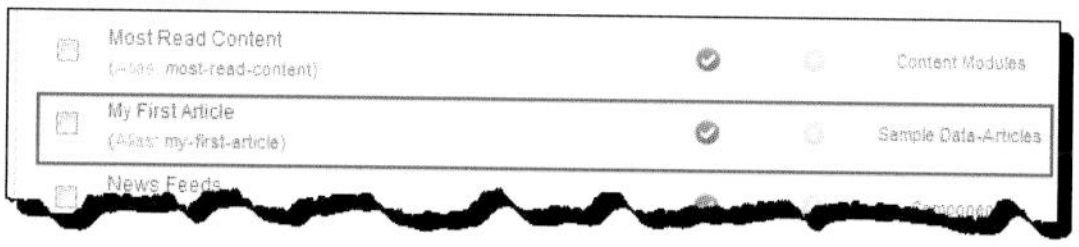

Figure 2-15
The newly created My First Article should appear as shown.

You have now added a live article to the category you created earlier and are well on your way to getting a grasp on the content management system of Joomla! 1.6. There's a lot more to learn about this process, so let's examine a set of parameters that affect every article on your site.

Article Parameters

When the Article Manager is open, the Options icon appears in the top-right control menu. Selecting this icon opens the Article Manager Options, wherein you can select parameters that affect all articles on your site.

If you explore the pop-up (see Figure 2-12), you will notice a number of tabs, each one applying a global option to the respective areas such as articles, categories, and more. We won't discuss those global settings in detail right now. Because of their complexity, global Article Manager Options are covered in depth in several later chapters.

Close the pop-up by clicking on the X at the upper-right corner.

Featured Articles

The designation of a Featured Article is just a fancy way of saying that the article should appear on the front page of the Website, assuming that the opening page contains visible articles. This brings up an immediate question: Can the front page display anything else? Well, yes, it can, and we'll clear that up shortly. But for now, let's assume that the front page consists only of articles.

In the Article Manager, you can create articles and assign them to their respective content categories. Articles that you created as regular, nonfeatured articles can be designated as Featured by selecting that option from the drop-down selector on the Edit Article screen or on the Article Listing table by toggling the icon. See the examples in Figures 2-16, 2-17, and 2-18.

Figure 2-16
In the Article Editor, toggle the Featured drop-down to have the article appear on the front page—or not.

If you are viewing the article list, you may also change the Featured status of individual articles by toggling the icon in the Featured column, as shown in Figure 2-17.

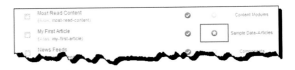

Figure 2-17
Click on the grayed-out icon to toggle it to blue and make the featured article appear on the front page. Click the blue icon to remove the article from the front page.

You can also create articles directly in the Featured Article Manager, which displays an article list that shows only those that appear on the front page of the site. This way, if you have many articles but only a few on the front page, you can access them quickly using a prefiltered display of the list. When the Featured Article List is displayed, a new article is created using the New icon at the top right. However, creating articles in the Featured Article Manager does not automatically assign them as such. You must still select Yes in the Featured drop-down.

Figure 2-18
The Featured Articles List and controls operate identically to the regular Article Manager.

There is also a bank of tabs that allows toggling between articles, categories, and featured articles. Toggle between those tabs and view the displayed lists. This is a handy feature if you are creating or editing a lot of categories and articles and need to flip back and forth repeatedly. Joomla! 1.6 is loaded with useful features of this type and, because we are fast tracking the content creation process, they will be explained in greater detail later on in the book as we apply their functions.

Viewing the Site Front-End

To view your Website's front-end, you can click the View Site link in the top-right part of the admin screens, or you can open a new browser window to the domain URL. You will be switching back and forth between screens in many of the exercises in this book, so once you have a browser window open to the Website, leave it open.

Creating a Menu Link Item

There is one more step to go to finish our fast track to creating content. There is now an article (My First Article) that you created in a category (My First Category). All that is left to do to make the article publically visible is to create a menu link item to it. Here's how.

Go to the Admin control panel and open the Menu Manager, as shown in Figure 2-19.

Figure 2-19
Use the Menu Manager icon to access the Menu Manager from the Admin control panel. You can also access the Active Menu list using the drop-down Menus tab at the top.

The result of clicking the Menu Manager icon is the display of existing menus being used on the site. (Remember: Sample data is installed with preconfigured menus.) Normally, at this stage, you would create an entirely new menu. However, because we are fast tracking this process, we will create a menu link item in an existing menu, rather than creating an entirely new menu and adding to it. That process will be covered in Chapter 15, "The Joomla! Menu System."

Menu Manager Top-Right Menu

As with previous menus that control administration areas, the control icons for the Menu Manager, at the top right of the screen, work in the same way as those for categories and articles.

EXERCISE 3: CREATING A MENU LINK ITEM

There are two ways of creating menu link items. Let's take the fast track method:

1. Open the main menu by clicking on its name or by clicking the box to the left and using the Edit icon in the top menu. Either action opens the main menu item list, as in Figure 2-20.

   Each menu has a corresponding display on one of the pages of the Website. In this case, the main menu is displayed on the front page with a heading of This Site, as shown in Figure 2-21.

2. Before adding a My Menu Link Item, change the screen from menus to menu items using the tab shown in Figure 2-20.

3. In the admin view, select the New icon from the top-right control buttons. This opens the New Menu Link Item Manager for the main menu, which you previously selected.

Figure 2-20
Main menu list view showing all menu link items assigned to the selected main menu.

Figure 2-21
Corresponding front page menu for the main menu as shown in Figure 2-20.

Figure 2-22
The New Menu Item window with only
the left side showing.

4. With the New Menu Item panel open, perform
   the following steps to create a new menu
   link item.

   a. Click the Select button to access the types
   of links available, and when the pop-up opens,
   select Single Article as the type of link to create (in the right column).

   b. Enter My Menu Link Item in the Menu
   Title field.

   c. On the right side, Select Article, open the
   selector box by clicking the Select/Change
   button, as shown in Figure 2-23.

   d. Scroll down and select My First Article on
   the alphabetized list.

   e. Click Save & Close in the menu editor.

The menu link item, My Menu Link Item, should
appear at the bottom of the list of items that are
part of the main menu. If you go to View Site
(top right), you see that item on the main menu
also. Click on the link to open the article. My
First Article should appear on the page, as
shown in Figure 2-24.

Figure 2-23
Open the Required Settings > Select/Change box to
select an article that attaches to a menu link item.
Scroll the list to find the article to assign.

Figure 2-24
View the menu on the front page, and you should
see the My Menu Link Item as the last item.

The article is now live content on the Website.
Congratulations! You did it!

Creating a category, an article, and then the
menu link item wasn't that difficult. Adding
more content becomes a repeat of the above
for each article added. Other content inclusion
might not be that easy and may require more
steps or a different approach by selecting the
type to be created and using administrator
controls in other areas, but it's pretty much the
same process with minor variations.

Following the steps and processes for creating
a specific type of content takes the mystery out
of doing it. The remainder of this book covers
those procedures again and illustrates much
greater detail on the whats and hows and a lot
more information about everything you can
think of relating to a Joomla! 1.6 Website. When
you reach the end of this book, your mastery of
Joomla! 1.6 should be complete.

Summary

In this chapter, you learned the following:

► The Administrator login gives you access to the Admin control panel.

► The Admin control panel accesses all the necessary management areas on the Joomla! 1.6 back-end.

► Content is organized as articles in categories.

► You create categories using the Category Manager.

► Categories store and help organize articles that appear on the Website.

► You can create subcategories within categories (nesting), to provide greater article cataloging if needed.

► You can create articles using the Article Manager.

► You must assign articles to a category when you create them. It is possible to have an article assigned to a category called Uncategorised if necessary.

► You can assign articles to only one category at a time.

► You can designate articles as featured to make them appear on the front pages of the site if that is how your front page is configured.

► You can toggle articles between visible states on the front page using the Featured column in the Article Manager.

► Articles designated as featured appear on the front page whether or not they are assigned to a menu link item.

► To display an article from a link item in a menu, you must create a menu link item that associates with the article.

Default

Joomla! Installation

CHAPTER 2, "FAST TRACK START," INTRODUCED the fast track method of creating categories, articles, and menu link items. This chapter delves deeper into the fundamentals of Joomla! 1.6 Websites and administration of the content. Some of the material here will be a repeat of Chapter 2, but it will be more in depth, with additional information you should know as a Website's Super User, or Webmaster if you like.

The site's Super User is the person who controls everything. There are many other levels of users and administrators you can create, but the Super User is at the top. It is the administrator who grants privileges and allows different access levels to be assigned to all other users. For the purpose of the materials presented in this chapter, the assumption is that you are the sole user, and you are the only one who will be making changes and adding and editing content as the Super User.

User management and access control are covered in Chapter 13, "User Management and Access Control."

Accessing the Admin Back-End

As you learned in Chapter 2, the administration of Joomla! Websites is through an admin back-end, or back-end for short. All actions to create and manage content and the Website overall are performed at the Super User level after login. However, keep in mind that other content management users may be created for editing certain parts of the Website or specific content if your site is a company one with many stakeholders who manage the content.

These other classes of administrators often do not have as much control over the Website as the Super User, who usually is responsible for installing the Website and setting the username and password during site installation. These administrators may access only the parts of the site to which they have been granted permission to access and modify.

Admin Control Panel

The Admin control panel is the hub of back-end activity. Everything you do as a Super User is started on this page after a proper login. It's the same with other users, but when they log in, parts of the back-end that they are not allowed to edit or modify are not visible to them. One example is the Global Configuration icon. Other users will neither see it nor be able to access it via the drop-down menus.

Mastery and knowledge of the admin back-end is essential for higher levels of Website administration. Spend some time looking over the Admin control panel screen on your site, and compare it to Figure 3-1 and the companion drop-down menus in Figure 3-2.

Figure 3-1
Admin control panel when you're logged in as Super User. Other administrators may not see all the manager icons shown, and they won't see the drop-down menus containing links to the nonaccessible areas.

Figure 3-2
Drop-down menus access the same control panel areas shown in Figure 3-1.

34

Use the Drop-Down Menus

When you are in the content area of the back-end, it is inconvenient to return to the control panel every time you want to access another admin area. The drop-down menus located to the top left, as shown in Figure 3-2, allow you to cross-navigate all functional areas of the back-end. Although the control panel is handy when you first log in to the back-end, it is much easier to work with the drop-down menus to access the rest of the management areas.

Different Monitor Resolutions

Depending on the resolution setting of your monitor, the Admin control panel shown in Figure 3-1 may have more icons per row or have a slightly different layout. Functionality, however, is not affected. Everything works the same, regardless of your monitor settings.

Let's look at each drop-down and discuss their link destinations and what you can expect to find there. As we get deeper into the book, each link will be explained in greater detail. In the end, you will be proficient in moving around the back-end with ease to access the management areas for each part of Joomla! 1.6.

The control panel provides the quick access links to the parts of the back-end you are likely to use the most. You will find that the drop-downs give you more options for accessing admin areas quickly when you are not in the control panel view. You should use the drop-downs as often as possible because they speed up transitions between the working areas of the back-end.

Although the explanations that follow will be helpful for defining what each menu does, you may want to take a few minutes to explore each drop-down and each submenu item to see what screen is displayed and look around. Most of the screens are filled with parameters from the default content that give you some insight into what to find and where to find it.

Access the Admin Back-End Help Area

You can extend the explanations that follow by visiting the Help area of the back-end and inspecting the topic areas. Screenshots have been excluded here because they are included in the Help sections. Visit that area if you want more information.

Site Drop-Down Menu

The following are the menu items that are accessible under the Site drop-down menu.

Control Panel. Takes you back to the Admin control panel.

My Profile. Allows changes to the logged-in user information. Allows all logged-in users to change their respective profile information.

Global Configuration. Accesses the Site, System, Server, and Permissions controls. This section is visible only to the Super User after login to prevent anyone who's not authorized from making changes.

Maintenance. Opens submenus. Note that the blue arrow indicates that there are submenus under this link. This is standard throughout all the drop-down menus in the back-end. Here are the fly-out items:

> **Global Check-In.** Checks in all content that others have checked out, making it available for editing. If others have edited content and not closed their screens or logged out properly, you can't open it unless you click Global-Check-In.

> **Clear Cache.** Clears all the files that are temporarily stored in the Website's cache, such as administrator actions. A cache with a lot of content may cause the site to run slower; clear the cache occasionally to keep the system operating efficiently.

> **Purge Expired Cache.** Checks the cache files and purges all those that are out of date. This is generally not an area of concern on personal or low-traffic sites. Higher traffic sites should periodically purge expired cache items.

System Information. Displays information relating to the server where the site is hosted. This is useful for troubleshooting issues that arise.

Logout. Lets you log out of the back-end, which you should always do before closing the browser window. There are several logout buttons on the back-end. Note that the one on the top right of the screen remains on all screens.

Users Drop-Down Menu

Users and their access to the site will be covered in Chapter 13. The general functions found under this menu perform the following actions:

User Manager > Add New User. Adds a new user with an access group designation. You must have at least someone's name, username, and e-mail address to create a new user, but you can select additional settings and options.

Groups > Add New Group. Adds a new group or subgroup as needed to further classify users for Websites that have many content contributors.

Access Levels > Add New Access Level. Creates a new user access level, or class of user, and then adds access or limitations to content.

Mass Mail Users. Opens a utility screen that allows sending of messages to classes of users. It's good for system alerts or other messages relative to their access to the site back-end.

Menus Drop-Down Menu

Other than the Menu Manager link, the other links are for actual menus that are part of the default content for the installation. If you recall, you selected that option when you installed Joomla! 1.6. We will be using the sample content for examples as we go along. The main menu is required, but you can name it something else. However, using the term *main menu* helps to identify which menu is the primary one for site navigation. It usually contains the default link item, which determines what is displayed on the front page when the site opens. You'll read more about that after our discussion of the administrator drop-down menus.

Reminder: The Default Content Must Be Installed

The menu link items that follow are shown based on the default content. If you install Joomla! without the default content, these items will not appear. Based on the content you have decided to include on your site, the menus and menu link items will likely be different. Because you can view the menus described here via the back-end, screenshots of each menu and sub-menu are not shown here.

Menu Manager Drop-Down Menu

Creating and managing menus and menu link items is discussed in Chapter 8, "Module Basics." Following are the general functions of the menu items in the Menu Manager:

Menu Manager > Add New Menu. This is the first step in menu creation. It adds a new menu for menu link items to link to site content.

The menus described next were created during the installation process when the sample content was added. They are explained here for illustration of their relationship to the sample content. If the sample content was not installed, the menus are not part of the admin back-end.

User Menu > Add New Menu Item. Adds a new menu link item in the User menu, which is accessible only after a registered user has logged into the site and depends on her user group assignment.

Top > Add New Menu Item. Adds a new menu link item into the top menu, which is the one located above the site banner. Again, it's selectively created as part of the default installation.

About Joomla! > Add New Menu Item. Adds a menu link item into that menu.

Australian Parks > Add New Menu Item. Adds a menu link item to the Australian Parks menu, which becomes visible when you click the Sample Sites menu link item in the This Site menu.

Main Menu > Add New Menu Item. The main menu is the menu into which you created the My First Article menu link item in Chapter 2. It is called the main menu because the default front page layout is controlled via one of the menu link items within that menu. *Main menu* is a standard term used in Joomla! content, but you can name it anything you want on your own Website. The menu functions just fine if it has another name.

Fruit Shop > Add New Menu Item. Adds menu link item to the Fruit Shop menu, which becomes visible when clicking the Sample Sites menu link item in the This Site menu and opening the appropriate tab.

Content Drop-Down Menu

The following are the menu items in the Content menu:

Article Manager > Add New Article. Adds a new article to the site and assigns it to a category for management and classification purposes. A category must exist before assigning an article to it.

Category Manager > Add New Category. Adds a new category or subcategory as needed to manage site content objectives.

Featured Article. Lists articles that are designated to appear on the front page of the site. You can remove this designation at any time by opening the article and changing the Featured status from Yes to No. The Featured option must be set to Yes for an article to appear on the front page, which will then assign it to the Featured Article listing.

Media Manager. Accesses the Media Manager of the site, where all graphics and images used in association with content are stored. The Media Manager is covered in Chapter 11, "Image Basics."

Components Drop-Down Menu

Banners are graphic panels or images that can be displayed on the site. You cannot create text panels. You can only use banners that are actual images (GIF, JPG, PNG). Banners may be advertisements or special promotional graphic panels assigned to banner positions.

Banners. Manages and configures banners on the site, including publish and unpublish dates. Banners may only appear in the module positions called Banners. The publishing dates are selected when the individual banner content item is opened.

Categories. These are categories for banners only. They are *not* the same as categories for content. Their hierarchy operates the same way but is limited for assignment related to the individual banners.

Clients. *Clients* are those individuals or companies that have placed banners on your site. You may note at this point that the banner process is purely a manual one under control of the Super User. Clients cannot put banners on your site unless you have specifically granted them proper access to do so.

Tracks. Monitors the statistical activities related to the banners and generates reports for clients and advertisers.

Contacts. Displays a list of contacts, creates contacts, and enters them into categories. There are many options for displaying this information, so spend some time looking around the Contacts Manager screen to become familiar with what can be displayed for each person.

Categories. Classifies contacts into groups, such as Sales, Marketing, and Support, on larger sites.

Messaging. A lightweight internal communication system between site users. It's helpful for the site administrator to send messages to other users about content or other site-relevant subjects.

New Private Message. Opens a screen to create a new message for the selected user.

Read Private Messages. Displays private messages sent to you.

Newsfeeds. This is content sourced from other sites and fed into your site for display. Many informational Websites offer feeds or Really Simple Syndication (RSS) from their sites that can be displayed using this component.

Feeds. Creates feeds onto your site from other sites.

Categories. Helps organize feeds by categorizing them as needed.

Redirect. Sends links from one URL to another or redirects the user somewhere else.

Search. When someone uses the Search feature of your site, assuming you have the Search module active and displayed in a module position, this component displays the search phrase used. Only site administrators can access this information.

Weblinks. Similar in concept to contacts but deals with URL links to other Websites. Chapter 7, "Component Basics," discusses some special features of this component.

Links. Creates the actual link. These links should always be assigned to a Links category.

Categories. Classifies the links by designated categories. If you have many links on your site to outside Websites, categories keep them organized and accessible via smaller lists.

Extensions Drop-Down Menu

This menu area is used to access the extensions and the various managers for them, as follows:

Extension Manager. Access point where extensions are added/uploaded and installed into the Website. Extensions are covered in Chapter 6, "Extension Basics."

Module Manager. Once installed as extensions, modules are managed through this administrator location. You can create, position, configure, or set existing and newly installed modules to display or not to display.

Plug-In Manager. When installed, the plugins on the site can be managed through this location. In most cases, plugins require no configuration other than being either enabled or disabled.

Template Manager. Manages all site templates after the Extension Manager installs them. Allows designation of the default template and template assignments to individual menu link items that change the page to a different template when clicked.

Language Manager. If your site is to display in multiple languages, this is where the language extensions are set and designated. Individuals around the world create language files in their native language and contribute the files to the Joomla! Extensions Directory (JED).

Help Drop-Down Menu

If you need help with anything, use this menu to access the Help pages, but don't be too disappointed if they are not complete. The Help pages for Joomla! take a long time to be filled with meaningful content by the folks who volunteer to create and maintain the pages.

Joomla! Help. When you need to know something, this is the place to find more information. Pick the subject and read the screen contents. It is always helpful to spend some spare time in the help screens when you're first experiencing Joomla! 1.6. There is a lot to learn, and every little bit of information, regardless of the resource, builds your knowledge of the platform, how it operates, and how you can make it work better for you.

Support Forum. Takes you to the Joomla.org forums. You need to create a user account there to be able to post forum topics. You can read all the topics, but you cannot be active with responses or create new topics without an account.

Documentation Wiki. Joomla! has an extensive, information-filled wiki page. When you visit the wiki, make sure that you are reading topics relative to version 1.6 and not 1.5. It is easy to view the wrong topics if you don't pay close attention to the navigation as you click through the content.

Useful Joomla! Links. Takes you to various destinations where you can download extensions and access an abundance of resources and information. Visit the links and spend time at each looking around. You can acquire a lot of knowledge on those Websites and pages.

In this chapter, as we did in Chapter 2, the menu items are explained for each section as they are used. From that point onward, we don't redefine similar menu items that perform in the same or in a comparable manner. Only new buttons that appear in the selected control areas are discussed. It will be easier and faster to learn Joomla! 1.6 if we don't repeat definitions.

Joomla! Extensions Defined

THE JOOMLA! 1.6 PLATFORM consists of the core platform, which is the code that makes a Website run, and extensions, which enhance or enlarge the ability to add more content. The extension types that come with the Joomla! core, shown in Figure 3-3, are described here.

Figure 3-3
You can add six types of extensions to the Joomla! 1.6 core program.

Components. Mini-applications that operate inside the Joomla! framework. An example of a component is a photo gallery that displays images in an orderly way from photos located in a folder on the Website. Another component that is often used is a contact form for site visitors to send messages to the site owner. There are many components, some of which are discussed in Chapter 7.

Modules. Visible areas on the page that contain flexible extensions that may or may not be associated with a component. An example is the login module for users. A module that displays the latest articles is another example. Modules can be positioned anywhere on a Website template that has a designated module position, such as left, right, top, and footer.

Plugins. Routines that are associated with triggered events. When a trigger event occurs, it executes a function if it associates with the plugin. An example is a plugin that allows the display of a module within an article by specifying the module using special code inserted into the article.

Libraries. Packages of code that provide a related group of functions to the core Joomla! framework or to the extensions and are installed, updated, and deleted in the extensions installer.

Templates. Controls the physical structure and the visual layout of the site pages. A template consists of the code necessary to display a Website in a certain layout, with module positions, style sheets for colorization, and other elements of content appearance.

Languages. Extensions that display Website content in other languages may be installed. You can install language extensions at any time and set them to the default or control them with a language selector that allows switching between languages based on user preferences.

Content found on Joomla! sites comes in four forms, as shown in Figure 3-4 and explained here. The majority of content on Joomla! sites is published via articles. Additional content is contained in modules located on the pages, content generated by components, or other specialized extensions, along with content generated by event triggers.

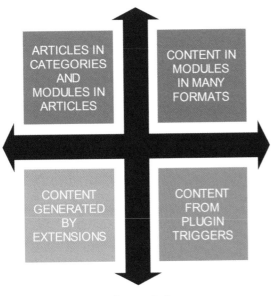

Figure 3-4
The main parts of Joomla! 1.6 that create or generate content visible on the site.

Articles in Categories and Modules in Articles

Content in Articles. This is the normal manner in which content is added to Joomla!. Articles can be anything, take on any format, and include text, images, tables, and other types of layouts. Articles are always viewed in the main content area. In the case of the default template, this is the center/middle area of the page, using the default templates. The actual layout of this area can be controlled and will be discussed here.

Categories collect and organize the articles. A hierarchy of categories can exist with subcategories to further organize content on Websites that have a lot of articles, or articles that are written by several authors. If you have a small site, only one or several categories may be sufficient to keep the articles organized without the complexity of using multiple subcategories. For more complex sites, you should give thought to the best way to catalog the content articles without creating a highly complex category structure.

Modules

Content in Modules. Similar to articles, content in modules takes on the same form with the exception of where it can be located on a page. The difference between content in modules and that within articles is the ability to locate module content anywhere on the page where a module position, or placeholder, is located. This feature provides great flexibility in laying out the Website pages. Additionally, you can assign modules to specific menu link items and set them to display, or not, based on which item is clicked.

Content Generated by Extensions

Content Generated by Extensions. Many extensions are specialized as to their contents and what they do or how they function and the manner in which content is displayed. For example, with an extension to display a photo gallery, content is controlled by the extension and not an article or module, although you may use a module to control the position on the page. Extensions can be components, modules or plugins. They are distinguished as being separate from the default installation. Extensions are thoroughly covered later in this book.

Extensions as Components

Content Generated by Components. Some components generate content in their own format and display it in the center content area. Some of these built-in default components follow:

Banners. Manages banners that you may want on your site. This component usually doesn't manage the page's top banner (site header).

Contacts. Creates and displays a list of contacts for your site. Typically not used on smaller sites, but is used on larger sites that have many people editing content, or a company that wants to list all its staff/ employees and contact information, such as Sales, Customer Service, and Support.

Messaging. Allows sending and receiving of private messages among users who have accounts on the site; it's good for large sites, but not for smaller, one-person Websites.

Newsfeeds. Lets you display newsfeeds from other Websites on your site. You can also set up newsfeeds in categories to keep them organized or display them selectively or under specific conditions.

Redirect. Creates a redirect from one URL to another. This is usually used internally to direct visitors to another location on the site, but you can use it for external links also. It has limited value with respect to site administration.

Search. Displays the searches that were conducted on the site by the phrase that was used for the search event. Search features are helpful in larger sites. Smaller sites, however, usually don't need for the Search module to be displayed.

Weblinks. Allows the creation of categorized Weblinks for site visitors to view other Websites you may want to reference for them.

Visit the Sample Content Pages

THE SAMPLE CONTENT ON THE DEFAULT Joomla! 1.6 installation illustrates how content can be organized and provides information about the way Joomla! operates. Take some time to visit the links in the left column and read the article pages. It is important for you to spend some time looking at the entire Website by following the links in the menus.

Start with the This Site menu and view Example Pages and the links under Using Extensions. There is some excellent information under each link that you should know as a Super User.

View the Components, Modules, Templates, Languages, and Plugin pages. The content on those pages is useful in helping you understand the various aspects of the Joomla! 1.6 platform.

Also, look at the sample sites and notice how the layouts change along with the positions of elements on the pages. These are but a few examples of the type of pages that you can create and modify for display on a per-link-item. This is where the true horsepower of the Joomla! platform surfaces. It allows you to create many layouts using the same template, or multiple templates, based on the needs of the content of your site.

Front Page Layout

FOR ILLUSTRATION PURPOSES, the way Joomla! 1.6 operates and functions will be explained using the template(s) that are included as part of the default installation. The default template used for the sample content is Beez_20 Default.

You can access the templates via the Admin control panel > Template Manager, or via the Extensions drop-down > Template Manager. The screen shows the installed, default templates that are assigned to a particular section of content. The gold star, as shown in Figure 3-5, in the right column indicates the default template for the site's home page. Also, if there is a green checked circle for any template, it indicates that somewhere in the menu system there is a menu link item that has that template associated with it. In other words, the template is assigned to a link item.

In addition, there are other parts of the default installation Website content displayed using the Beez5 template assigned to different content areas, such as the Parks Site and the Fruit Shop.

There is also a template called Atomic-Default, which is included as an example for the viewing of the template. No content areas are assigned to it.

One of the great features of the Joomla! template and menu system is that you can assign different templates to different menu link items to provide different layouts, appearance, and content configurations. This topic will be covered in greater detail in Chapter 10, "Template Basics."

In most Joomla! 1.6 installations, the default administrator template is used and rarely changed. We will use the default template on the admin or back-end of the site in our explanations. We can change both template types, but at this time, the Hathor template will not be used. For discussion purposes, we'll use the default Bluestork administrator template throughout this book.

Location	Template	Default	Assigned	ID
Site	atomic		✓	3
Site	beez5		✓	6
Site	beez_20		✓	114
Site	beez_20	★	✓	4
Administrator	bluestork	★		2
	hathor			

Figure 3-5
The gold star indicates the default template in use for both the site and the admin back-end.
The green checkmarks indicate that the template is "assigned" to a menu link item on the site which, when clicked, displays the layout for that template rather than using the default to display content.

What Are Modules?

Modules are placeholders on a page that have a certain format based on the type of module used. The term *positions* typically describes module locations. Modules will be explored in depth in Chapter 8.

The modules listed next are the defaults. You can view the list in the Module Manager by selecting the New icon in the top-right menu and viewing the resulting pop-up window, where you can select the type of module to include on your site when adding a new one to the layout.

Archived Articles. Shows a list of the articles that have been archived, or saved historically.

Articles Categories. Shows a list of the categories that contain articles. This is referred to as a Category List view.

Articles Category. Displays a list of articles from one or more categories. This is referred to as a Category Article view.

Articles – Newsflash. Displays a fixed number of articles from one or more categories by designation.

Articles – Related Articles. Shows a list of articles that "relate" to the current article being displayed.

Banners. Displays ad panels that contain graphics elements that you want to appear in selected module positions called "banner" within the template.

Breadcrumbs. This module displays your location information for the current page. It's helpful for sites with a lot of content in many areas, but it isn't used much on smaller, less complicated sites.

Custom HTML. Allows content to be displayed in module positions that contain custom HTML code, which is the code that creates physical (or module content) layouts.

Feed Display. Can generate RSS feed displays in module positions on the site with many controls on how/where the display is to appear.

Footer. This module appears in the footer position on the site and typically contains copyright and other information, such as how to contact the Website Manager.

Language Switcher. If invoked, changes the display to another language.

Latest News. Displays the latest content published on the site.

Latest Users. Shows which users have logged in to the site recently.

Login. Standard user front-end login module. It's not usually needed on sites that only have one Super User and no other content editors.

Menu. Can be a menu of any type or style and can be located in any module position desired. You can set it to hide or display based on which menu link item you associate with it.

Most Read Content. Shows which site content has been read the most. This is sometimes referred to as the "most popular" content on a site.

Random Image. Displays a random image array and is linked to an image folder that the Media Manager manages.

Search. This is the basic site search module you use to find site content.

Statistics. Shows information about your server installation, along with statistics on the site users, number of articles in your database, and number of Weblinks.

Syndication Feeds. Creates an outbound RSS feed for the article on the page displayed where the module is located.

Weblinks. Displays the Weblinks created in the Weblinks component.

Who's Online. Shows which users are currently logged in to the site.

Wrapper. This allows the display of another Webpage from an external location within the main content area, or a site that is "wrapped" into the Joomla! 1.6 Website page. Many users expect too much from this Wrapper module, and its limitations will be discussed in Chapter 8.

As you can see, there are a number of modules, depending on what you want to present and where on the page. You can add more via the Extensions Manager, depending on what kind of additional content you want to display on the site.

Other than the main (center) content area, everything else on a page is located within, or its position is controlled by, the location designation of the module. Modules, for example, can be assigned the left or the right position. You can also assign them as a footer, a banner, or any-thing else, provided there is a placeholder desig-nated at that location on the page. Remember that Joomla! 1.6 calls many module positions simply "positions" with an assigned number and not by an actual physical location.

You can set modules to show or not show during certain types of events that result in clicking menu link items. For example, if you click a link to an article or a Category Blog layout, different modules can be triggered to appear only upon that link's execution. Likewise, you can set modules to be hidden under the same set of conditions. This feature in Joomla! 1.6 allows some creative horsepower to be added for special page layouts.

This extraordinary feature applies only to link items that are created and held in system-generated menu modules. It does not work for hard-coded links within an article unless there is a menu module inserted into the article. In that case, you can invoke the show/not show.

Anatomy of the Front Page

To better understand how Joomla! 1.6 structures visible content, let's look at the front page and how it is structured with the default installation and templates. Shown in Figure 3-6 is the front page with content areas identified and explained.

Figure 3-6
Default installation front page with content areas and module positions using the Beez2 template.

You may note that only a limited number of modules contain content. When you view the module positions, you will see many more additional positions where you can place modules on the same page. Joomla! sites are typically laid out in this manner, where the main content area holds the articles and the modules place additional content around it. You will see that happen when you view the other parts of the Website, the example pages, and sample sites (Australian Parks and Fruit Shop).

Actually, when you select Example Pages, you will see another menu appear above the This Site menu that opens the About Joomla! menu with the links to the example pages. This is a good example or relationship you can make between modules and, in particular, menu modules.

How to View the Actual Module Positions in Templates

You can view the positions for modules in templates via the Template Manager in a few easy steps. This will give you the exact module positions in any template that might be installed on your site.

Here's how you can view the module positions in a template:

1. Open the Template Manager.

2. Select the Options icon, top-right menu.

3. In the Templates tab, set Preview Module Positions to Enabled.

4. Select Save and Close.

5. In the Template List view, select the Templates tab in the top-left area of the page. Each template now has the word *Preview* under its title.

6. Click the `Beez_20 Preview` link. A new Web browser opens with the Template's front page displayed. The labels in red are the module positions available for the template, whether it is being occupied with a module or not. Note that in the module positions shown, there are individual positions, and there are multiple modules assigned to the same position. This is explained in the later section titled "Stacking Modules."

7. Close the browser window and return to the Template list by selecting the Styles tab at the top left.

8. Note that the gold star in the right column indicates which template is the default, or the one that is assigned to the Home menu link item.

STACKING MODULES

More than one module may occupy the same module position. This is called *stacking*, and it allows efficient use of template space by allowing modules in the same location to be arranged or "ordered" in any manner to control appearance on the page.

Modules and ordering are covered in Chapter 8.

Types of Content Layouts

THE JOOMLA! STRUCTURE ALLOWS Website owners the option of displaying article content in several ways. The default front page, as you have learned, may contain articles that are sourced from different categories if that is how the site's content structure is set up. But the front page is not limited to displaying only articles. There are many options, which are controlled by which menu link item and its assigned format are designated at the default home page layout.

Let's examine the different types of layouts you can create within Joomla!. First, recall that you got a glimpse of these in Chapter 2 when you created the menu link item for an article. The other options were not explained then, so this is a good place to list the types of link items you can create, or more accurately, the types of content you can create to connect with menu link items.

The types of layouts that you can create are selected via the Menu Link Item Manager. This may sound a little strange, but if you recall, after an article is published, unless it is designated as featured, it must have an associated menu link item to show it. But the menu link item isn't limited to being associated with single articles. There are more options, such as what is shown when you open the Menu Manager > Main Menu > Menu Link Item > Select button. The types of content that are possible will be explained in greater detail in Chapter 5, "Content Management Basics."

Changing the Front Page Content Area Layout

Now that you have an idea of the architecture or layout of the front page, let's change the way the front page articles are displayed. Note that the front page of the layout type selection is "Featured Articles," which was previously explained as the designation for articles that are to appear on the front page or appear in categories *and* the front page, based on designation when added to the site.

The next part of the front page layout, in addition to the featured articles, is "how" the articles are displayed. Let's quickly review some terms that apply to the physical layout of the front page:

Leading articles. Indicates the number of articles in the "lead" before the columns begin. This is usually an article display that spans above the columns, but you can configure it to 0, which displays all articles as intro articles in column format.

Intro articles. Number of articles to appear in the columns.

Columns. Indicates the number of columns for the intro articles. If you set it to 0, all articles display the full width of the content area.

Links. Creates links for additional articles within the selection bounds instead of showing the article.

Multi Column Order. Sets the way articles are displayed in the columns.

Category Order. Can be used to set the order of the article categories that are being displayed, which can be articles from several categories being featured at the same time.

Article Order. Determines how the articles are displayed, such as by latest, by author, and by titles. Several options are available.

Date for Ordering. Sets the ordering based on article date information, such as created, modified, or published.

Pagination. If many articles or links are displayed, Pagination can create multiple pages rather than one long page.

Pagination Results. Can show or hide the results of multiple link paginations, which can make the page look less cluttered.

Front Page Can Be Anything You Want

The front page content of your site does not need to be articles. You can display other content and associate it with the Home menu link item or the default for the site, such as a photo gallery.

Figure 3-7
Area of the home (default) menu link item that controls the article layout of the front page.

Changing the Front Page Article Arrangement

To change the front page layout, you will log in as the Super User and follow these steps:

1. Access the Menu Manager.

2. Open the menu that displays the gold star icon, indicating that the home default is in that menu.

3. With that menu open, open the menu link item that has the gold star shown in the right column with the heading of Home.

4. Open the menu link item by clicking on it or selecting the check box and opening it with the Edit icon in the top-right menu. Both methods produce the same result.

5. With the menu link item open, look to the right, and you should see the area of the screen shown in Figure 3-7.

6. Make the changes desired to alter the layout.

7. Save. Remember, Save keeps the page open so you can make further changes. Save & Close takes you back one viewing level.

You can change the actual layout of the front page anytime you want. Remember that the front page layout always takes on the characteristics of the layout specified as the site's home page, or the menu link item that is designated as the default.

Summary

In this chapter, you learned the following:

- ▶ The site's Super User controls all administrative functions and access.
- ▶ The Admin control panel is the starting point for all administrator management activities.
- ▶ The Admin control panel has companion links in the top menu that take you to the same points of access.
- ▶ The drop-down menus take you to the control or admin locations for the back-end.
- ▶ The sample content has drop-downs and special menus created to manage the overall content.
- ▶ Six types of extensions are used in Joomla! 1.6.
- ▶ Components are mini-applications that operate within the Joomla! framework.
- ▶ Modules are content that can be placed into module locations or module positions on a template.
- ▶ Plugins are routines that are associated with triggered events.
- ▶ Libraries are packages of code that provide groups of functions.
- ▶ Templates control the style and layout of the site.
- ▶ You can add languages to sites using language extensions.
- ▶ Content generally comes from four sources: articles, modules, extensions via components, and plugins.
- ▶ Content can be created using the default components.
- ▶ Content can be created using the default modules.
- ▶ You should review the sample content pages to get an idea of what Joomla! can do and how to arrange pages.
- ▶ You control the front page layout by the Home menu link item.
- ▶ You can modify the front page layout to display any type of content desired.
- ▶ If the front page layout is composed of articles, you can easily modify their physical layout.
- ▶ Templates contain a main content area and module positions that allow the placement of content using modules.

Joomla!

Website Content

NOW THAT YOU UNDERSTAND THE FUNDAMENTALS of Joomla! 1.6 Website administration, let's move into content planning. Because of the way Joomla! 1.6 is built, using a core platform and add-ons called *extensions*, you can create all manner of Websites. Extensions take the Joomla! format beyond the basics and shape the nature and content of the site. To describe it another way, the content shapes the form of the Website and the kind of extensions to be installed. Everything hinges on a plan for content, so let's start there.

Determine Your Website Objective

BEFORE DECIDING EVEN THAT Joomla 1.6 is the right Website platform to use, you should determine the objective of the Website. What is the site's purpose? What will the main content be? Who will administer the content?

The purpose of the Website is the most important factor, not how to make it look good. That's why you should follow the fundamental rule of establishing a content plan before a design plan.

If your content will consist of only a few articles with a photograph or two, the basic Website configuration is fine. But if you plan to have an extensive amount of content, such as photo albums instead of just a few photos, or other dynamic content such as informational articles or a blog, the selection of Joomla! extensions to fit the content plan becomes important.

Using that as a foundation and having answers in hand to the fundamental questions, what kind of Website do you plan to build? Here are some classifications of Websites that fit the Joomla! 1.6 profile:

- ▶ Personal or family
- ▶ Photo-sharing
- ▶ Community-building
- ▶ Blog format
- ▶ Informational
- ▶ Small business
- ▶ Large business
- ▶ Large business subsidiary
- ▶ Online business brochure/catalog
- ▶ E-commerce and online store
- ▶ Product showcase
- ▶ Forums
- ▶ Social networking
- ▶ School, church, organization, and club
- ▶ Industry-specific (real estate, hotels, others)

There are many more types of Websites that can be created by combining Joomla! 1.6 and its available extensions, some of which are highly specialized, such as a Website for a real estate business. This type of site would rely heavily on a specialized extension built specifically for managing real estate listings. In essence, the content determines the format and extensions needed.

What's the point? You can use Joomla! 1.6 to create different types of Websites through a combination of the core features and the many available extensions found in the Joomla! Extensions Directory (JED) at Joomla.org.

We'll discuss extensions in greater detail in Chapter 6, "Extension Basics."

Decide on the Content

NOW THAT YOU'VE DETERMINED the type, you need to decide the various parts it will contain. Who will create the content? Who will maintain and keep it current? How often will it be updated? Having a good grasp on content and how it will be managed should also be a primary consideration when building a Joomla! 1.6 Website.

In Joomla! 1.6, content is generally contained in articles that are published in categories and opened for viewing using menu link items. Articles are created in the back-end, by an administrator or an editor who has been granted permission to do so.

Once you've created an article, you need to add an associated menu link item to a menu that connects to the content article. From that point, adding content is a matter of repeating the previous actions and depends on how you would like the content presented for access by site visitors. A menu link item that links to a category content layout of some sort after a few clicks makes the article viewable.

The content management methodology for Joomla! 1.6 occurs through the use of extensions. If you want to have a page that links to other Websites, you *could* do that in an article and create all the links manually, including the page layout. However, the more efficient way is to use the Joomla! 1.6 Weblinks component and streamline the process of categorizing and displaying the links. All you have to do is add the link in the admin part of the component and let Joomla! do the rest. This is an effective use of a default component extension that comes with the platform.

Components are available for photo albums and various content types, both general and specialized. The JED has thousands of extensions you can use to collect and display content or do something on a Website in a somewhat automated process.

Reminder About Extensions!

Make sure the extensions selected for your site are identified as Joomla! 1.6 Native. Joomla! 1.5 extensions will probably not work in 1.6; there may be exceptions, but don't count on it. To ensure extensions work on your site, use only those that have the 1.6 Native designation.

Plan Your Site

BEFORE YOU BEGIN CONSTRUCTION of the site, spend some time making an outline of the intended content. Depending on the type of site, as mentioned earlier, the content will vary. Following are some of the content areas that are essential on a good Website:

- ▶ Something on the opening page of the Website that gets attention
- ▶ A plan for the overall concept of the site before a plan for the detail pages
- ▶ Content relative to the main site's purpose
- ▶ Meaningful pages/articles of relevant subject matter
- ▶ Subject matter that is displayed via specialized extensions
- ▶ Terms and conditions of Website use, if needed
- ▶ Disclaimers, if needed
- ▶ A means of easily navigating around the site
- ▶ A means of getting back to the home page from interior pages
- ▶ Contact information
- ▶ Contact form to send e-mails to you

Excerpts on Website Design from SmashingMagazine.com

"So many of us design too fast. You need to make so many decisions before working on a visual wireframe or pixel-based mockup. If you start designing before understanding the breadth and depth of the content that your website will contain, you'll inevitably have to cram stuff into places that it doesn't fit."

"Building a website is like telling a good story. It starts with a cohesive outline and clear plot. No matter how fantastic your website looks or works, eventually someone will read it. Someone will have to navigate it. Truly great Websites pay attention to content and organization. There's no way to fake that late in the game. Greatness comes from a solid plan."

It's not reasonable to attempt to identify every content element that may appear on a Website. Websites can contain anything and everything, based on the initial objective of the site, the content plan, and the ongoing content that appears as the site matures. If you start out thinking in simple terms about content, you will build a better and more content-rich site than what you imagined. Websites are built in parts, so build your content one area at a time. Before long, the job will be done, and you will be able to "go live" or deploy the site for public viewing. You can also build the most important content first, take the site live, and add to it later in smaller parts.

Define Content Type Formats

JOOMLA! HAS AN ABUNDANCE of horsepower for creating a range of content formats. Within the Joomla@ framework are many possibilities of how to present content to site visitors. Keep these content formats in mind when planning your Website.

Shown in Figure 4-1 is the relationship between menu link items, which associate with content, and the type of content that can be included on the site from the default Joomla! 1.6 installation.

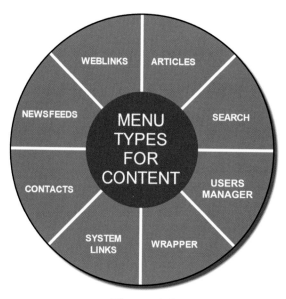

Figure 4-1
Menu link items and relationships to content types for the default installation.

Here are a few things to keep in mind when selecting the type of content to display, which depends on the type of menu link item that is created:

- ▶ **Content Format.** Can be different for each menu link item based on type of content selection.

- ▶ **Content Format per Menu Link Item.** May call up a new template with a completely different layout, look, and colorization scheme than the main site pages.

- ▶ **Modules Associated with Menu Link Items.** May display certain modules in module position based on hide/show attributes selected for the module and its associated menu link item.

- ▶ **Combinations.** A combination of components, modules, and templates that can be configured for all or any part of a Joomla! 1.6 Website.

Here are some content layout options you might select for your site:

- ▶ **Featured Articles.** Default view for the Front Page menu link item designated as Home. Displays articles designated as featured regardless of their actual category assignment, because all articles may be designated as Featured.

- ▶ **List All Categories.** Displays a list of all the categories and subcategories that are published on the site.

- ▶ **Category List.** Displays a list of subcategories in a specific upper-level category.

- ▶ **Category Blog.** Displays a list of articles in a single category. This layout has controls similar to those of the Featured Articles, or the front page if so designated.

- ▶ **List All Contact Categories.** Displays a list of the categories created in the Contact Manager.

- ▶ **List Contacts in a Category.** Displays a list of all the contacts that are assigned to one category.

- ▶ **Single Contact.** Displays an individual contact from among all contacts—perhaps the Website Manager, as an example.

- ▶ **List All News Feed Categories.** Displays a list of all the categories from the Newsfeed component.

- ▶ **List News Feeds in a Category.** Displays a list of the newsfeeds from a single category.

- ▶ **Single News Feed.** Shows one newsfeed from among all configured feeds.

- ▶ **List All Web Link Categories.** Displays a list of all the categories in which there are Weblinks.

- ▶ **List Web Links in a Category.** Displays a list of all Weblinks assigned to a single Weblink category.

- ▶ **Login Form.** If user registration is active, displays a login module. This can be displayed in the content area or in a module position, depending on which type is created.

There are other types of content display formats you can apply, but the preceding ones are the most likely to be used on an average Website. You can configure additional content display layouts with the installation of additional extensions that consist of different components or modules. These may be a shopping cart or an affiliate display of information from Amazon.com, for example. A photo gallery for the front page could be an extension that replaces the front page featured articles layout. You will have a better understanding of the display and content variables as you progress though the other chapters.

Generate Content via Components

COMPONENTS THAT INSTALL with the program can generate content. Components are essentially "mini-applications" that run inside of Joomla!. Components only display in the main content area of the template.

Shown in Figure 4-2 are the components, some of which are described earlier, that are available in the default installation upon which you can build site content.

Figure 4-2
Drop-down menu showing Components installed with the Sample Data option selection during install.

Following are some relevant things you need to know about the components:

Banners. Allows banners to be placed in the Banner module position on the site. Although modules in every sense, the banners are limited to the positions on the template designated to display them.

Contacts. Creates a contact list that displays on the site. You must create a menu link item for this content to display.

Messaging. Allows messaging. It has nothing to do with content and cannot be displayed. This is strictly something that operates on the admin side of the site.

Newsfeeds. Newsfeeds can add much content to a Website by pulling content generated on other sites and displaying it on your site. If your site is devoted to something like tourism in a local area, you can pull feeds from other sites that have the same kind of information. It is free content you can add to your site without updating on your part. The feeds update when the remote site updates the content you are pulling into your site.

Redirect. Not really so much of a content component but a functional one that redirects site visitors to a specific page if the one they are seeking is no longer published. Rather than displaying an error page, the redirect initiates the process of "if pages no longer exist, go here." The redirect is helpful if visitors have bookmarked pages that no longer exist.

Search. This is another non-content component. It lets you identify the items that site visitors have searched for on your site. If you have a lot of searches for a certain content term, you can adjust your content to give users more or specific search results.

Weblinks. Can be collected in categories and display links to other Websites. In this component, the categories are relative only to Weblinks and should not be confused with categories that contain articles. This is great to use if you have a knowledge-based site and want to reference materials relative to the topics located on other sites.

Generate Content via Modules

WHEN PLANNING CONTENT, here are the modules that come with the Joomla! 1.6 program and allow the insertion of content in module positions designed in templates. The list shown in Figure 4-3 is visible by going to Extensions > Modules and then clicking on the New icon in the menu bar.

Because of the complexity of modules and their configuration and management, they are covered in detail in Chapter 8, "Module Basics." Use of most modules is intuitive, but each has its own degree of complexity for displaying content properly.

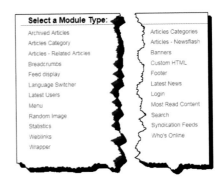

Figure 4-3

Note that there is a similarity between some content display formats and modules, which allows placement of the content in different locations on the template. The relationship is formed using a combination of menu link items and module position locations and their respective assignments.

Add New Content

NOW THAT YOU KNOW which content you can include on a Joomla! 1.6 Website, let's add some.

In Chapter 2, "Fast Track Start," you created a category (My First Category), an article (My First Article), and a menu link item (My Menu Link Item). The link opens the article directly. Within the menu item type scheme of things, you created one called Single Article.

In the following exercises, you create menu link items of different types, and the content displays in the main content area with preset formats for the default installation. After you create the content, it is suggested that you read the resulting Webpage. The text and content contain valuable information about the Joomla! system and the parts of it you are currently working with.

Also, when various menu link item creation screens are open, you should take the time to view the parameters in the drop-downs in the right column area.

The Menu Manager: New Menu Item screen is shown in Figure 4-4. All new menu items are created using this manager screen.

To complete the exercises that follow, log in to the Website Back-End as the Super User. Use the Menu Manager in the Admin control panel to access the main menu, or use the top-left drop-down for Menus > Main Menu, shown in Figure 4-5, to create the menu link item and type of content selection.

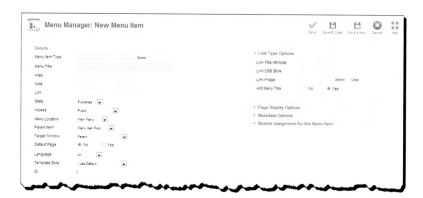

Figure 4-4
This is the screen you will view for the exercises to add content items.
After you click the Select box and make the content type selection, the
right side of the page changes to show configuration parameters
based on the type of content creation you have selected.

Parameters for Content Items

Most content items have parameters that can be configured to further refine the content display or set other conditions about the content as may be desired. In the exercises that follow, the default parameter conditions are being used. For future reference, open the drop-down sections and view the options available for each type of content item.

The parameters are not changed during the exercises. Only the main content item creation steps are covered.

Figure 4-5
Access the Menu Manager via the top-left menu when you're logged in as the Super User.

At the end of each exercise, open a new browser window, view the front-end of the site, execute the link item in the This Site menu, and click the menu link item that was created for that type of content. View the displayed page to get a better understanding of what was created and how the content is being displayed using the default Joomla! 1.6 configuration.

Let's work through the exercises and create different types of content layouts.

EXERCISE 1: ALL CATEGORIES LIST VIEW

Purpose: Creates a view of a list of all the categories on the Website. If a description was created of the categories, it too will be displayed. This allows all categories to have a descriptive text associated with it, and the option to display or not display it.

How to Accomplish It:

1. Open the Menus drop-down, mouse over to the main menu, and select Add New Menu Link Item. The Menu Manager: New Menu Item page will open, as shown in Figure 4-4.

2. Enter this into the Menu Title field: My All Categories List.

3. Click on the Select box above the title. This opens a pop-up box that displays the list of content type options.

4. From the list displayed, in the right column, select List All Categories. The pop-up box closes, and the Menu Manager: New Menu Item page changes, displaying all parameters relative to the type of content item selected.

5. On the right side, under Required Settings, select Root in the drop-down, which shows all categories of content that contain articles. No other parameters should be selected.

6. Click Save & Close.

7. Go to the Website Front Page in a second browser window, and refresh the screen. The new menu link item My All Categories List should be displayed in the This Site menu.

8. Click on the link. The result displays all the categories and their subcategories, along with the site's article information. The text shown is the description of the categories entered when created.

9. If you scroll to the bottom of the page, you see the My First Category link, which is the category that you created in the Chapter 2 exercise.

10. Click on the link. The page opens to the My First Article page you previously created.

11. Click on the My All Categories List menu link item in the This Site menu.

12. Click on any category name link.

13. This displays all the articles that are within that category. The text shown comes from the actual article and can be controlled via the parameters for this content item.

EXERCISE 2: CATEGORY LIST VIEW

Purpose: Create a view of all the subcategories in a single category.

How to Accomplish It:

1. Open the Menus drop-down and select Main Menu > Add New Menu Item. The Menu Manager: New Menu Item page opens, as shown in Figure 4-4.

2. Enter this into the Menu Title field: My Categories List.

3. Click on the Select box. This opens a pop-up box that displays the list of content type options.

4. From the list displayed, in the right column, select Category List. The pop-up box closes, and the Menu Manager: New Menu Item page changes, displaying all parameters relative to the type of content item selected.

5. On the right side, under Required Settings, select Extensions in the drop-down. This shows that category and any subcategories under it. No other parameters should be selected.

6. Click Save & Close. This creates a display of all the subcategories that are assigned to the parent Extensions category.

7. Click on the category named Modules to view the list of subcategories assigned to the next level of category. This is a category within a category within a category (a third-level category). Remember what we discussed about limited user drill-downs being three clicks or fewer.

8. Click on the link named Display Modules and view the resulting list, which is a list of the articles within the Display Modules category.

9. Click on the Custom HTML Module link, which displays the actual article. Note the Prev and Next navigation links that allow navigation to view other articles within the category without going back to the previous viewing level.

Exercise 3: Category Blog View

Purpose: Create a view of all the articles in a single category. Joomla! calls this a Category blog because it shows the text of articles.

How to Accomplish It:

1. Open the Menus drop-down and select Main Menu > Add New Menu Item. The Menu Manager: New Menu Item page opens as shown in Figure 4-4.

2. Enter this into the Menu Title field: My Category Blog.

3. Click on the Select box. This opens a pop-up box that displays the list of content type options.

4. From the list displayed, in the right column, select Category Blog. The pop-up box closes and the Menu Manager: New Menu Item page changes, displaying all parameters relative to the type of content item selected.

5. On the right side, under Required Settings, select Display Modules in the drop-down, which shows only the content in that category. No other parameters should be selected.

6. Click Save & Close. This creates a Category Blog Display of all the articles in the Display Modules category.

7. View the page in a second browser window.

8. Note the similarity in layout of the content compared to the default front page layout for the site. The content presentation structure is controlled the same way because both are blog layouts. If you open the menu link item in the Main Menu Manager and the parameter drop-down in the right column named Category Options, you find the controls for the layout of the page. These controls are the same as the Home page Featured Articles Layout.

Exercise 4: User Registration Form

Purpose: Creates a registration form for users to register on the site. For this function, you can also use a Login module with user registration turned on. Chapter 8 discusses this method.

How to Accomplish It:

1. Open the Menus drop-down, mouse over to Main Menu, and select Add New Menu Item. The Menu Manager: New Menu Item page opens, as shown in Figure 4-4.

2. Enter this into the Menu Title field: My Registration Form.

3. Click on the Select box. This opens a pop-up box that displays the list of content type options.

4. From the list displayed, in the right column, select Registration Form. The pop-up box closes, and the Menu Manager: New Menu Item page changes, displaying all parameters relative to the type of content item selected. Note the content in the right column. Application of the parameters is discussed in Chapter 8 and Chapter 13, "User Management and Access Control."

5. Click Save & Close.

6. View the resulting page by clicking on the My Registration Form link item in the This Site menu.

7. View the resulting page. It is a simple user registration function.

EXERCISE 5: LOGIN FORM

Purpose: If user registration is part of the site, create a Login Form page that opens with a menu link item. You can use a Login module for the same purpose.

How to Accomplish It:

1. Open the Menus drop-down, mouse over to Main Menu, and select Add New Menu Item. The Menu Manager: New Menu Item page opens, as shown in Figure 4-4.

2. Enter this into the Menu Title field: My Login Form.

3. Click on the Select box. This opens a pop-up box that displays the list of content type options.

4. From the list displayed, in the right column, select Login Form. The pop-up box closes and the Menu Manager: New Menu Item page changes, displaying all parameters relative to the type of content item selected. Note the content in the right column. Application of the parameters is discussed in Chapters 8 and 13.

5. Click Save & Close.

6. View the resulting page by clicking on the My Login Form link item in the This Site menu.

7. View the resulting page. It is a simple Username/Password login feature.

EXERCISE 6: CONTACT CATEGORY LIST

Purpose: Displays a list of all the categories and subcategories of contacts on the site.

How to Accomplish It:

1. Open the Menus drop-down, mouse over to Main Menu, and select Add New Menu Item. The Menu Manager: New Menu Item page opens, as shown in Figure 4-4.

2. Enter this into the Menu Title field: My Contact Categories.

3. Click on the Select box. This opens a pop-up box that displays the list of content type options.

4. From the list displayed in the right column, select List All Contact Categories. The pop-up box closes, and the Menu Manager: New Menu Item page changes, displaying all parameters relative to the type of content item selected.

5. In the parameters area, select the Root as the top-level category.

6. Click Save & Close.

7. View the Website in another browser window, and click on the My Contact Categories link in the This Site menu.

8. Click on several of the links to see the resulting page displays of contact information as it has been classified and organized.

Exercise 7: Contact Single Category List

Purpose: Displays a list of contacts in a single contact category.

How to Accomplish It:

1. Open the Menus drop-down, mouse over to Main Menu, and select Add New Menu Item. The Menu Manager: New Menu Item page opens, as shown in Figure 4-4.

2. Enter this into the Menu Title field: My Contact Category.

3. Click on the Select box. This opens a pop-up box that displays the list of content type options.

4. From the list displayed in the right column, select List Contacts in a Category. The pop-up box closes and the Menu Manager: New Menu Item page changes, displaying all parameters relative to the type of content item selected.

5. In the parameters area, select Sample Data-Contact as the top-level category.

6. Click Save & Close.

7. View the Website in another browser window, and click on the My Contact Category link in the This Site menu. Viewed in the browser window, this displays a list of the individual contacts within the top-level category called Sample Data-Contact. Because there are subcategories assigned to this category in the Contact Manager, they are shown also.

8. Click on the Contact Name Here link. It opens the listing information for the individual contact.

9. Open the drop-down panels to view what is in each section. The information in these panels is derived from the information that was entered in the Contacts Manager.

Exercise 8: Single Contact Display

Purpose: Displays all the information for an individual contact that has been entered. It also includes a contact form, links (Twitter, Facebook, and so on), and additional information if included.

How to Accomplish It:

1. Open the Menus drop-down, mouse over to Main Menu, and select Add New Menu Item. The Menu Manager: New Menu Item page opens, as shown in Figure 4-4.

2. Enter this into the Menu Title field: My Single Contact.

3. Click on the Select box. This opens a pop-up box that displays the list of content type options.

4. From the list displayed in the right column, select Single Contact. The pop-up box closes and the Menu Manager: New Menu Item page changes, displaying all parameters relative to the type of content item selected.

5. In the parameters area, click the Change Contact button and select Contact Name Here as the individual contact.

6. Click Save & Close.

7. View the Website in another browser window, and click on the My Single Contact link in the This Site menu. Viewed in the browser window, this displays the contact information for the contact selected.

8. Open the drop-down panels to view what is in each section. The information in these panels is derived from the information that was entered in the Contacts Manager for that individual.

Exercise 9: News Feed Single Category List

Purpose: Displays a list of all News Feed Categories created to gather content from other Websites.

How to Accomplish It:

1. Open the Menus drop-down, mouse over to Main Menu, and select Add New Menu item. The Menu Manager: New Menu Item page opens, as shown in Figure 4-4.

2. Enter this into the Menu Title field: My Feeds Category List.

3. Click on the Select box. This opens a pop-up box that displays the list of content type options.

4. From the list displayed, in the left column, select List News Feeds in a Category. The pop-up box closes and the Menu Manager: New Menu Item page changes, displaying all parameters relative to the type of content item selected.

5. In the Parameters area, select Sample Data-Newsfeeds as the News Feeds category.

6. Click Save & Close. When viewed in the browser window, this page displays a list of all the news feeds that come from the sites selected that provide outbound RSS data feeds for selected content.

Exercise 10: Web Links Category List

Purpose: Shows a list of all the categories of Weblinks into which links to other Websites have been organized.

How to Accomplish It:

1. Open the Menus drop-down, mouse over to Main Menu, and select Add New Menu Item. The Menu Manager: New Menu Item page opens, as shown in Figure 4-4.

2. Enter this into the Menu Title field: My Weblinks Category List.

3. Click on the Select box. This opens a pop-up box that displays the list of content type options.

4. From the list displayed, in the left column, select List All Web Link Categories. The pop-up box closes, and the Menu Manager: New Menu Item page changes, displaying all parameters relative to the type of content item selected.

5. In the parameters area, select Root as the top-level Web Links category.

6. Click Save & Close. When viewed in the browser window, this page displays a list of all the Web Links Categories from the Web Links component.

7. Open any of the category links and view the results. The Links page opens and shows the links that have been created within that category or subcategory.

Exercise 11: Web Links Single Category List

Purpose: Displays individual links to Websites within a single category of Web Links.

How to Accomplish It:

1. Open the Menus drop-down, mouse over to Main Menu, and select Add New Menu Item. The Menu Manager: New Menu Item page opens, as shown in Figure 4-4.

2. Enter this into the Menu Title field: My Weblinks Category.

3. Click on the Select box. This opens a pop-up box that displays the list of content type options.

4. From the list displayed, in the left column, select List Web Links in a Category. The pop-up box closes and the Menu Manager: New Menu Item page changes, displaying all parameters relative to the type of content item selected.

5. In the Parameters area, select Joomla! Specific Links as the category of Web Links.

6. Click Save & Close. When viewed in the browser window, this page displays a list of all the Web Links with the category or subcategory that was selected.

The menu previously called Main Menu should now be called This Site, with the menu link items added. See Figure 4-6.

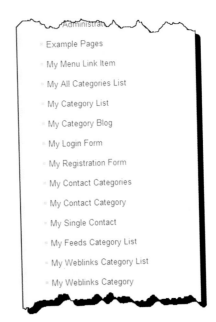

Figure 4-6

After completing these exercises, the menu called "This Site" should have the links that begin with "My" in place as shown.

Get There from Here

As MENTIONED EARLIER, a Website needs a good navigation scheme so you can get around and view the content. Joomla! 1.6 has a tremendously powerful and flexible menu system that is based on modules that are classified as menus. They can be displayed in different ways on the Website.

The Main Menu and the Home Link

Joomla! sites generally have a main menu that contains the Home button. However, there are exceptions, and any menu created can have a menu link item designated to be the default or Home button. This button dictates what is shown on the front page of the Website and the layout. It's something that you determine based on content and the way you want to show it to site visitors. This is an important item, so consider it when planning site content.

For example, you can simply have an article that has been designated to appear on the front page of the site and leave it at that. Or you can set the default link item to be, let's say, a Category Blog layout, which would then display the articles that have been created in a particular category. Anything you create in Joomla! can be the default or the home page. Make it an array of photos generated by a photo gallery component if you like. All manner of front page layouts is possible. It's entirely up to you and what you want on your Website.

Other Menus

By default, Joomla! typically installs only one menu during the installation process, unless you install the sample data, which we strongly suggest you do—initially—so you can visit the Example Pages and Sample Sites areas.

If you install the sample data, the menus that will install are shown in Figure 4-7.

Figure 4-7
Note the gold star indicating which menu contains the menu link item to the default home page layout. Only the main menu is included if you do not install the sample data.

As you can see, the content for the Joomla! 1.6 sample site has been thoroughly planned and well-executed. Use this as a model for building your own Website.

New Menus

You can create a new menu from scratch and give it any name you want. The menu can be vertical and appear on the sides of the site in module positions. Or the menu can be horizontal and appear at the top, middle, or bottom of the site. Different menus can appear at different locations. Multiple menus can appear on any Website. Menus may be set to hide or show based on which menu link items are clicked in other menus.

Look Over the Sample Content

When installing Joomla! 1.6, you should install the sample content and look it over before beginning to add your own content. There is much to be learned by looking at the menus, extensions, modules, and plug-ins in the default content. The content can be removed, deleted, or unpublished at any time, but it's a good idea to install it and tour all the content and functional areas. The chapters that follow reference the default content.

Remove the Sample Content from Your Website

ONCE YOU HAVE PROWLED around the sample content and visited the example pages and sample Website, you will want to remove that content and begin adding your own. Figure 4-8 shows the Trash icon to use when removing article content. Figure 4-9 shows the Delete icon to be used when removing categories.

Read the following sections to learn how to remove the sample articles, categories, and menus from your site.

Figure 4-8
To remove either an article or a category from the site content, use the Trash icon in the top-right menu.

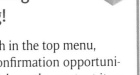

Important Warning About Trashing!

When you select Trash in the top menu, there will not be a confirmation opportunity. Executing Trash deletes the content item completely. Once the content is gone, it is permanently lost! Be careful!

EXERCISE 12: REMOVING ARTICLES

1. Access the Admin control panel.

2. Open the Article Manager.

3. Browse the article list, and find the article to delete.

4. Select the check box to the left of the article name. You can delete multiple articles at the same time. There is no confirmation message before deleting via the Trash icon.

5. Click on the Trash icon in the upper-right menu. The article is now deleted permanently.

EXERCISE 13: REMOVING CATEGORIES

1. Access the Admin control panel.

2. Open the Category Manager.

3. Browse the category list, and find the category to delete.

4. Select the check box to the left of the category name.

5. You can delete multiple categories by selecting multiple check boxes at the same time. Be careful, though, because deleting a category also deletes all the articles that the category contains. Also, there is no confirmation message before deleting via the Trash icon.

6. Click on the Trash icon in the upper-right menu. The category and all the articles it contained are now deleted permanently.

EXERCISE 14: REMOVING MENUS

1. Access the Admin control panel.

2. Open the Menu Manager.

3. Scroll to the menu that you want to delete.

4. Select the menu using the check box next to it.

5. Click on the Delete icon in the top-right menu, as shown in Figure 4-9.

6. A confirmation box appears asking you to confirm your intent to delete the menu.

7. Confirm your intent to delete the menu.

8. The menu, all menu link items, and the menu module in it have now been deleted.

9. Even when the menu and menu link items are deleted, the categories and articles remain available for additional content display. They are not deleted.

Figure 4-9
To remove a menu from the Menu Manager, use the Delete icon link in the top-right menu.

You can't remove or delete components as you can articles, categories, and modules. You must uninstall components from the system, which is similar to deletion but removes a good number of files and database tables that are associated with the component extension.

We will cover removing components and other extensions in Chapter 6.

View Content and Visitor Access

YOU CAN CONFIGURE VISIBILITY of content on a Joomla! 1.6 Website in any number of ways, depending on how you want visitors to view it. Basically, without some sort of user structure and registration system, all content that you have published is visible to anyone who visits the Website.

Joomla! 1.6 has a new and powerful User Management and Access Control System (ACS) that can allow (or prohibit) access to various areas or content sections of the site based on the parameters established for their respective levels of user access. Chapter 13, "User Management and Access Control," is devoted to the topic of user management.

In most installations, there is only one user, the Super User (you!), who has access to everything and is the only user allowed to post content. This is how a personal or small business Website is typically configured. Websites with multiple content managers are rare in the area of small business. Larger businesses usually have a number of content managers, so some method of access control is essential if the Joomla! 1.6 platform is used.

For other Websites, such as for a church or club, there may be several people adding and editing content, but you may want to prevent one group of users from editing the content assigned to another group. You can also restrict the level of tasks and access these same authors have regarding site administration. All this is possible in the Joomla! User Management System that is built into the default installation. User management is covered in Chapter 13.

Register—or Not

WHILE WE'RE ON THE SUBJECT of content planning, a discussion of the Joomla! 1.6 "registration" feature is in order. Joomla! has a built-in registration system whereby site visitors can create a username/password to access your Website contents. There is a built-in validation of the e-mail that requires registered users to confirm their e-mail by clicking on a link in an e-mail your system sends to them. If they do so, their registration is validated, and they can log in and access portions of the Website.

Is registration on your site necessary to begin with? Way too many Joomla! Websites ask for registration for no functional purpose beyond collecting e-mail addresses. There are times when registration is advisable; there are other times to forget all about it.

If your site operates with any of the conditions listed here, by all means, maintain a registration system. However, if you respond with a "No" to each of the elements that follow, forget the registration process altogether and disable the module that controls it.

Here the list of "Yes" items requiring registration:

▶ Will anyone else, such as editors, edit content? (See "Suggestion When Creating Users," which follows.)

▶ Is there more than one administrator or Super User?

▶ Will any content be private, viewable only to approved site visitors?

▶ Will any content be viewable only under certain conditions?

Suggestion When Creating Users

You can create users in the Users Manager yourself and give the username/password to whomever you want without having the Registration module in operation. These people do not physically need to register. You create their account in the Users Manager yourself. The Registration link in the Login Module would not be visible; only the login part would be.

Designate Menus to Specific User Groups

MENUS ARE MODULES and can be designated for viewing by specific users or user groups. They can be set to show, or not, based on what other menu link item was executed. The combinations are endless and depend on what kind of content you have, how you have it organized, and how you want it to be accessed and displayed.

When menus are restricted to user groups, only those authorized users can see the menu that appears and can access the content associated with the menu link items on that menu.

Menus and their link items are basically just a way to get from one part of a Joomla! 1.6 Website to other parts or access other content areas. Make sure you use these properly and they're not too complicated or confusing to site visitors. Give some thought to how *you* would like to navigate around the site, and then put that into action through the menu system. And, of course, remember the three-click rule to good Website navigation.

The complete Joomla! menu system is covered in Chapter 15, "The Joomla! Menu System."

Summary

In this chapter, you learned the following:

- ▶ Websites should start with a definitive plan for the content.
- ▶ You should determine content before you determine design.
- ▶ Joomla! extensions for version 1.6 should be native to Joomla!.
- ▶ Extensions for Joomla! 1.5 will probably not work with 1.6.
- ▶ Planning the site by making an outline helps site development work.
- ▶ Many content display options come with the default installation.
- ▶ You can create content using default components.
- ▶ The Admin area Menu Manager is the starting point for most content that is not an article.
- ▶ Content types are created by making the selection at the menu link item level.
- ▶ There are a number of options to select for content types.
- ▶ The front page of the site can be a layout other than the Featured Articles Category blog.
- ▶ Designation of the Home menu link item defines the front page layout.
- ▶ You can easily remove the sample content after learning the Joomla! system administration.
- ▶ You should delete the articles first when removing the sample content.
- ▶ You should delete the categories after the articles.
- ▶ You should also delete menus other than the main menu.
- ▶ There is *no* confirmation message when deleting articles and categories.
- ▶ There *is* a confirmation message when deleting menus.
- ▶ A user registration system can be used with a registration page and login area.
- ▶ Small Websites usually don't need a user registration/login feature.
- ▶ Larger or business Websites probably *do* need a user registration/login system.
- ▶ You can assign menus and therefore, content, to specific registered user groups.
- ▶ Articles, components, and modules can comprise content areas that can be either publically viewable or restricted to certain types of registered users.

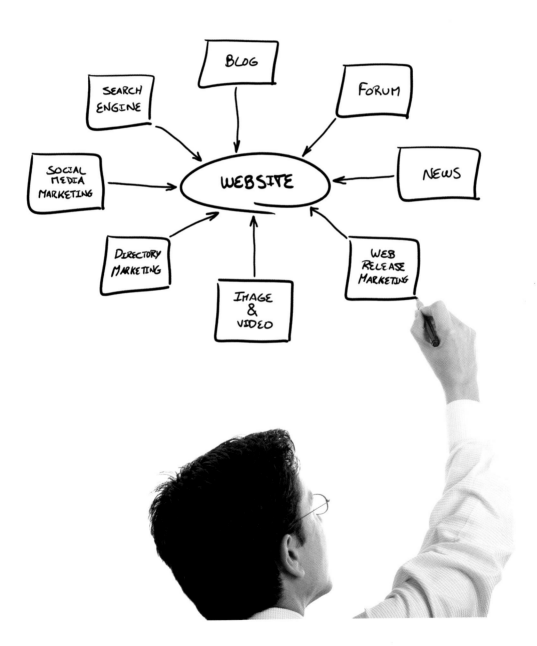

Content

Management Basics

C ONTENT IS THE CORE OF A WEBSITE. Depending on the type of Website, as discussed in the previous chapters, content will be displayed or presented in certain ways. This chapter focuses on developing content that will appear in articles and modules.

Brief Review

BEFORE BEGINNING, LET'S DO a brief review of some information that we covered previously and add to your Joomla! 1.6 knowledge base. Although some of this information may seem redundant, it's essential that you master the management of content in Joomla! so you can build good Websites; information is being repeated to get you to that level.

Articles

The bulk of Website content is contained in articles, so we will review their significant points first:

▶ Articles are created via the Article Manager in the Admin control panel.

▶ Articles display only in the main content area of the site.

▶ Articles can contain text, graphic images, photos, data tables, links to other sites, and more.

▶ Articles may be individually viewed by clicking on menu link items.

▶ Articles in categories may be viewed as lists or blog formats.

▶ Articles can be featured on the front page of the Website.

▶ Articles may be published, unpublished, or archived.

▶ Articles are not visible if their associated menu link item is unpublished.

Modules

▶ Modules are created via the Module Manager in the Admin control panel.

▶ Modules can be of two types:

- The type that contains custom content

- The type that places predetermined content on the page

▶ Modules can be displayed in any location on a template page where there is a module position, or placeholder, for the module.

▶ Modules can contain text, graphic images, photos, data tables, and more.

▶ Modules can be associated with menu link items that control the conditions of display.

▶ Modules can be placed in a published or unpublished state.

▶ Modules are not visible if their associated menu link item is unpublished.

Article Manager

WITHIN THE ARTICLE MANAGER are settings called Options that set the parameters for all articles on the Website. Figure 5-1 shows the Article Manager control menu with the Options icon highlighted.

Figure 5-1
Access Article Manager Options via the top-right menu Options icon.

The Article Manager Options have a considerable number of site-wide parameters that can be configured. The settings are "global," which means that, when changed, they affect every item on the Website for which the parameters are applied. The individual items are shown in Figure 5-2.

Essentially, the Article Manager Options set the parameters across the Website so that they will not need to be set or designated when each article, or content item, is created. This saves a lot of work and allows content creators and editors to work without distraction over how content is displayed. After all, the purpose of a Content Management System (CMS) is to separate the content from the design or, in this case, the content from the "how" of its display.

Figure 5-2
The tabs shown here open to the individual global parameters for the items. Remember to click Save or Save & Close after you have set the parameters. Save keeps the window open; Save & Close returns to the Article Manager page.

Here are the general Global Parameter areas you can set in the Options area:

Articles. Set all parameters that apply to every article that will be created on the site.

Category. Applies to the Articles category from the content types discussed in Chapter 4, "Joomla! Website Content."

Categories. Also apply to the category layouts discussed previously in Chapter 4.

Blog/Featured Layouts. Set the default format for the feature articles front page and the category blog layouts if that menu item type is selected to display content.

List Layouts. Lists are displayed in table formats. These controls set the manner in which the table-formatted information is displayed on the page.

Integration. Sets parameters for outbound newsfeeds from your site at the article level.

Text Filters. Limit text that may be applied within content by contributors/authors.

Permissions. Control how each user group can access, create, edit, or otherwise modify content on the site.

Option Parameters in Detail

LET'S REVIEW EACH OF THE GLOBAL parameters that you can set and discover what each one does at the content item level. You may also want to mouse over the items and read the tool tips.

Articles

Title. Article titles can be hidden or shown automatically.

Linked Titles. Titles may or may not have active links on the site.

Show Intro Text. Intro text is the beginning text of an article that a marker can designate. When the article title or a Read More link is clicked, the intro text shows or doesn't show based on this setting. This setting allows teasers for articles that do not reappear when the article is opened.

Show Category. Shows the category to which the article is assigned. This is good for sites with a lot of text and categories. It's not appropriate on smaller sites with limited content.

Link Category. If a category is linked, this item opens the category and shows the articles within it when you click it.

Show Parent. Shows the parent category if an article is in a subcategory.

Link Parent. Makes the parent category a link to the parent to show the articles therein.

Show Author. Shows the author's name. This is good for large sites, but it looks a bit goofy for sites that have only one person who writes all the articles. This can get repetitious and should be set to Hide.

Link Author. Same deal as for Show Author. This makes the author's name a link that opens a list of all the articles by that author. It's helpful for sites that have a lot of content by many authors.

Show Create Date. Displays the date the article was created. This isn't necessarily the same as the publish date, because an article can be written ahead of time and published.

Show Modify Date. Displays the date the article was modified or edited after publishing.

Show Publish Date. Shows the actual date the article was published.

Show Navigation. Shows Prev, Next icons under the text area, which allows navigation to the next article in sequence in the category.

Show Voting. If invoked, shows readership voting on the content of the article. This invokes the rating system for all articles; it can be shut off at the individual article level.

Show "Read More." If the article text is long, a Read More insert stops the text from showing beyond the point of the marker, and a Read More button is inserted that opens the entire article for viewing.

Show Title with Read More. Shows the article title with the Read More feature.

Read More Limit. Limits the number of title characters to appear in the Read More button.

Show Icons. If Show Icons is selected, the articles show the Email and Print options as icons; otherwise, they're shown as text.

Show Print Icon. Sets the display of the Print icon.

Show Email Icon. Sets the display of the Email icon.

Show Hits. Shows how many times the article has been read or opened.

Show Unauthorised Links. Shows links to all items, even those limited to registered users. Link destinations cannot open/read the content unless the user is registered.

Category

These settings apply to the display of an individual category and its default parameters.

Choose Layout. Sets the default category layout to Blog or List.

Category Title. Shows the category title on the page as a tagged head. You'll read more on that topic in later chapters.

Category Description. If a description has been written for a category, you can display or not with the title category.

Category Image. Each category can have a unique image. This sets the image to display or not.

Subcategory Levels. If a category has subcategories or sub-subcategories (or more!), the value in the box sets the number of "subs" to show.

Empty Categories. If a category does not have an article, only the title displays. Selecting this item hides category titles if they're devoid of articles.

No Articles Message. If Empty Categories is set to Show, this displays a message that there are no articles within it, which eliminates confusion if categories are empty. This happens frequently if articles pass their publishing dates and stop being displayed, which can create empty categories.

Subcategories Descriptions. If subcategories have descriptions, this hides or shows them. This option can be helpful if content is complete and the subcategories need definitions for viewers.

 # Articles in Category. Can be set to limit the number of articles to be shown in a category. If articles exceed the number, automatic navigation links appear to access those articles.

Categories

If a Website has a large collection of categories and content is displayed using categories as the primary display layout, setting the global parameters will save repetitive tasks as content is created.

Top Level Category Description. On a subcategory level, this hides the description of the top-level category, if there is one, for the subcategory display.

Subcategory Levels. Sets the number of subcategories to display. This is useful for content areas that have many embedded categories of related content.

Empty Categories. If categories have no subcategories or articles, this option can be set not to show.

Subcategories Descriptions. If subcategories have descriptions, they can be hidden or shown, depending on your preference.

 # Articles in Category. Sets the number of articles to be shown in the categories.

Blog/Featured Layouts

If you recall, this topic was addressed when setting the Home menu link item for the Category Blog layout for the front page of the site. If other link items are set to Category Blog, you can configure the global parameters or settings to set up each one the same way. This saves a lot of work if the site will contain a considerable number of category blog layouts on a per-category basis.

 # Leading Articles. Sets the number of articles that appear above the column selection.

 # Intro Articles. Sets the number of total articles that will appear after the leading articles and within the column layouts.

 # Columns. Determines how many columns the layout will contain, after the leading articles. If set to 1, the articles appear left to right, one above the other.

 # Links. These are links to articles in the category after the number of intro articles. If there are 10 articles in the category, with 1 leading and 5 intro, the number of links to the remaining articles will equal 5.

Multi Column Order. If set to Down, articles will go down column one, pick up on the top of the next column, and so on. If set to Across, the first article appears in column one, the second in column two, and so on.

Include Subcategories. Deals with display of only articles in the category, or you can include subcategories in the display.

Category Order. Determines how the categories will be displayed in order of content. If Category Manager Order is selected, the order is manually controlled with the up/down arrows in the respective top-level category manager area.

Article Order. These parameters are highly variable in application. This is a default setting that can be overridden at the individual category level if desired.

Date for Ordering. Allows the ordering of the content by published, created, or modified dates.

List Layouts

Whenever lists are selected as a layout format, they adhere to the parameters set in this tab for page appearance. When lists are created, they are set up in a table format with column heads. Setting these parameters controls their initial display.

Display Select. Options to show the number of items to display. This is helpful if the lists are long and you want visitors to view the entire list rather than using the navigation process.

Filter Field. Sets the manner in which the list is initially filtered.

Table Headings. Set table column headings to show or not. If the list is obvious about what it displays, it appears cleaner.

Show Date. Kills the date column in the list.

Date Format. Allows setting the date to US (month day, year) or European format (day month year), along with minutes and seconds if desired.

This field uses PHP code. For example: M D, Y shows the date as December 25, 2011. You can also designate short dates such as Dec 25, 11 using the correct PHP code.

Show Hits in List. If article hits are active, this will show, or not, that number in the list.

Show Author in List. Includes option to show or not show the author in the list.

Pagination. Deals with the way multiple lists are displayed, which allows the lists to be smaller; however, the user must page through them to reach the end.

Pagination Results. Shows which page the viewer is on and how many pages are in the navigation sequence.

Integration

Show Feed Link. Shows or hides a standard RSS feed link for the content.

For Each Feed Item Show. Allows you to limit the content to show in the feed. Less content encourages people to view the entire content via a link.

Text Filters, Permissions

The use of text filters and permissions is covered in Chapter 13, "User Management and Access Control." They are not important parameters to set at this point, but they will play a role later, especially for Websites that have a lot of content and many content contributors. A small or personal Website usually does not need text filters or permissions set to anything other than the default settings.

Overriding the Global Options

Sometimes the preset global options are not desired on single items of content. Each content item has, at the item level, most of the same parameters that can be set at the global level. This allows you to override the global parameter on a one-time basis for the individual content item.

Example: If the global parameter is set to Show Create Date on all articles, but on one particular article you do not want to show that date, you can set the parameter to a different state for that item. The override of the global parameters is set in the drop-down menus on the right side of the individual Article Manager, as shown in Figure 5-3.

Figure 5-3
Article Manager panel with the Article Options override settings open. Select the override value, and click Save & Close. Note all the other parameters that can be selected on a per-article basis, which overrides the options applied globally.

The Content Editor

Joomla! installs the Content Editor, which is visible when creating and editing categories, articles, modules, contacts, and Weblinks. This editor does not typically appear for any other component, or extension, for managing the content. It is similar to a typical text editor you might find on your computer system.

Editors Are Extensions

The editors that are part of the Category, Article, Module, Contact, and Weblinks Manager are identical. The Content Editor is an extension that comes bundled with the Joomla! 1.6 installation. Because it is an extension, you can replace it using any of several high-quality editor extensions available in the Joomla! Extensions Directory (JED). Three editors are worth mentioning as exceptional performers to replace the default editor.

Figures 5-4 and 5-5 show the button bars for the JCK and FCK editors.

JCE Editor. At the time of writing this book, JCE was *not* Joomla! 1.6 Native, but this editor has long been the favorite to add to Joomla! Websites. If you want to explore this editor, visit the JED and search for JCE, or visit the Website link in the JED listing to download the extension.

No JCE Screenshot

No screenshot for the JCE Editor is being shown, because the version for Joomla! 1.6, when released, may be different from the one for Joomla! 1.5. Visit the JCE Website for updates. Make sure the JCE is showing JCE Editor as being 1.6 Native before downloading.

JCK Editor: Joomla! 1.6 Native

Figure 5-4
Shown is the JCK Editor will all four rows of button bars visible above the content editing area.

FCK Editor: Joomla! 1.6 Native

Figure 5-5
The FCK Editor button bars. JCK and FCK perform the same functions, but with different visual layouts.

Installing a New Editor

BECAUSE THE EDITORS DESCRIBED earlier go beyond the default editor in terms of features, controls, functions, and the like, let's install and configure a new one into your administrator back-end. This will replace (technically, disable) the default editor and replace it with a third-party extension.

Regardless of which editor you may choose to install, provided it is a Joomla! 1.6 Native version, it will install the same way. In fact, all extensions that you may install on your Website install in the same sequential manner, as explained next.

This will be your first experience at installing a Joomla! 1.6 extension. Follow the step-by-step instructions in each section that follows to accomplish the installation. Extensions and their installation are covered more thoroughly in Chapter 6, "Extension Basics."

Exercise 1: Downloading the JCK Editor Extension

Follow these steps to download the JCK Editor:

1. Go to the JED at Joomla.org.

2. Search for JCK Editor.

3. Scroll down the list until you find the item shown in Figure 5-6.

> ### 1.6 Native Icon
>
> All Joomla! extensions that are 1.6 Native have the blue icon shown in Figure 5-6, which indicates its compatibility. Some extensions may work with 1.5 and 1.6 but are not likely to be the same file. Therefore, when downloading, make sure the correct version is selected.

Figure 5-6
Always select extensions that are identified as 1.6 Native, as shown for the JCK Editor.

4. Click on the word Editor. A new browser window opens.

5. Click on the Download button. This takes you to the JCK Editor Website.

6. At the top, select Register to create a user account on that site.

7. Log in to the site with the username and password you just created.

8. Select the Downloads > JCK Editor > Download link in the top menu.

9. Select the `plg_jckeditor3.4.5.zip` file to download to your computer. Another screen opens, with the Download button at the bottom of the content area.

10. Execute the download, and note where it installed on your machine.

11. Browse your computer and locate the file to verify its download and location.

This completes the downloading part of the JCK Editor Extension installation.

Exercise 2: Installing the Extension

Follow these steps to install the JCK Editor:

1. Open the Admin control panel, and open the Extensions Manager, as shown in Figure 5-7. When the Extension Manager is open, the Admin panel in Figure 5-8 should appear.

Figure 5-7
The Extension Manager is accessed via the Admin control panel or via the Extensions drop-down menu.

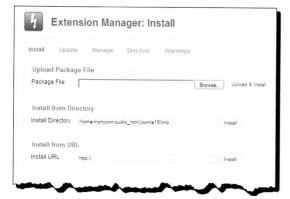

Figure 5-8
All extensions are added to Joomla! 1.6 using the Install manager as shown here.

2. Click on the Browse button, find the file you downloaded on your computer, and click on it, or select Open in your file manager. The filename is `plg_jckeditor3.4.5.zip`. When installing extensions, it is not necessary to "unzip" the files. Joomla! performs the unzipping during the installation process.

The filename should show up in the Package File field if you have selected it.

3. Execute the Upload & Install button to the right of the filename. If the install was successful, you should see the screen shown in Figure 5-9, which is the typical screen that appears after the successful installation of a Joomla! 1.6 extension. In this case, it was a plugin.

Figure 5-9
After a successful installation of an extension, this is the screen that should appear.

The installation process for adding the JCK Editor Extension to the back-end is now completed. Make a note that the extension plugin was automatically enabled upon install. Some extensions do this; others do not. For this extension, look in the Extensions Manager > Plug-In Manager > for Editor – JoomlaCK, and verify the status of the plugin as being enabled.

Always Check the Extension Status

After installing an extension, it's a good idea to check the Extension Manager to ensure the extension has been enabled. If it has not, select the Enable option in the column by clicking on the red circle icon. Extensions may consist of a component, a module, and a plugin.

Exercise 3: Configuring the Editor for Use

Now that the editor is installed, the administrator system must be configured to use the new editor and not the default one that was installed.

Configuring the JCK Editor for use is a two step process that involves invoking it as the default editor and assigning the JCK Editor to a specific user (you). Follow these steps:

1. Open the Admin control panel as the Super User.

2. Open the Global Configuration Manager.

3. Change the Default Editor to the Editor – JoomlaCK, as shown in Figure 5-10.

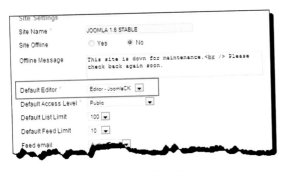

Figure 5-10
This sets the "default editor" selection for the entire site. It can be overridden at the user level.

4. Click Save & Close to shut the window. The JCK Editor has now been designated as the default editor for the entire Website.

5. The Admin control panel opens following the Save & Close action.

6. Open the User Manager in the Admin control panel. The next screen is a list of the site users. There should only be one: the Super User.

7. Click on the Super User name. View the screen in Figure 5-11 and the Basic Settings panel.

Figure 5-11
This panel allows the setting of the default editor for this particular user. In this instance, JoomlaCK is the selected editor.

8. In the Editor drop-down, select the Editor – JoomlaCK option.

9. Click Save & Close.

10. Go to Article Manager > Add New Article.

11. Verify that the new editor replaced the default one.

Let's do a review of what just transpired with respect to changing the default editor to help you install a new editor and install extensions in general.

1. The JCK Editor Extension was downloaded after locating the extension in the JED and linking to the developer's Website, where a user account was created and the plugin file downloaded. This is the usual process, but sometimes you must buy an extension as a product or buy a membership on the site to download the extension(s).

2. The file was download to your computer.

3. The file was located in the download area of your computer.

4. The Extension Manager was used to install the extension.

5. The JCK Editor was designated at the default editor in the site's Global Configuration panel.

6. The JCK Editor was designated as the default editor for the Super User.

7. The plugin was checked to see if it was enabled in the Extensions Manager > Plug-In Manager.

8. The JCK Editor was verified as the editor that appeared in the appropriate manager panels.

Acquiring Extensions

Some extension developers list their extensions in the JED as "noncommercial." This means, according to JED policies, you are not supposed to pay for them as extension programs. You may occasionally be fooled by the noncommercial tagging because the site of the download may require a stiff membership fee or a time-limited fee to access the extension download area. Technically, you are not being charged for the extension *per se.*

Before committing to using an extension, check whether the extension is, in fact, free and noncommercial, or whether you need to pay for it per extension or become a paid member of a Website.

Content via Articles

ARTICLES ARE DESIGNED to contain just that: text that conveys information. This usually consists of paragraphs of text that may be enhanced with additional content such as photos, images, tables, and other relevant content. Articles always appear in the main content area. They cannot be located anywhere else.

Articles can take on a range of different display formats. The most popular of these is the category blog layout, which shows articles from only one category. For a front page layout, all articles designated as featured may appear in that location regardless of their category assignment.

Construction of content in articles, as well as modules containing text, is a mechanical process of typing in or pasting the content, as well as adding photos, images, tables, and lists.

Use of the Article Manager Editor for these functions will be explained later.

Content via Modules

MODULES ARE SIMILAR TO ARTICLES in terms of their content. However, modules can contain more variations to content type than standard articles. In addition, modules can be placed anywhere on a template page where there are module positions.

Modules can contain the same content that is placed into articles with the one advantage of locating it in an area on the Webpage other than the main content area. Modules, of course, can contain generated content, as a login module does, in which case, there is little control over what the actual content of the module contains. Modules can be simple, such as one containing a few lines of text or an ad panel, or complex, such as one containing forms or other advanced content elements.

In the explanation of the use of the Article Manager Editor that follows, keep in mind that the same editor is used for modules, contacts, and Weblinks. All functions apply equally and do the same thing in all the editing modes.

Using the Editor to Create Content

YOU WILL LIKELY NOTICE that the JCK Editor is similar to the content controls found in a word processor, including those that manage layout and appearance, such as bold and italic. Given that most of the controls are similar and intuitive in nature, the following explanations deal more with peculiarities that apply to using the editor in the Joomla! environment.

Tool Tips Show the Way

When you mouse over any of the items in the Editor menu bar, tool tips pop up giving a short term for the function of the button. After you've had a little practice, these buttons will become intuitive, and your proficiencies will increase.

To help you understand the various buttons that make the JCK Editor apply primarily to the Joomla! environment, study the explanations associated with Figure 5-12, which shows the editor with callouts and notations for specific control buttons. The Word theme is used to better display the color of the button bars. You can change to the Kama style in the Plug-In Manager for the editor if you want to. The buttons function the same way, regardless of the display color or style.

Style Sheets Control Visual

With respect to the default content, the template style sheet, which will be covered in Chapter 10, "Template Basics," controls almost everything. When you type in text, regardless of how it looks in the editor, it appears with the attributes assigned to it in the style sheet. For example, text that is typed into the editor automatically takes on the parameters of the HTML style tag called <p>. If you select text in the editor and then select other attributes for it, those "locally assigned" attributes override those from the style sheet.

Figure 5-12
The JCK Editor with the Word design/colorization option selected via the extension's plugin.

Here are the unique aspects that apply to Joomla! 1.6 and which are identified in Figures 5-13 through 5-16. Most of the other buttons and features of the editor replicate the word processor functions you are already familiar with.

Before beginning, take a few minutes to explore the JCK Editor controls. Mouse over all the icons.

Click on some of them to see what pops up, and study those screens. Knowing where to do things in the editor speeds up content creation and display.

Let's look at the special functions available in the JCK Editor.

BUTTON ROW 1

Source. This icon toggles the viewer window between the Editor view and the Code view so that you can view and modify Hypertext Markup Language (HTML) code. HTML does not show as code in the regular Editor view. Bold text in Code view, for example, is enclosed in code like this: <strong>text<strong>. You cannot see this in the Editor view. It is helpful if you need to tweak text content or put in special code.

Paste from Word. This feature is like gold! When you copy text from a Microsoft Word document, it contains some code that you cannot see and don't need. When you paste the text into the editor, that code goes in also. So, copy the text from Word, click the W icon, and then paste the text. All that extraneous code simply goes to "Code Heaven" and is never seen again. Just paste the text into the little window that pops up.

BUTTON ROW 2

This button row contains configuration choices that are found in all word processing and text editing programs for changing the weight, alignment, and other text parameters, as shown in Figure 5-14.

Toggle this to view the HTML code of the article   If text is being pasted from Word, click this to insert into article content

Figure 5-13
JCK Editor, button row one. Two special functions are typically used: the "source" to view source code and the Word input filter that removes extraneous code from the pasted content.

Make text bold, italic, underlined   Create numbered or bulleted lists   Set text indenting

Figure 5-14
JCK Editor, button row two. These are typical text enhancement, format, and positioning controls. This row contains normal word processing functions that can be applied to text when selected.

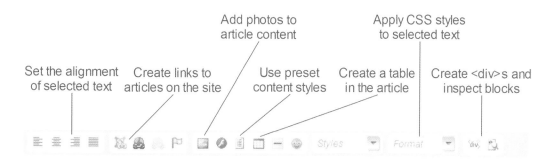

Set the alignment
of selected text

Create links to
articles on the site

Add photos to
article content

Use preset
content styles

Apply CSS styles
to selected text

Create a table
in the article

Create <div>s and
inspect blocks

Figure 5-15
JCK Editor, button row three. Text alignment, photo insertions, styles, tables,
and styles from Cascading Style Sheets (CSS) are applied. The JLink icon
allows in-article links to other articles on the site.

Button Row 3

Paragraph Alignment. As in a word processor, sets the alignment of the selected paragraph, overriding the default alignment in the style sheet.

JLink Properties. Another cool feature in the Editor. JLink allows you to link text within the article to other articles on the Website. Enter the text, select it, click the JLink icon, and type in the first couple of characters of the article you want to link to. Then make the selection for the article you want linked to it. This is great for cross-linking between a series of related articles.

Link. Works like JLink, but doesn't link to internal articles. This feature is primarily to link to other Websites. Enter the URL of the destination site. When you create external links, make sure you open the Target tab and select New Window (_blank) in the drop-down. If you do not select this option, visitors who click the link are taken to the new site in the browser window where your site appears. That's not good. Set the link to open a new browser window so you don't lose your site visitors if they chase links on the other site. As a rule, make external links open a new browser window (target = _blank).

Unlink. You can undo any links created using Link by using the Unlink feature. Select the text that is link highlighted and click the Unlink icon. The link ceases to be connected to the text. It is not recoverable, so once it's unlinked, you must manually relink it. If you have not saved, just close the article or module, and the change will not be affected.

Images. Inserts images into the content.

Content Templates. Another unique feature. Several in-article template formats are available. Open the icon and select the layout you want. After it appears in the article, enter the editing area and make the changes desired. Adding more content templates isn't a task for the faint-of-heart or beginning Website administrators. A good working knowledge of JavaScript and code is required.

Tables. If you need a layout that contains data in a table, click the icon to open the Table Editor to set the table properties.

Styles. Generally not used for content editing. This is only for advanced users, so just ignore that function option for the time being.

Paragraph Format. A useful feature. Let's say you have text with a main heading and then some subheadings between paragraphs. You can select the subheading and quickly assign a CSS-style tag to it.

Create Div Container. In HTML parlance, a <div> is a layer, or a container element. You can loosely consider it a block, but that might be a bit confusing with other terminology, so just call it a <div>. You can enclose content items in <div> codes, and these <div>s may have an associated style sheet attribute. This topic is covered in Chapter 19, "CSS-PHP-HTML Basics," which addresses HTML and CSS coding.

Show Blocks. Essentially, every content element in the text area is part of, or surrounded by, some sort of tagging, be it <p>, <div>, <table>, and the like. By selecting Show Blocks, these areas are identified and displayed. This is extremely helpful if the content consists of stacked <div>s or embedded tables.

BUTTON ROW 4

Font. With text selected, you can choose any of the typical system fonts available for the text, as is accomplished in a word processing editor. Remember that you are limited in the direct fonts you can use. However, there are other methods of using almost any font on a Website. These are discussed in Chapter 17, "Advanced Topics."

Font Size. With the text selected, you can change the size of the font. This selection overrides the default font size in the template style sheet. The number displayed is the font size in screen pixels. Most Webpages use 12 or 14 pixels for the default size. Don't make the fonts too small or too large; the former can be difficult to read, and the latter produces garish-looking pages.

Figure 5-16
JCK Editor, button row four. Selects the font, font size, and colorization
as overrides to the default CSS for body text.

Summary

In this chapter, you learned the following:

► Articles can be displayed in many different content formats.

► You can only display articles and their content formats in the main content area of a template.

► Modules can contain content similar to articles but are limited in the format they display.

► You can place modules containing article-like or module-specific content anywhere on a template page where there are module positions or placeholders.

► You can set global options that predetermine what format the content on the site will be assigned as attributes when it is created.

► You can set global options not only for articles, but for all other content formats.

► Global options have different attributes for different content.

► You can override globally applied options at the individual item level by setting the parameters in the Item Manager.

► The default content editor in the system is an extension that can be replaced by another.

► Extensions are downloaded from the Joomla! Extension Directory or from the developer Websites.

► Some extensions are free (noncommercial), but others require payment per extension or a membership on a Website to download them.

► Extensions are easy to install, as illustrated when you installed the JCK Editor extension.

► You need to select the installed editor extension in the site's global configuration as the default for the site.

► The editor is assigned to a user. You can assign different editors to different users.

► After the global user assignment, the JCK editor is the one used to edit article and module content.

► Special buttons on the editor allow special actions, such as importing content that is copied from Word documents into Joomla! without extra hidden codes.

► When selecting the extension, make sure it has designated Joomla! 1.6 Native compatibility.

Extension Basics

EXTENSIONS ADD HORSEPOWER TO JOOMLA! 1.6. They change Joomla!'s initial 6-cylinder engine to 8 cylinders and add the power needed to create literally any kind of Website from the basic foundation. Extensions do that—they extend the use and function of Joomla! beyond the basics.

Third-party developers usually create extensions. For the most part, these developers create extensions as personal projects and contribute them to the open source community. Other developers create extensions specifically to sell them. Some extensions are excellent and do a great job of adding functionality to Joomla! Websites. Some are not quite as good.

Using Extensions as Needed

JOOMLA! 1.6 EXTENSIONS COME IN six classifications: components, modules, plugins, templates, libraries, and languages. Each type of extension has a specific operating characteristic and method of access in the administrator section of the Website. Most sites probably won't have an application of the library or language templates. The others, however, can be applied for many of the content areas found on a typical site.

Components, by far, are the most available and most used type of extensions. These "mini-applications" are programs within themselves that run inside Joomla!. Components are individual functional features that reside in the back-end and display content in the front-end. As an example, the Contact Us component, which is part of the default, displays information relative to contacting the Website operators. You can install many components into any Joomla! Website. However, multiple instances of components usually cannot be installed, that is: cannot be added two or more times to the same site.

Components available for Joomla! number in the thousands. Because Joomla! 1.6 is relatively new, the number of components that are native to 1.6 might be somewhat limited in 2011. However, be assured that the Joomla! 1.6 compatible extensions will be on a rapid increase as version 1.6 is used more and more.

Modules are extensions that display information on your Website in one manner or another. They are unique because they can display content without being attached or associated to a component. They may also display content in areas of the page other than the main content area, provided there are module positions (placeholders) coded into the template.

How modules work isn't as important as what they do on your Website. Sometimes extensions consist of both a component and a module, and both must be installed and configured for proper content display. Others include a plugin along with the component, or a component and a module.

Modules can be controlled as to their location on the pages of your Website and be selective in when they appear. That feature is explained in great detail in Chapter 8, "Module Basics," which also discusses how to create modules with different suffixes that can take the same two modules and make them look different.

Plugins add extra functionality to the core platform. They are complex extensions that operate in different ways. Plugins generally are triggered into action by events, such as clicking on a menu link item.

Generally, as a Website Super User, you will not do much to plugins other than install them, toggle them on or off, or remove them. Perform the later action, removal, with great care and with certainty that it is the action you want to take.

Templates allow Joomla! administrators to change the look and layout of the Website. The entire visual presentation of the Website is controlled through specific templates you have chosen. In fact, you can use completely different templates in different parts of your Website. You can find instructions for doing that in Chapter 10, "Template Basics."

The default installation contains templates for the front-end and a separate one for the back-end. There are more templates available for the front-end than the back-end from a range of resources. Replacement administrator back-end templates are now starting to be developed and made available via the Joomla! Extensions Directory (JED).

Use Caution!

Uninstall only plugins that you have installed as extensions. The plugins that install with Joomla! breathe life into the program and should not be uninstalled. Doing so may permanently crash the Website. If you didn't install it, don't uninstall or remove it! It's fine to disable a plugin. If doing so affects operation of the site, however, re-enable the plugin immediately.

Libraries are something that site owners and administrators really don't need to be concerned about. They are a new kind of extension in Joomla! 1.6, designed to allow different components and plugins to share the same code libraries. With that said, unless you are a developer creating a Joomla! 1.6 extension, libraries need not be discussed further.

Languages internationalize Joomla! through translation features. Joomla! provides an extensive selection of languages that comes with the core installation. If you recall, it is the first selection you make when installing the program on your server. You were asked which language you wanted to be the default language for the site.

You can add language extensions any time you want to change the site's languages or add language options for site visitors. This is covered in Chapter 16, "Additional Content Topics."

Every language used in Joomla! has a file that contains the words that are displayed (not the actual content, of course). All the default terms that display on the site are contained in a file that you can edit and change terms to suit your own site. Chapter 17, "Advanced Topics," includes a section on this resource.

Using Open Source Extensions

The Joomla! Extensions Directory

divides extensions into two types: noncommercial or free, and commercial, which means some payment is required to obtain or download the extensions files. When searching the Extensions directory, be mindful of this fact. You might find an extension that you think might work for you, but you can't test it without laying out some money. Also, developers should have a full working sample of their extension on their Website, or a demo Website you can view. If they charge for their extensions and do not have a sample you can view, including the administrative side, give serious consideration to bypassing the purchase.

This does not imply that you might be cheated or anything. It simply means you have no way of knowing what you are buying. Good extension developers have a sample that you can access to see what the front-end looks like and how it works. They also give you back-end access so you can see how that side of the extension works. At the very least, they give you screenshots of the extension's manager screens. There is nothing worse than going to a developer's Website, supposedly created in Joomla!, that looks like a train wreck, has an extension demo that doesn't load properly or work at all, and doesn't allow you to access the admin side for. Given all those issues, do you really want to shell out money for it? Probably not!

Good English, Bad English

Joomla! is a global community, and many extension developers are located in foreign countries. Sometimes their grasp of English isn't that good. Their extensions and code may be great, but their description isn't. When you run across one of those extension's descriptions, the language problem will be obvious. Do not let that deter you from downloading a good extension that will do what you want on the Website. Just because the developer can't put the extension's description into fancy verbiage doesn't mean the extensions are not high quality.

You should be able to do the following when evaluating an extension:

- ▶ Read a description of functionality of the extension.
- ▶ See it in action at a demo location.
- ▶ Access the admin side of the extension.
- ▶ Evaluate the way it configures and works.

Noncommercial (Free) Extensions

Within the Joomla! Open Source Matters (OSM) community, extensions that are free and comply with OSM requirements are classified as non-commercial. This means they are free to use and obtain. The JED identifies extensions by their noncommercial or commercial status in the listing. OSM is a not-for-profit that provides organizational, legal, and financial support for the Joomla! Project.

Many sites that give extensions away free require the downloader to register or create an account on their site before allowing access. Go ahead and fill out the registration form and verify the link in the e-mail address when you get the e-mail.

Have a Separate E-mail Account

For consistency and to keep your personal e-mail from vulnerable spamming following registrations, create a separate e-mail account for extension registrations. Indicate the same e-mail address and the same username and password for every site where you register. That way you don't have a collection of usernames and passwords for the accounts. Just use the same for all of them. It's easier to remember them in the long term.

Commercial Extensions

Opposite noncommercial extensions is the pay-to-use type. These are commercial products from which developers expect to earn money and charge accordingly. There are many available, so ensure that the extension is what you want and that it will do what you expect before purchasing.

Sometimes extension developers get the non-commercial designation by using a "free to download" term. It may be free to download, but only after you have purchased a subscription or access to the Website from which the free down-load can be obtained. Don't be disappointed if this happens more than you want for some of the more desirable extensions.

Some of the pay-to-access-download sites offer more than one extension for the subscription price. If so, you get the bonus of downloading all the extensions they offer. Some of these sites have levels of membership that allow downloads of extensions based on the level of membership and the varying amount you paid to subscribe.

Just make sure the extension you "must have" is worth the return in value on the site for what you paid for it.

Using Legacy Mode for Special Extensions

Joomla! 1.5 had a legacy mode you could activate to allow some extensions created for previous versions of Joomla! to operate in version 1.5. Joomla! 1.6 does not have such a feature. In other words, there is no "Joomla! 1.6 Legacy" equivalent to Joomla! 1.5.

Downloading and Installing Extensions

ALMOST EVERY EXTENSION AVAILABLE for Joomla! is listed in the JED. About the only ones that are not listed are templates, which you can find if you search for `Joomla templates` in Google. Many sites offer both free and fee-based templates for Joomla!. They are not singularly listed in a category in the JED. If you search for templates in the JED, you get results, but not thousands of listings for individual templates. None of the items are marked as Joomla! 1.6 Native, which you know is a requirement for use with Joomla! 1.6 installations.

One nice thing about the JED is that the extensions are classified into categories of use or type of application, so searching for them is reduced to looking at those listed in the category. However, the category names in the JED may make finding extensions more of a "treasure hunt" than an absolute extension finder.

If you view the JED page, you will note a list of categories on the left side, then Joomla! 1.6 in the directory below it, as seen in Figure 6-1.

Unfortunately, the Joomla! 1.6 directory will take a while before subcategories are added. For the time being, subscribe to the Really Simple Syndication (RSS) for 1.6 compatible extensions. Also, visit the JED regularly to review the new releases under the category.

Figure 6-1
The JED with a link to show all Joomla! 1.6 Native extensions and an RSS feed link to receive updates when new extensions are added to this category.

Once you've found an extension that will do the job, you need to download it. Do so by saving it into the directory created in Chapter 1, "The Basics: Installing Joomla!," and put it in the `Joomla! Extensions` subdirectory. If your system saves download files into a specific directory by default, simply move it from there to the `Joomla! Extensions` directory when the download is complete. This way you will have all the extensions in the same location on your system. Extensions usually do not have large file sizes, so the downloads go pretty quickly.

Extensions Are Reusable

Although templates may be sold that are specific to a domain, few extensions require the domain to be identified. Therefore, once you download an extension, you can typically use it on multiple Websites. There are exceptions to this, but as a whole, extensions are universal, pretty much in the same manner that other open source programs are: download once, and use it many times.

EXERCISE 1: DOWNLOADING AND INSTALLING AN EXTENSION

There are thousands of extensions you can download. So you fully understand this process, an extension will be downloaded and installed. This is what you did in Chapter 5, "Content Management Basics," when you installed the JCK Editor Component. You download and install all extensions in a similar manner.

In this exercise, a free extension that allows a module to be located anywhere will be downloaded, installed, configured, and applied in an article. This extension allows you to include a module within an article. Normally, modules must occupy a fixed module position on a template. This extension breaks that rule and allows you to place a module anywhere that suits the needs of your site.

In this exercise, let's download the Load Module in Article extension, which is available via the JED, in the Joomla! 1.6 directory. This will be a plugin-type extension.

EXERCISE 2: DOWNLOADING THE EXTENSION

1. Go to www.joomla.org and open the Extensions section in the top Do More menu.

2. Select the Joomla! 1.6 Compatible link in the left menu, as shown in Figure 6-1.

3. In the Joomla! 1.6 category Search box, enter load module into an article, as shown in Figure 6-2, and execute the search.

Figure 6-2
Use the Search feature after the Joomla! 1.6 directory is open.

You should find the online summary of the extension, as shown in Figure 6-3. Most extensions include some sort of brief description of what they do, along with other information. The most important piece of information is the usability icon that indicates 1.6 Native compatibility. Also, the star ratings give you an idea of what other users think about the extension. This extension averaged 4.5 stars out of 5 among 37 users.

1. Click on the article title to open the information page.

2. Click on the Download button, which takes you to the developer's site and the download area.

Figure 6-3
All extensions have a summary page on the JED
with information and links to the download,
demo, and other information about the extension,
including the developer's Website.

3. Scroll down the page and select the plugin
   download file for the Joomla! 1.6 Native
   version. Note the content of the page, which
   contains instructions on how to use the
   plugin.

4. Bookmark the page for future reference.
   Instructions on using the plugin are covered
   in the next section.

5. Save the extension to your computer, noting
   where it copied if you do not have it set up
   to go to a specific directory.

That completes the first phase of extension
installation: acquiring the extension. Next, the
extension will be installed via the Extension
Manager in the admin back-end.

EXERCISE 3: INSTALLING THE PLUGIN EXTENSION

1. Log in to the Admin control panel of your
   Website.

2. In the top menu bar, open Extensions >
   Extension Manager.

3. The Extension Manager opens. This screen
   is used to install *all* Joomla! 1.6 extensions,
   regardless of the type. Recall what was done
   in the previous chapter when you added the
   JCK Editor extension.

4. Click Browse, and drill down until you find
   the Joomla! Extensions directory.

5. Open it.

6. Select the plg_module-in-
   article_v2.0.0_j1.6.zip extension file.

7. Click on Open on the window. The extension
   zip filename then appears in the Extension
   Manager in the Upload Package File text
   area. The path to the extension file also
   appears in the box.

8. Click on Upload & Install to begin the
   process.

   If the install was successful, you see the message Installing plugin was successful.
   This page may be different among extensions
   and contain additional instructions. Before
   proceeding, read the page content and follow
   the instructions.

9. Go to the Extension Manager > Plug-In
   Manager, and find the extension to make
   sure it is enabled. This is a Content extension
   that should have a green circle check in the
   Enabled column.

10. Click on the Content - Load Module in Article
    extension in the left column. The plugin
    admin panel opens, as shown in Figure 6-4.

11. Read the Description section at the bottom.

Figure 6-4
Note the specific instructions in the Description section about how to use the plugin code to make a module appear in an article. When using these types of modules, make sure you enter the implementation-use syntax correctly.

Referring to the drop-down in Figure 6-5 and viewing it on your screen, here are the options that you can select for this plugin. Normally, plugins do not have options. However, the developer saw fit to include module display options in this extension as follows:

Xhtml (wrapped by `divs`). This wraps the module insertion in an HTML `DIVS`, which then allows parameters to be assigned to it in terms of "styles" that modify the visual part of the display.

Rounded (wrapped by multiple `divs`). Automatically adds the necessary `DIVS`, which are required to enclose the module content in a box with rounded corners.

None (raw output). This is the default selection, which means it inserts the module "as is" without particular visual modifications.

In this extension installation, nothing more needs to be done at this stage. The installation is complete. What remains is configuration, publishing, and locating the extension on the Website.

Figure 6-5
These options allow the inserted module to acquire style characteristics that may control the appearance via HTML and CSS.

EXERCISE 4: FINDING A MODULE ID NUMBER

To use this extension, you must find the ID number of the module you want to insert. Each extension, article, menu link item, and so on in Joomla! 1.6 has an ID number, which you can use in one way or another to make specific content selections. In this case, the plugin code requires the ID number of the module to be inserted. Let's find the Feed Display module and its ID number so we can add an external RSS feed to the article.

1. Go to Extensions > Module Manager and open it.

2. Filter the Select Type—by Feed Display. This shows a list of the modules of that type that are active on the site, published or unpublished.

3. Look to the far right, as shown in Figure 6-6, and find the ID number for the Feed Display module.

4. Make a note of the module's ID number.

5. Open the module by clicking on its name, and explore some of the configuration parameters and options that may be selected for the display.

6. Close the Module Manager.

Figure 6-6
Module listed with ID number in the
far-right column.

EXERCISE 5: USING THE EXTENSION

Once an extension is installed, enabled, and configured (if required), the next task is to start using it, which will include some steps to make it work properly on your site. The plugin extension is now ready for use. Follow these steps to add a module to an article.

1. Go to the Article Manager.

2. Filter the list of articles by going to the Select Category—pull-down filter; then click on My First Category, which you created previously.

3. This should show a list with only the My First Article showing.

4. Open the article.

5. After the last line of text, insert the cursor.

6. Type this in exactly as shown:

   {module [30]}

7. Click Save & Close.

Figure 6-7 shows the resulting page output when you go to the site front-end and click on the My Menu Link Item link previously created in the This Site menu. The red boxes and notes have been added.

Figure 6-7
This is the resulting article page with a Feed Display
module added to the article using the
Load Module in Article extension.

Configuring Extensions

ALL EXTENSIONS HAVE SOME TYPE of
configuration that can be applied by setting
parameters or options. Each extension has its
own settings, depending on what the extension
is used for, or what type of content is being controlled or displayed, as explained in this section.

Components

Components do not have a manager like the
modules and plugins have in the back-end. You
access them via the Components, which is a
menu group by itself. Components and their
configuration parameters are controlled in two
ways: via the component itself in the individual
component's manager, and via the menu link
item that "calls" the component to display on
the page.

For example, in the Components menu, look at
the options for the Weblinks component. There
are only two: Links and Categories. (These are
relative to the Weblinks component only.) Only
those content controls are directly available via
the component. The menu link item creation
options create another scenario.

Figure 6-8 shows the available options and
parameters for the same Weblinks component
when accessed via the menu link item creation
process. Explore the drop-downs in the right column, and view the available optional parameters.

They are considerable for this component and
allow a high degree of customization. You can
configure two links to two different Weblink
displays to be completely different, even if both
originate from the same component.

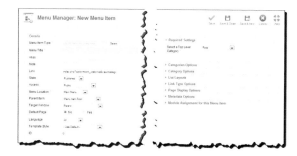

Figure 6-8
The Weblinks component configuration accessed
via the menu link item creation function.

The Weblinks example is not necessarily true
across the board for all components. The Weblinks
component was selected to demonstrate the
possible variations between component controls
and menu link item controls. Many components
have everything within the component manager,
and almost none at the menu link item level.
The way the developers wanted their component
to be controlled or managed determines the
"how" by the end user.

Every component has its own manager and may, or may not, have additional or more configurable parameters via the menu link item creation process. And then, within that process, it may vary between the types of components. The best thing to do after a component is installed is to visit all parts of the component manager to get a feel for what controls are there. Then you can go to the menu link item level, connect it to the component, and explore those options.

In the Module Manager

In many instances, extensions have both a component and a module so that they can be further configured and located in template module positions. Once you have configured the component side, you may need to access the Module Manager for a final step in making it visible. Other modules have extensive customization possibility via their parameters.

As an example, let's look at the standard Joomla! 1.6 Login module, as shown in Figure 6-9.

On the left side, you can set start and finish publishing dates and other configuration parameters, along with the module position assigned. Many modules have similar configurable options. Some have more, based on the function of the module.

Note the Basic Options on the right where text can be added above and below the actual login and password fields, the redirection pages that users can be sent to after login/logout, the display of a greeting, and the user's name.

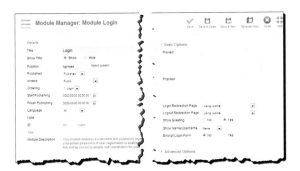

Figure 6-9
The Login Module Manager with the Basic Options that can be configured for it.

In the Plug-In Manager

Most plugins have no configuration parameters beyond enabled or disabled. They are either on or off. But even a simple plugin, like Load Module in Article that was explained previously, can have configuration parameters at the plugin level. In that instance, the "how" of the plugin's appearance was controllable to a degree. If you look at the plugin Content-Load Modules, you will find the same type of options, but more of them. Looking at Button—Readmore, you will find no options that may be set, so this plugin is either enabled or disabled.

The short of it for plugins is that you need to look at them to see if you can control anything, and if so, what that is.

Making Extensions Display

AS EXPLAINED, YOU ACCESS components by creating a menu link item to the component or to the content that the component creates. In Contacts, for example, you can create four different views that are generated by the component. Weblinks and newsfeeds have three different layouts, and so on. Chapter 7, "Component Basics," explains components in greater detail.

Plugins are either enabled or disabled and present their display based on a triggered event. They depend on the event, the trigger, or their default intended use. Plugins are explained in Chapter 9, "Plugin Basics."

Modules, on the other hand, have some unique display choices. You can set them to be associated with an individual menu link item. In other words, the module only shows up on the page when you click a specific menu link item. Chapter 8 covers more about this feature.

Summary

In this chapter, you learned the following:

▶ You can enlarge Joomla! 1.6 through the use of extensions.

▶ Extensions add and expand Website content.

▶ The most used extensions are components, modules, plugins, and templates.

▶ Components are mini-applications that operate within Joomla! 1.6.

▶ Modules are content elements that you can position anywhere on a page.

▶ Plugins create content or cause content to be displayed when events are triggered.

▶ Templates control the look and feel of a Website.

▶ You can add extensions to display content in other languages.

▶ Extensions can be open source (free) or noncommercial.

▶ Extensions can also be commercial and require payment to download or access.

▶ There is no legacy mode for using extensions built for previous Joomla! versions.

▶ You can easily download extensions via the JED.

▶ Extensions are always installed via the Extension Manager.

▶ Some extensions, after installation, require enabling before use.

▶ Some extensions have configurations within the Extension Manager.

▶ Extensions can be configured when the menu link item is created to show or display the item.

▶ Some component extensions have parameters that can be configured within it, which is part of the component's operation as a mini application.

▶ Components, depending on their function, have different display options to select when creating the menu link item.

▶ To hide components, you must disable the link item.

▶ You can disable modules and plugins to prevent them from showing or triggering.

▶ Take care when uninstalling extensions.

▶ Before uninstalling, disable extensions and test the site.

Component Basics

I N PREVIOUS CHAPTERS, COMPONENTS WERE DISCUSSED and
identified as "mini-applications" designed to reside within a Joomla! 1.6
installation to manage the presentation of information. Components
are not stand-alone products that can operate by themselves. They require
the Joomla! 1.6 platform and core functionality to operate. They rarely
need attention once they have been installed and configured, however.
After that, the trick is to use the components in the manner in which the
developers intended them.

Components take up the bulk of Joomla! extensions. Although modules
do a lot of neat stuff, and plugins contribute in their own "triggered" way,
components are the meat and potatoes of a good Joomla! stew. Components
do everything from creating links and directories to creating forms,
allowing users to register for events, and so on. Just surfing the Joomla!
Extensions Directory (JED) is enough to convince anyone that components
are the "rock stars" of Joomla!.

Before we begin, a brief reminder: the only type of extensions you should
consider for use on a Joomla! 1.6 site are those that are 1.6 Native designated.

Default Components

WHEN YOU PERFORMED the installation procedure, Joomla! 1.6 automatically added a group of components. Let's review the components as described in Chapter 4, "Joomla! Website Content," and accessed via the Components drop-down menu bar in the admin back-end, as shown in Figure 7-1.

Figure 7-1
Components drop-down menu in the admin back-end showing the default components and the CKE Editor installed in a previous chapter.

Here is a quick review of the default components and what they do:

Banners. Allows banners to be placed in the module positions on the site. Although they are modules in every sense, banners are limited to the positions on the template designated to display them. In this component, the categories are relative only to banners and should not be confused with categories that contain articles.

Contacts. Creates a contact list that displays on the site. A menu link item must be created for this content to display. In this component, the categories are relative only to contacts and should not be confused with categories that contain articles.

Messaging. Allows messaging. It has nothing to do with content and cannot be displayed. This only operates on the admin side of the site.

Newsfeeds. Newsfeeds can add content to a Website by pulling content generated on other sites and displaying it in module positions on your site. If your site is devoted to something like tourism in a local area, you can pull feeds from other sites that have the same kind of information. It is free content you can add to your site without updating on your part. The feeds update when the remote site updates their content you are pulling into your site. In this component, the categories are relative only to newsfeeds and should not be confused with categories that contain articles.

Redirect. Not so much a content component as a functional one that redirects site visitors to a specific page if the page they are seeking is no longer available. Rather than just throw up an error page, the redirect allows you to initiate a process that "if pages no longer exists, go here" and it takes the visitor to that page. The redirect is helpful if visitors have bookmarked pages that no longer exist.

Search. This is another noncontent component. It lets you identify terms that site visitors have "searched for" on your site. If you have a lot of searches for certain content terms, you can adjust your content to give users more or specific search results.

Weblinks. Can be collected into categories and display links to other Websites. In this component, the categories are relative only to Weblinks and should not be confused with categories that contain articles. Weblinks are great to use if you have a knowledge-based site and want to reference materials located on other sites.

Installing Additional Components

SO FAR, SEVERAL EXTENSIONS have been installed to your Website. The JCK Editor was installed, along with the Load Module in Article plugin. To help you get a good, solid understanding of the component installation process, let's install another. Let's install an extension and then remove it from the site, so you can gain some experience in doing that as well.

Download the Extension

This extension is a component that displays a category with photos, text, and other content. The extension is called Category Block and is downloadable via the `Extensions` directory, as follows:

1. Go to the JED.

2. Filter the extensions by the 1.6 Compatible link in the left menu.

3. Enter `Category Block` in the search box.

4. Execute the search.

5. The extension description shown in Figure 7-2 displays.

Figure 7-2
JED search results for the extension used in this exercise. The actual screen may be slightly different; developers often change their page layouts.

6. Click on the extension's title.

7. The extension details/comments page opens as shown in Figure 7-3.

8. Click on the Demo button if you want to view the developer's demo site.

9. Click on the Download button to access the Download link on the developer's site.

10. The page shown in Figure 7-3 displays.

11. Click on the link button outlined in red in Figure 7-3. You can click on either the file-name or the button.

12. Save the extension to your computer's `Joomla Extensions` folder.

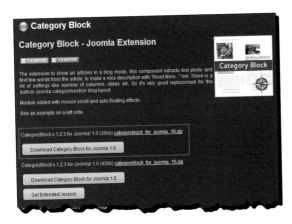

Figure 7-3
Extension download page on the developer's Website for the Category Block component.

Install the Component Extension

After downloading the extension, you must install it:

1. Go to the admin back-end of your site.

2. Go to the top menu: Extensions > Extension Manager.

3. Select Browse, and find the file you down-loaded:
   (`categoryblock_for_joomla_16.zip`).

4. Select Open to add the filename to the form field.

5. Upload and install the extension.

6. The resulting Success Page should be the one as seen in Figure 7-4. This is the page typically displayed after a successful exten-sion install has completed.

Figure 7-4
Message page that is displayed after successfully installing an extension. A similar message is displayed for most extensions. There may be instructions on this page, so please read it before exiting.

The Category Block extension now appears in the Components drop-down menu. If you click on it, you will note that there are no parameters to set or configure. If you recall from previous exercises, this is not important when it comes to extensions. In fact, it's a clue as to where the parameter controls might be. That's correct! The parameters and selections are set via the menu link item created to display the Category Block.

Let's look at them.

1. Go to the Menus drop-down and select Main Menu > Add New Menu Item. The Menu Manager: New Menu Item Manager panel opens.

2. Click the Select button.

3. Find the Category Block content type and note the two options available, as shown in Figure 7-5.

4. Click on the Category Block – Default link.

5. Enter `My Category Block` in the Menu Title field.

6. Click the Save icon in the top-right menu. Clicking Save keeps the page open for further editing. Clicking Save & Close exits the manager page and requires you to open it again to continue.

Figure 7-5
The menu link "type selector" with the component's options shown. The component adds this information to the Select pop-up page for choosing the type of menu link item to create.

At this point, the component extension has been downloaded, installed, and connected to a menu link item for display. The component must now be instructed on what content to display from which category. Let's do that now.

1. Go to the right column and open the Required Settings drop-down.

2. Select the Components category in the drop-down.

3. Click Save.

4. Go to the site's front page and click on the new My Category Block menu link in the left This Site menu.

5. View the content area of the page and note that the articles that appear come from the Components category. Also note that there is a category description and an icon for the category. Finally, note that the layout is somewhat lacking in style and appearance.

6. Go back to the parameters section of the component in the menu link item manager.

7. Open the General pull-down parameter.

8. Change the Number of Columns to 2.

9. Click Save.

10. Go back to the front page and refresh the browser window. Note the layout is now in two narrower columns rather than one wide column.

11. Go back to the menu item manager for the component.

12. Open the Extended drop-down parameter. Note that all the elements that affect the design, layout, and style of the component output display have been restricted For Extended Version Only, which means that to fully use this extension, you must purchase the advanced version.

13. Click Save & Close.

This is as far as this extension can be configured because of the way the developer made it a non-commercial extension, allowed users to install and configure it, and limited the ability to configure the visual aspects of the component.

So, based on that, you decide you don't want to purchase the extension and don't plan on using it on your Website. Okay, let's remove it. Here's how that is done:

1. In the admin back-end, open the Extensions drop-down menu.

2. Select and open the Manage tab, as shown in Figure 7-6.

Figure 7-6
Use the Manage tab to administer the extensions installed on your site.

3. When the Extension Manager: Manage panel opens, note that the upper-right menu has changed and that the Uninstall icon is now present, as shown in Figure 7-7.

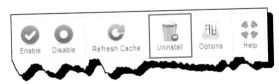

Figure 7-7
The Uninstall icon is used to remove extensions from the Website.

4. Go back to the list of extensions and click the Name column head to sort the list alphabetically. You can also filter the list by extension type in the Select Type drop-down under the top-right menu.

5. In that drop-down, select Component, and the list will only show components.

6. Select the Category Block by checking the box next to the name.

7. With that box, and only that box, checked, execute the Uninstall process by clicking on the icon in the menu bar. If the uninstall was successful, the next page displayed indicates as much.

8. Go back to the front page of the site.

9. Click on the My Category Block menu link item. The display of the page fails. Why? Because the component was uninstalled, no longer exists on the system, and is no longer part of the menu link item.

10. Go to the main menu manager and check the box next to the My Category Block menu link item name and, this time, select the Trash icon in the top-right menu, as seen in Figure 7-8. If the menu link item is not showing, increase the number of items viewable in the Display # selector underneath the columns.

Figure 7-8
The Trash icon, when it appears in the menu bar, is used to simply delete content items. It does not actually uninstall extensions, so use it appropriately.

11. Go back to the front page and refresh the browser window (F5). The menu link item should no longer display in the left menu.

When using Joomla! 1.6 for your Website platform, you will go through the preceding exercise many, many times. Just make sure that when you pay money for extensions, you have already determined you want the extension to display content on the site.

Most components install in the same manner— by going through a download and installation process. After installation, a component must either be configured within itself or via the menu link item that calls the component to display in the main content area. Some components have complex configuration details, such as a forms component that requires you to design a form top to bottom. Each component requires its own level of skill sets from the Website manager to make it work properly.

What Components Should You Add?

THE ANSWER TO THAT QUESTION is simple: only add components that contribute to the display of content on your site. Adding components just for the heck of it isn't the way to manage your site's content. If you don't need a user community, there's no sense in adding the Community Builder extension. If you are not going to sell anything, you don't need the VirtueMart Shopping Cart extension. If you are not going to blog, you don't need to add that extension. Anyway, you get the idea.

On the other hand, if you are going to be managing a Website that sells real estate, by all means, add the extensions that allow you to do that in the best way possible. If you are running a Website for your church or community group, look at the Event and Calendar extension as a way of presenting your content to your fellow members. It's all about the content and the best way to display it.

Overkill! There Oughtta Be a Law

JUST BECAUSE A COMPONENT exists doesn't mean you should install and use it. Way too many Joomla! 1.0 and 1.5 sites have visual clutter because they use too many components that don't add value to the Website. A good example is games. If you have an informational site or a small business site, it is doubtful that site visitors are interested in being side-tracked by some *World of Warfare* game playing. In fact, having such "content stuffers" on your site may be the factor that keeps visitors away after their initial visit.

Because there are so many extensions available under the JED noncommercial provisions, some Website administrations are obsessed with including as many of them as possible on their sites, which end up looking like train wrecks when you arrive on the home page. Be judicious in using extensions by making sure they fit your site's content appropriately.

Another reason not to keep unused extensions is that they are a liability when loading the site. You can improve the time it takes for the Website to load with many extensions by uninstalling those that you're not using. If you install an extension and find that it does not meet your content needs, uninstall it. You can easily reinstall it at a later date should the need to use it arise again.

Your content is what's important, not the gizmos and distractions you can add with too many extensions and components. Use a conservative approach, and make sure that any additions relate to what your site is all about. Perhaps "underkill" might be a good term to keep in mind when you run across components that are neat but not needed to enhance the content of your Website.

Summary

In this chapter, you learned the following:

▶ Components are mini-applications that run within Joomla!.

▶ Components make up the bulk of Joomla! extensions.

▶ You should carefully select extensions to complement your site's content.

▶ You should not install and use extensions just for the heck of it.

▶ Management of individual components is via the Components drop-down menu in the admin back-end.

▶ There is a group of select specialized components that come with the default installation.

▶ You can install components via the admin back-end Extension Manager.

▶ Extensions, including components, are obtainable via the JED.

▶ You must download most extensions directly from developers' Websites.

▶ After a successful installation, a page displays indicating that the extension has been properly installed.

▶ You should read the "success" pages for additional information or instructions on the use of the extension.

▶ To display components on a page, you must create a menu link item that selects the component.

▶ You must configure some components to operate within the component.

▶ Some components have their main configurations accessed when the menu link item is created to invoke their display on the site.

▶ Some components have configuration settings in both internal and menu link item parameter settings.

▶ You micromanage extensions in the Extension Manager using the Manage tab.

▶ You must uninstall extensions to remove them properly from a site.

▶ You should take care when uninstalling any extension to ensure that it does not affect the function of the Website.

▶ It is better to initially unpublish or disable an extension and then test the site to make sure it still functions properly so that you can restore the site if issues arise.

Module Basics

MODULES, IN PREVIOUS CHAPTERS, were defined as content elements that can be placed anywhere on a template page where there are module positions (or targets). Modules can display a wide range of content or make it possible for content to be inserted into the module. For example, if you want to display a collection of YouTube videos, it will require some heavy-duty coding to make it work in a regular module. By using a specialized content module that has been programmed for that purpose, adding videos requires nothing more than identifying them by their URL in the module parameters. Another example is a digital clock. There are modules that display various styles of clocks and, after installation, can be placed in any module position and configured to display the current time in different formats.

There are hundreds of modules in the Joomla! Extension Directory (JED) that are available in noncommercial, commercial, or pay-to-subscribe versions. Remember our previous cautions about Joomla! 1.6 Native requirements.

Obtaining Modules

THE MODULES INCLUDED in the default installation were discussed in Chapter 3, "Default Joomla! Installation." Refer back to that chapter to review the modules and their functions.

This chapter discusses the mechanics of modules and how to use them. It also includes a review of some of the modules and their particular functions. Remember, many of the mechanics of module management apply to all other modules, except for the configuration of their specific function for content display.

Modules are obtained via the JED and from developer Websites, just as all other extensions. Modules, when saved to your computer, usually have a mod_ prefix to their names. Components have a com_ prefix, and plugins have a plg_ prefix. This helps separate them when viewed in an alphabetical list of files.

Explore the JED and look at some of the modules that are available for such things as a Facebook icon display, specialized content, different types of menus, and more, based on what you want to display on your site.

Module Naming Variations

Some modules do not start as mod_ files. They may have another, more common name, but are usually zipped files. Some may say Unzip First in their name, which means that after download you must unzip the file and upload the contents separately— sometimes as several extension files. Just be aware that you may need to perform an additional step or two before you actually install the module extension.

Installing and Positioning Modules

MODULES ARE EXTENSIONS. They install easily using the Install feature in the Extension Manager. You install a module the same way you install a component, which you have already done several times. All extensions install the same way.

However, you can install and configure modules as nonvisible. When a module is disabled, it will not show or appear in a module position on a Website. When you configure a module to display and set the parameters for its content, remember to implement the visibility feature by publishing the module.

In short, you install modules like all other extensions. You must publish them, or set them to publish on a certain date, before they will display.

Modules are placed on a Webpage via the template used for the site or the page. Every template has built-in module positions, or placeholders, that modules are assigned to for display. Some templates only have a few module positions, as shown in Figure 3-6 in Chapter 3, whereas others have a good number of them based on the design and layout the template created, as in Figure 8-1.

Figure 8-1
This template has an abundance of module positions to assign modules to. This image is from the free template (JM-0013) found at the Joomla-Monster.com Website. Templates with many more module positions are available.

Module Position Names

There is no standard for naming module positions, although many template designers collectively adhere to similar names for module positions. Note the module positions in Chapter 3, Figure 3-6, which are generically called position #. Most templates have names for module positions, as in Figure 8-1. Be aware that not all templates will have the same name for module positions used for the same content display. When in doubt, use the module position preview in the template manager to locate a name.

Study the Module Manager

Before we discuss how modules are "stacked" in the same module position, let's take a look at the entire module assignment process. Because modules are the Post-it notes of Joomla!, it is important to have a thorough understanding of the power of modules, how you can use them for content display, how you can use them within pages and templates, and how you can manage them.

SOME BASIC RULES OF MODULE MANAGEMENT

- ▶ Multiple modules may occupy the same module position.

- ▶ You can order modules within individual module positions.

- ▶ Modules may have multiple instances on a site.

- ▶ Similar modules, with different module suffixes, can appear on the same page or on the same site.

- ▶ Modules may appear differently based on their menu link item assignment.

- ▶ Modules may be assigned to display (or not) for any menu link item in any menu.

- ▶ Modules may appear differently on different pages, and in different positions.

- ▶ Modules may appear differently on separate templates assigned to menu link items.

- ▶ The menu assignment for the module controls where it appears.

- ▶ Modules and their display have many variables based on the desired page view.

Stacking Modules

More than one module can be located in the same module position. For example, four or five modules can be assigned to the left module position at the same time. Within that module position assignment, the modules can be stacked in a certain order. Stacked modules can be arranged in whatever order suits the needs of your site. A Login module, as an example, can be located at the top, middle, or bottom of a group of modules in the same module position.

Before we begin the next exercise, study Figure 8-2 to familiarize yourself with the different parts of the Module Manager.

So, the question is, "How do you stack modules?" Here is how it's done using the sample content and the default modules and their positions as examples.

If your site has a lot of active or published modules, it is easier to work with them if you narrow down the displayed list by using the drop-down filters, such as the Select Position filter shown in Figure 8-3. Even though the order of the modules is displayed by position (alphabetically), and then their order within the position, it is easier if you have less to look at when setting the ordering for a single module position. Using the drop-down filters lets you narrow down the modules to view while you're reordering them.

More Uses of Filtering

You can use the filtering drop-downs to select the exact display desired (Type = Menu). If you're viewing articles, they may be filtered by category assignment. When in those sections of the admin back-end, take a few minutes to explore the drop-downs in the manager windows. There are some differences between them on the manager screens.

Sort the List to Narrow the Selections

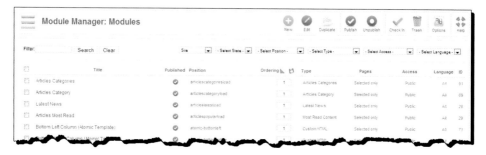

Figure 8-2
The drop-down filtering controls are above the module list column heads.
Pull each one down and view the available options for filtering the list.

Figure 8-3
Filter the module list display by selecting the
module position they are assigned to.

1. Open the Module Manager and filter the
   modules according to the position you want
   to reorder them by using the Select Position
   drop-down selector.

2. For this exercise, select position-7, which is
   the left column on the front-page display.

3. To display the order of the modules within
   position-7, click on the Ordering column
   head.

4. Study the filtered layout and the information
   displayed in Figure 8-4.

When a filtering action is triggered (by clicking
the column head), the up/down arrows display
along with the order number in the adjacent
boxes. Ordering may be changed using either
the arrows or the numerical values in the boxes
as explained in the following two methods.

METHOD 1: ARRANGE USING THE ARROWS

Objective: Move the Login module to the top
position.

1. Click the left blue arrow on the Login Form
   line. It moves up one location order each
   time it is clicked.

2. Click it repeatedly until the module is at the
   top of the list of published modules.

3. Click the Disk icon in the Ordering column
   head.

4. View the front-end of the site and note the
   position of the Login module. It should be at
   the top of the left column.

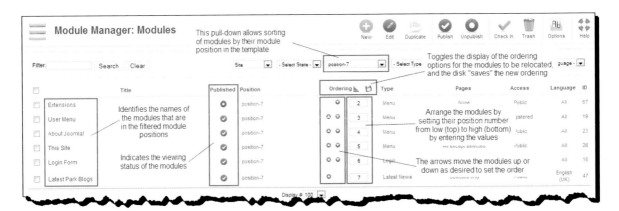

Figure 8-4
With the modules in position-7 filtered and ordering activated, there are two ways to reorder them.
First, you can use the up/down arrows. Second, you can simply change the numbers in the boxes.
The Disk icon saves the order in which the modules were stacked.

Method 2: Arrange by Numbers

Objective: Move the This Site menu module to the top-most position, above the Login module.

1. First, notice that the number values order the modules from low to high. Unpublished modules may be ordered but they do not display.

2. In the box for the This Site menu, enter 1.

3. In the box for the Login Module, enter 2.

4. Click the Disk icon in the Ordering column head. The module now appears at the top of the list.

5. View the front-end of the site and note the position of the This Site menu module. It should be at the top of the left column, above the Login module.

Leave the Login module and the This Site menu module in their new ordered locations in the module positions.

Put Unpublished Modules at the Bottom

If you have modules (or articles, menus, and so on) that are not published, give them high numbers to position them at the bottom of the list. This keeps them out of the way if you are doing a lot of work with the content items. Lock the ordering in place by clicking the Disk icon.

Creating Duplicate Modules

MORE THAN ONE COPY of a module may exist on a site or on a page within the site. This feature is helpful for displaying different content in the same manner. For example, two different RSS newsfeeds from two different sources may show on the same page in a selected module position. This allows a lot of content to be displayed in an orderly manner. Multiple Custom HTML modules may also be displayed on the same page. The same goes for any other type of content, where more than one display is logical.

There are some modules, however, where duplicates would not make sense, such as those for login modules, the latest news, searches, breadcrumbs, and the like. Common sense should prevail regarding "how many of what" appears on a site.

Here is how modules are duplicated and displayed. Refer to Figures 8-5 and 8-6 for this exercise.

1. Filter the module list by choosing Feed display in the Select Type drop-down. The results should be a list of feed display modules.

2. Select the module to be duplicated via the check box next to the name.

3. Click on the Duplicate button in the top menu. The module is duplicated with the same name and with a (#) to indicate which copy it is, as shown in Figure 8-5.

4. Open the module to change its parameters or configuration.

5. Change the title of the module to Feed Display (2). Do not make any other changes to the duplicated feed module.

Figure 8-6
The new, duplicated module assumes the same name as the original, but adds a number, (2) in this case, to the name for identification. If you perform multiple duplications, the numbers increase accordingly.

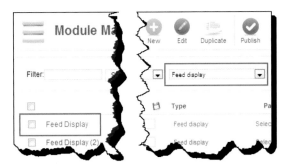

Figure 8-5
The Duplicate icon in the top menu bar is used to copy selected modules.

Applies to Menu Link Items, Categories, and Articles

The same ordering process for modules can also be used to order articles within their respective categories, and in menu link items in menus and categories, which will allow them to be displayed in any order desired. The filtering process via drop-downs, which includes using arrows to change the order or changing the order by the numbers and then locking in the new ordering, is identical.

Using Modules

NOW THAT YOU HAVE a good understanding of extensions, and modules in particular, let's apply some of this "modulizing" to your Website. For the next exercise, let's summarize the steps where we go to the JED to download and install a module extension and instead pick up from the Installing Component Was Successful screen.

Remember, you should use only 1.6 Native extensions. Make sure to download only the 1.6 type.

EXERCISE 1: YOUTUBE GALLERY FOR JOOMLA! 1.6

This is one those extensions you must unzip after downloading it. This is because the developers included both the 1.5 and 1.6 version of the module in the same download. The one for version 1.6 is clearly named.

Let's begin by going to the JED, opening the 1.6 Compatible extension list, searching for `YouTube Gallery`, downloading the extension, and performing the install. Now we can pick up from the Installing Component Was Successful screen. The name of the zipped extension file to install is `youtubegallery_for_joomla_16.zip`.

This is a unique extension in that it not only uses a module to position a YouTube video, it also uses a component to manage galleries you may want to display on your site.

1. Go to Extensions, Module Manager and open it. The new extension should be at the top of the list, unpublished.

2. If it is not at the top, filter the list by Select Type with YouTube Gallery Module to display the list with only that module visible.

3. Open the module and study the parameters. Note the right side in the Basic Options. There is no gallery name in the drop-down.

4. Close the module for the time being.

5. Go to the Components menu, open the YouTube Gallery, and click on New in the top menu, as shown in Figure 8-7.

5. Enter `My First Gallery` into the Gallery Name box.

6. Click Save to create the gallery with that name.

Figure 8-7
The New button icon creates a new gallery. In other managers it will create a new content item within that manager.

The next step in configuring this component/module is to add a list of YouTube videos, so open a new browser window, go to YouTube.com, and enter `joomla 1.6 modules` in the search bar. A list of available videos will display.

7. Open the Joomla! 1.6 Tutorial – Modules video.

8. Underneath the video is the Share button. Click on it.

9. Select the link URL and use Ctrl+C to copy it.

10. Go to the Gallery List in the component and insert the link by using Ctrl+V.

11. Repeat this with several more videos from the list. Your component should now look like the one shown in Figure 8-8. Each URL for a video should be on a separate line in the Gallery List.

12. Although you can change other settings, leave all the default settings for this exercise.

13. Click Save & Close.

Now that we have the gallery configured to display videos, we need to make it display on the page. This can be accomplished by placing a module in a module position and associating the module with a menu link item, or by creating a menu link item to the component and the specific gallery.

Figure 8-8
The videos added in the Gallery List create thumbnails underneath the video player in the page that is opened from the menu link item. There are parameters that may be set to manage how the gallery and video player are sized and appear on the page.

Because this is a training exercise on using modules, let's try the first option and assign the module to a module position and connect it to an existing menu link item.

1. Open the Module Manager.

2. Select the YouTube Gallery module and open it. Note how, on the right side, the gallery created in the component is in the drop-down list. Because there is only one, that is the only one shown. If you had several galleries, they would all be in the drop-down list and you could select any one of them. Duplicates of this module could be created to add other galleries in other locations.

3. Assign the module to position-12 by clicking the Select position button, scrolling down the list in the pop-up window for this module position, and selecting it.

4. Publish the module. The module parameters should appear as in Figure 8-9.

5. In the Menu Assignment selection, go to the Main Menu tab (see Figure 8.10).

6. Make the following selections:

   a. Module Assignment – Only on the pages selected.

   b. Check the My Single Contact check box.

   The menu assignment parameters should appear as in Figure 8-10.

7. Click Save & Close.

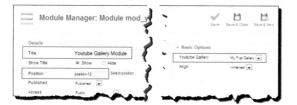

Figure 8-9
Your screen should look like this for the module
title, position, and gallery selected.

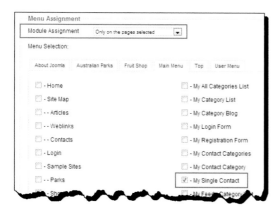

Figure 8-10
By only selecting one menu link item assignment,
the module will only display when this item
is clicked on the This Site menu.

When you view the front page of the site, the YouTube Gallery should now appear when you click the My Single Contact menu link item in the This Site menu. The gallery only appears on this particular page of the site because that is how it was configured in the exercise.

Showing the YouTube Gallery Component

The YouTube Gallery component can be displayed on a page by itself by creating a menu link item to the YouTube Gallery as the menu item type. When clicked, this will open the gallery component with the selected gallery displayed on a blank page, and it is only associated with its own menu link item.

Exercise 2: Latest News, Using the Default Module

This exercise uses the default Latest News modules to display the latest news articles in a module position. The list of article titles appears in the left column, which is module position-7. There are some additional steps in this exercise to help demonstrate some of the other features of module display management.

1. Open the Module Manager under the Extensions menu item and select the New icon.

2. From the pop-up list, select the Latest News type to create.

3. When the module opens, enter My Latest News as the title.

4. Assign the module to position-7.

5. Make sure the module is set to Published.

6. On the right side of Basic Options, choose Joomla! as the category to display the article titles. The screen should now look like Figure 8-11.

Figure 8-11
You must select an article content category to show the latest articles published within it. More than one module may be used to display latest articles from different categories.

The next series of steps involve assigning the module to various menu link items. If the module is not assigned to a menu link item, it will not appear on the pages. The module can be assigned to any number of menu link items. In this part of the exercise, let's assign the module to all of the menu link items in the main menu, except one (My Single Contact). There is no particular reason for not assigning it to My Single Contact, other than as a demonstration of the variables that can be employed in menu link assignments.

7. Go to the Menu Assignment parameters at the bottom of the page.

8. Designate that this module should be displayed Only on the Pages Selected in the drop-down.

9. Select and open the Main Menu tab.

10. If all the check boxes are not checked, use the Toggle Selection button to select all the items displayed. All the check boxes should be checked.

11. Go to the My Single Contact item and uncheck the box.

12. Click Save & Close.

Now if you look at the front page after refreshing it (Shift+Screen Refresh) in the browser location control bar, you should see the module displayed with the listed articles, as shown in Figure 8-12. If another item is clicked in the This Site menu, the Latest News module appears, but selecting My Single Contact actually hides it from view.

Figure 8-12
Each link connects to the respective article within the Joomla! category designated in the Basic Options - Category Parameters module.

As is the case with all modules, more than one instance of the same module may appear on a site or in the same module position. The module may also be styled separately using the Module Suffix feature discussed later in the section "Module Class Suffix."

Exercise 3: Feed Display, Using the Default Module

In this exercise, let's pull in an RSS feed from another Website via the Feed Display module and display it conditionally with a specific menu link item. This means that it will only display when that link item is clicked. Let's display the module, for convenience, in position-12, which is above the main content area. The feed will originate from the Joomla! Website.

1. Open the Module Manager under the Extensions menu item and select the New icon.

2. From the pop-up list, select the Feed Display type to create.

3. When the module opens, enter `My First Feed` as the title.

4. Assign the module to position-12.

5. Make sure the module is set to Published.

6. Click on Save.

    Next, go to the Joomla.org Website and grab an RSS feed from it.

7. Go to the Joomla.org Website and open the JED.

8. Click on the RSS feed icon next to the 1.6 Compatible link in the left, bottom menu.

9. When the screen opens, go to the browser location bar and copy the URL, which is http://feeds.joomla.org/Joomla16Compatible Extensions.

10. Return to the Module Manager and go to the right site.

11. Paste that URL into the Feed URL box.

12. The number of feed items can be designated. Leave it at the default value 3.

13. Click Save & Close.

If you performed the steps properly, the module window should appear as shown in Figure 8-13. The mechanics of the feed are now established and ready to be displayed on the site.

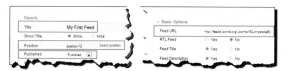

Figure 8-13
After you obtain the URL of the feed content, insert the entire link into the Feed URL box in the Basic Options area.

The next step is to assign the Feed module to one specific menu link item so that it will only appear when that item is selected. In this instance, let's use the My Menu Link Item.

1. With the My First Feed module open, go to the Menu Assignment parameters.

2. Select the Only on the Pages Selected option.

3. Open the Main Menu tab.

4. Make sure all the check boxes are unchecked.

5. Select the My Menu Link Item check box. It should be the only one checked.

6. Click Save.

7. Go to the site's front page and refresh the browser window.

8. You should not see the RSS feed on the page. If you do, review the module settings pertaining to the menu assignment and correct the settings as needed.

9. Click the My Menu Link Item in the left menu.

10. You should see a heading blurb and three articles displayed above My First Article, which the menu link item is connected to from previous exercises. Postion-12 is above the content, so the feed appears above the article.

11. Go back to the module and change the number of feed items from 3 to 1.

12. Click Save.

13. View the results on the site after refreshing your browser window. Only one feed item should now display above My First Article.

14. Go back to the module and select No for both the Feed Title and the Feed Description.

15. Click Save.

16. View the results again, after refreshing your browser window. Only the single article should display above the My First Article content.

17. Click Save & Close.

In the preceding exercises, we looked at many different ways to display content via modules. One of the main features that wasn't mentioned, but implemented during the menu assignment steps, was the ability to hide/show modules by associating or disassociating them with menu link items and assigning them to certain page displays on the site. This might be confusing, so let's clear it up.

The module assignment page displays are actually those pages that associate with the menu link items for the respective menus. If you recall, an article must be assigned to a menu link item to display, which then becomes the "page" shown in the main content area of the pages.

The tabs actually represent the menus in which link items are created that display their associated pages.

So, the hide/show process simply becomes one of associating (or not!) a module with a menu link item, regardless of the item's menu location. When the module is assigned and the link is clicked, the module will appear in the module position to which it was assigned. That's it, plain and simple.

Throw in a little imagination with this great Joomla! 1.6 feature, and you can see how it is possible to create unlimited types of page layouts for an entire site by using a combination of components, articles, and modules and using menu link items to control what displays and where.

Module Class Suffix

WHILE LOOKING AT THE PARAMETER panels for modules, you may have noticed a field called Module Class Suffix and wondered what that was all about. Well, one of the great features of Joomla! 1.6 is that most content items have configurable parameters that can be modified to change looks and appearances down to the individual content item level, otherwise known as "individual styling."

The details of Module Class Suffix implementation are not covered here. They are discussed in Chapter 19, "CSS-PHP-HTML Basics." But let's define Module Class Suffix implementation here and explain how it is used.

The Website template has a style sheet that contains all the code that affects the display of the site. The site's index.php page and the CSS (cascading style sheet) define the structure of the site along with how it looks.

Within the CSS, there are parameters for modules that control how they appear, for example: with or without a border, white or color background, and so on. So, let's say your default setting for modules shows a white background but you want this particular module to have a red background.

You can go to the CSS file and modify the code to add a suffix to the basic module CSS code that specifies the red background. You may call this suffix _redone when you create the new style for the module. Then, in the Module Class Suffix box, you simply enter _redone, and that module, and only that module, will pick up the coding to make the background red.

While it sounds somewhat confusing at this point, when the CSS style sheets are covered in Chapter 19, there is an exercise that will explain how this is all accomplished.

Adding New/More Module Positions to Templates

This is a task for administrators who understand HTML and PHP code. It should not be attempted if you do not have the skills or experience in changing coded PHP files. But, if you want to do it, this subject is covered in Chapter 17, "Advanced Topics."

Summary

In this chapter, you learned the following:

► Modules, like all other extensions, are obtained via the JED or from developer Websites.

► Modules files have mod_ as part of their filename for installation; however, the download may require unzipping before doing the actual install of the module.

► You can only place modules on template pages that have module positions for them.

► A number of rules apply to how, when, where, and by what manner modules may be displayed.

► More than one module may occupy the same module position in a template.

► Within module positions, modules may be ordered to arrange how they appear.

► Modules may be ordered by using control arrows or by numerical values.

► The Module Manager has drop-down filters so you can narrow down the list of modules by type and other factors.

► More than one of the same module may appear on a Website, or duplicates may be displayed that show different content.

► Modules can contain a wide range of content, some manually entered in a manner similar to articles.

► Most modules generate the content they display based on the developer's programming.

► Modules may or may not have configurable parameters within the Module Manager.

► To be displayed, modules must be associated with a menu link item or menu assignment.

► Modules may be assigned to any number of menu link items to display properly.

► Modules may be assigned to a single menu link item for specialized display characteristics.

► Modules may be deleted without uninstalling them.

► A module class suffix may be applied to modules on an individual basis to change the appearance of how it is displayed.

► The appearance of modules can be controlled via the CSS associated with the template being used for the site.

► Modules have global characteristics but may be overridden on the individual module level.

► Templates may be modified to add module positions.

Plugin Basics

PLUGINS OFTEN DON'T GET THE ATTENTION they deserve, because once installed there isn't much that needs to be done to them—other than enabling them. But plugins do serve important functions with regard to how a Joomla! 1.6 site operates and displays content.

What are plugins? If you recall in Chapter 6, "Extension Basics," plugins were defined as complex extensions that operate in many different ways. Plugins generally are triggered into action by events, such as clicking on a menu item.

An example of a plugin that is triggered by an event is the Load Module in Article extension that you installed previously. The plugin displays a designated module content. In this case, it is within an article that has the code used by the plugin. What's the trigger? The trigger is the page load event, which is started by clicking the menu link item that opens or calls up the page.

Plugins are no simpler or more complicated than that. Plugins cause something to happen or content to display when something else is executed to put the plugin into action. Some of the more common uses of plugins are explained in this chapter.

Plugins are not the most exciting Joomla! 1.6 topic to discuss, so this chapter only covers the highlights, along with the application of some of the more common plugins that you may use in the development and management of site content.

Default Plugins

PLUGINS ARE DIVIDED INTO TYPES. These types pertain to their use on the Website and are broken down according to their application. Each type of plugin serves a specific role associated with its name prefix. It is not important for Website administrators to know the detailed programming functions associated with each plugin, just how they can be utilized to enhance content and how content displays. The following is a list of default plugin prefixes:

- ▶ Authentication
- ▶ Button
- ▶ Content
- ▶ Editor
- ▶ Extension
- ▶ Search
- ▶ System
- ▶ User

Relative Importance of Plugins

Although plugins play an important role in the operation and function of the Joomla! 1.6 core platform, the lack of a Plug-In Manager link box in the Admin control panel indicates that there isn't much to configure in a plugin once it's installed and enabled. When you consider the functions of plugins, this omission is understandable.

Obtaining and Installing Plugins

PLUGINS ARE OBTAINED via the Joomla! Extension Directory (JED) and from developer Websites, just as all other extensions. The prefix for plugins is plg_. When viewed in an alphabetical list of files, plugins are usually gathered together.

Plugins install using the Extension Manager. Once installed, plugins should be checked in the Plug-In Manager to make sure they are enabled. This step is often forgotten, and Website administrators can't figure out why the plugin isn't doing what it is supposed to do. If that happens to you, check the status of the plugin in the Plug-In Manager.

Some plugins come bundled with components and are installed at the same time as the component. Some are also bundled with modules. (Remember the Load Module in Article extension from a few chapters back?) But, for the most part, plugins are stand-alone extensions.

Also, if you have an extension that instructs you to unzip first, there may be a component, module, and plugin included in the set of files. Each needs to be installed separately.

The Plug-In Manager is somewhat limited with respect to controls compared to other content managers, as shown in Figure 9-1. This is because plugins usually do not need much attention with respect to their configuration or parameters. It's smart management to limit plugin control to the site Super User.

Figure 9-1
The Plug-In Manager controls are limited to those shown because there isn't a need to perform additional management tasks to plugins.

Use the Check In If You Check Out

When you open content and don't close it properly, it may be checked out, which means another administrator or user cannot open it. Remember to close content items properly, or select the item and check it back in to resolve the issue.

Using Plugins

THERE ARE SEVERAL PLUGINS that you are likely to use on a recurring basis as you learn to insert and display content into the site. The following exercises explore four commonly used plugins that are most likely to be used regularly. These plugins are primarily used in content generated as articles, although you may also find them in the Custom HTML module, because it creates article-like content.

For these exercises, open My First Article in the Article Manager you created earlier.

EXERCISE 1: ADDING A LINK TO AN EXISTING ARTICLE IN AN ARTICLE

The following steps add a link to another article on the site using the Article plugin, as shown in Figure 9-2. This is useful if you want to refer visitors to another article or to other articles related to the one currently on the screen.

1. Insert the cursor one line below the module code.

2. Click on the Article button at the bottom of the content window. A pop-up appears containing a list of all the articles on the site and their location.

3. Select the Beginners article. The name of the article should appear as a blue, active link.

Figure 9-2
The buttons that appear under the content area editing window are plugin-generated and display content when the article is opened.

4. Enter a new line under that link and do the same thing; this time select the Directions article.

5. Click Save & Close.

6. Go to the front page of the site and click the My Menu Link Item, which links to My First Article in My First Category. At the bottom of the article, you should see the two links shown in Figure 9-3. Clicking on the links in the article takes you to their respective pages.

7. To remove the article link, simply highlight the word and delete it.

Figure 9-3
The two link items automatically generated by the plugin.

Exercise 2: Adding Images to Articles

This exercise adds a photo to the article from either the existing images in the Media Manager (Chapter 11, "Image Basics") or from your computer to the site's media folders.

Method 1: Using an Existing Image

Let's insert the Powered by Joomla! 1.6 image from the Media Manager.

1. With the article open, add a line under the previously created article links.

2. Click on the Image button at the bottom of the content window. This opens the media content area as shown in Figure 9-4 and shows all the image files and other folders containing images on the site.

3. Select the Powered By image shown in the red box.

4. Click the Insert button in the top right of the window. The image should appear in the content window.

5. Click Save.

Figure 9-4
Select the image indicated in the Media Manager.

6. View the page on the site's front-end, using the link to open the article. The logo should appear on the page.

Method 2: Uploading an Image

1. With the article open, add a line under the previously inserted image.

2. Click on the Image button at the bottom of the content window. The Media Manager opens in a pop-up window.

3. Near the bottom of the window, click the Browse button, which opens a screen to access the folders on your computer.

4. Select any photo on your computer and click the Start Upload button. Select a small photo because it goes into the page at its actual size. A 250-pixel-wide photo was selected for this method. When the image uploads, it should appear in one of the small windows in the manager.

5. Select the image.

6. Click Insert to add the image to the article.

7. Click Save.

8. View the results on the front page by refreshing your browser window. The result should look similar to Figure 9-5.

Figure 9-5
Screenshot showing article links, an on-site inserted photo, and an external photo that was uploaded and inserted into the page using the Image feature.

141

Exercise 3: Adding a Page Break to Long Articles

You can add long articles; however, viewers lose interest if they have to continually scroll down the page to read one. The Pagebreak feature lets you break up an article into smaller parts and create a navigation box with links to open the next page of the article in sequence.

This exercise uses the Getting Started article. Preview it by using the Getting Started menu link item in the My Latest News module display we created earlier. There are six subheadings in the article that can be broken down into the main article page and five subpages using the Pagebreak feature.

1. Open the Getting Started article via the Article Manager.

2. In the content area, go to the Site and Administrator heading and place your cursor at the beginning of the line.

3. Click the Pagebreak button below the content editing area.

4. In the pop-up window that opens, enter `Site and Administrator` in the Page Title box. Ignore the Alias box.

5. Click the Insert Page Break button. This takes you back to the content screen where a horizontal rule is now above the heading. This is not an ordinary horizontal rule, it is one coded with the page break instructions from the plugin.

6. Repeat this for each of the remaining headings in the article.

7. Click Save.

8. Go to the front-end, click on the link for the article again, and you should see the same results as shown in Figure 9-6, which shows the first paragraph, a box with links to each article page, and a Prev-Next navigation at the bottom. Note that the option to view All pages still exists.

Figure 9-6
After adding multiple page breaks, the system generates a box with navigation links and adds a navigation system under the content.

Exercise 4: Adding a Read-More Break in an Article

This feature works in conjunction with other parts of Joomla! that display content. If you insert a read-more break into an article, just that part of the article before the break displays and the viewer must click the Read More link or button (depending on the template) to read the rest of the article. The text before the break now appears in the reading-more part of the article.

This exercise uses the Joomla! article that appears on the site's front page. Go to the front-end of the site and view the original display of the article.

Let's add a read-more break after the first paragraph.

1. Open the article in the Getting Started Article Manager.

2. Place your cursor between the two paragraphs and insert a new line.

3. With the cursor on the blank line, click the Read More button at the bottom of the content window. Note how a horizontal rule appears at the point of insertion. Link the page break rule above, which is a nonvisible horizontal rule coded to create a break in the content, and insert a button into the article.

4. Click Save.

5. View the front page after refreshing the browser window and the Read More button should appear at the bottom of the article with the name of the article shown.

6. Go back to the article and open the Article Options drop-down. At the bottom, there is a data field for the Read More Text to override the default text with custom text specific for this article.

7. Enter `Special Article about.` (Enter a space after `about` when you enter this text.)

8. Click Save & Close.

9. Refresh the front-end screen again and view the results, which should be the same as in Figure 9-7.

There are other plugins that have configuration controls and that perform special functions; there is rarely a need to modify them. When we discuss user management, in Chapter 13, "User Management and Access Control," we will return to plugins and use one in relation to the user profile listings.

Figure 9-7
The article with the read-more added using custom versus default wordage for the button.

Plugins react to something else that is going on in Joomla! 1.6, which "triggers" them into action, so keep that in mind. Plugins are rarely visible elements of themselves; they are always used in association with, or in relation to, some other content, such as articles, components, and the like.

Read More: Important to Know

The Read More plugin inserts a break into articles to create a "display the text above only" situation. However, the Read More button link only appears in articles assigned to a category blog style layout. It does not work for single articles. You cannot create an article that is opened directly by a menu link item that has a Read More link. The Pagebreak plugin function is used for that display. The button also inserts a logical content break point that other displays use to limit what text is displayed directly from the article, such as the *Articles-Articles Category* or *Articles-Newsflash* modules, where the option is available in the Display Options. The Read More break must be physically inserted into the articles to be implemented in the parameter options.

Summary

In this chapter, you learned the following:

- ▶ Plugins are extensions triggered into action by some other event.
- ▶ Plugins are obtained via the JED or developer Websites.
- ▶ Plugins are installed the same way as all other extensions.
- ▶ Plugin files have the `plg_` prefix.
- ▶ Plugins are managed via the Extensions > Plug-In Manager section of the back-end.
- ▶ To operate, plugins must be enabled in the Plug-In Manager.
- ▶ Plugins typically do not have configurations settings, although some do require set parameters before they can function. This varies between plugins and their application.
- ▶ Plugins may either come with or be installed with components and modules.
- ▶ The Article plugin lets you place links within an article to other articles on the same site.
- ▶ The Image plugin lets you insert photos into articles directly from the Media Manager, or via an upload procedure.
- ▶ The Pagebreak plugin lets you insert breaks into long articles, create a subdirectory of the article parts, and add page navigation to the article.
- ▶ The index created by the Pagebreak plugin lets you name the sections of the article.
- ▶ The Read More plugin breaks an article at a certain point and inserts a button that must be clicked to view the remainder of the article.
- ▶ The read-more leading words may be changed in the parameters when inserting the marker.
- ▶ Read-more breaks only work with a category blog style layout and other special layouts used to display content in a blog style.

Template Basics

S O FAR, THE FOCUS OF THIS BOOK HAS BEEN ON the back-end and administration of the site and its content. Let's refer to those processes as the "mechanical part" of managing the Website. Now let's switch gears and address some of the visual aspects of a Joomla! 1.6 Website, beginning with templates. Templates control how the site looks in the browser window.

Templates bring to life all the other tools we discussed previously, such as the layout options, components, modules, and plugins, by managing how they are displayed through page layouts, color, graphics, look, feel, appearance, and anything else that contributes to the "visual part" of the Website.

Joomla! is a Content Management System (CMS), which is just a short way of describing a platform where the mechanical and content management is separated from the visual, as illustrated in Figure 10-1. A CMS typically allows editorial types to enter content changes without dealing with the design issues involved. Content is added, and it appears just the way it was entered. It's the site's Super User who ties it all together.

A CMS also helps implement visual standards on a site. Can you imagine five content contributors all configuring their own style and layouts? The site would be a visual train wreck. But, by creating templates that can be applied to five different content layouts, different visual standards can be established.

For a business-type site, for example, sales and marketing could have their own page, with its own look and feel, while the corporate site could have its own design with a more "techy-looking" page. That's the idea behind templates. Joomla! 1.6 offers the means and methods for implementing templates in many different situations.

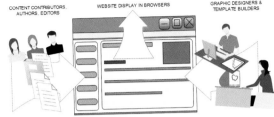

CONTENT MANAGEMENT SYSTEM

Figure 10-1
In a CMS, the content of the site is separated from the "look and feel" of the site by using global and content-specific templates.

Template Types

TEMPLATE DESIGNERS ALWAYS try to create the best combination of design, layout options, colors, and more into their products to sell them. There are several top-notch template companies that produce templates for Joomla! 1.6.

All templates are pretty much the same in what they do. The differences are in how they manage the content display. Here are some things to consider when selecting templates, especially commercial types. Some of them can be expensive, so you want to make sure you don't waste money buying a template that doesn't fit your site's content goals and objectives.

▶ Is the template a fixed-width, fluid-width, or combination-width layout?

▶ Is the template sufficient for the Website layout?

▶ Is the template too complicated for the Website, or can you scale it down?

▶ Does the template have preset selectable color options?

▶ Are there collapsible module positions if no modules are assigned?

▶ Can the template assign presets to individual pages (that is, link 1 = red page theme, link 2 = blue, and so on)?

▶ Does the template have special modules and plugins that install with it?

▶ Is the template specialized for ecommerce, general content, blogging, or some other format?

▶ Are template overrides available?

The default installation with the sample data also installed the templates used on the site. The installed templates are listed in Extensions > Template Manager and indicate Beez2-Default as the front-end template, Bluestork-Default as the back-end template, a variation of Beez2 used for the Parks pages, and another Beez5 template used for the Fruit Shop pages. The Atomic template is used on a couple of demonstration pages.

Obtaining Templates

IT'S A JUNGLE OUT THERE! Joomla! templates are everywhere. Are Joomla! 1.6 Native templates available? Yes, they are. Search Google for Joomla! 1.6 templates, and you could spend days looking at them. Let's find a template to download and install.

EXERCISE 1: OBTAINING TEMPLATES FROM ONLINE RESOURCES

1. Go to Google.com and search for free Joomla 1.6 templates.

2. Select the joomlathemes.com link from the search results. You might have to scroll down for it.

3. Scroll down the page on that site to see a lot of different template images.

4. Click on the Read More button for the Hotel theme Website template.

5. When that page opens, scroll down to an image of the module positions used on the site.

6. Look at the live demo, if you like.

7. Download the jt005_j16.zip template file.

Installing Templates

At the risk of repeating ourselves, templates are extensions. Extensions all install the same way via the Extensions Manager: Install screen by browsing your system for the appropriate file and click the Upload & Install button.

After you install the jt005-j16 template, go to Extensions > Template Manager to verify that the template has, in fact, been installed. That's all that you need to do for the moment.

Even though you are not a hotel or a business site, the same installation process applies to all templates used in Joomla!. We are using this example because it visually contrasts with the default templates.

After installation, anything else done with a template is done via the Template Manager, which can be accessed from the Admin control panel or via Extensions drop-down menu > Template Manager.

Exercise 2: Assigning Templates to Menu Link Items

Let's assign a separate template to a menu link item.

1. Open the Template Manager.

2. Find the jt005_j16-Default template you just installed.

3. Open the template file by clicking on the template name in the Style column or by clicking the box next to the name and selecting Edit from the top-right menu. This opens the template information and menu assignment page.

4. Check the box next to the My Category Blog link under the Main Menu heading.

5. Click Save.

6. Go to the site's front page and refresh the browser window. The menu link item has been reassigned, and the change will not go into effect until the browser is refreshed.

7. Click on the My Category Blog menu link item in the left menu. The displayed page should be a blog listing using the newly installed and assigned template to display the content. Note that the menus are missing on the left site. This is explained in the next section, along with how to fix that problem.

Module Positions

IF YOU RECALL, the module positions on the left side in the default templates were identified as position-7 and position-5. In an earlier exercise, we stacked modules in the position-7 module position. The new template, if you look at the module positions after completing the following steps, will have differently named positions. Let's check that out.

EXERCISE 3: LOCATING MODULE POSITIONS IN TEMPLATES

1. Open the Template Manager.

2. Click on the Templates tab to open a table view of the installed templates.

3. Scroll down to jt005-j16 Details and click on the preview link. Note that there is no position-7 in that template, but the module position is called left on that side, which is a logical name considering the site layout. Also note that there is a right location. This means that modules assigned to position-7 will not display, because there is no location for them to do so in this template.

4. Close the Template Manager.

Now that we identified the module positions in the new template, let's configure the Main Menu to display on the left module location rather than position-7, as it was in the site default template.

To do this, we create a duplicate of the Main Menu module and assign it to the left module position of the new template. Let's do that now.

EXERCISE 4: CREATING DUPLICATE MODULES

1. Open the Module Manager.

2. Filter the list of modules by type = Menu.

3. Open the Main Menu.

4. In the top-right menu, select Save as Copy. A copy is made to preserve the original module for display on the default Beez2 template. The new module should display on the screen, provided that the module has been set to the "published" state.

5. Change the name by adding - JT after Main Menu in the Title box.

6. Click Save.

7. Open the Select Position option box.

8. Scroll down until you find left in the left column. Note which templates have the left module position.

9. Select left.

10. Save.

11. Go to Menu Assignment > Module Assignment and select Only on the Pages Selected, which narrows the display conditions.

12. In the Main Menu tab, select the My Category Blog menu link item. See Figure 10-2 for which options to select.

13. Click Save.

14. Go to the front-end home page and refresh the browser.

15. Click on the My Category Blog link and the page should appear as in Figure 10-3.

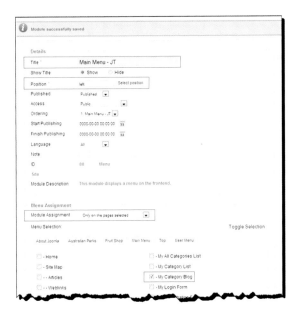

Figure 10-2
Settings to assign a module to a separate template and a specific menu link item. The menu name can also be changed in this step to identify the template.

Multiple Module Position Assignment—Nope!

You cannot assign a single module to multiple module positions. However, templates may have module positions with the same name, in which case a module assigned to the `left` module position would appear in the same module position on other templates. Keep this in mind when switching templates within a site and keeping the display. It may be a good practice to have similar module position naming conventions employed in the templates being used, but this may not be under your control, so make position assignments on a per-template basis.

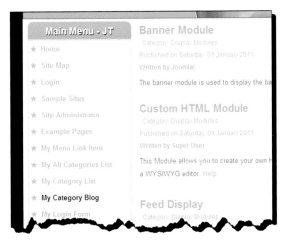

Figure 10-3
The resulting menu module is displayed in the left module position for the new template, which is only assigned to the My Category Blog menu link item.

To help understand this process better, let's take a quick review:

- ► A new template was downloaded and installed.

- ► The module positions in the new template were identified.

- ► A duplicate copy of the Main Menu module was created.

- ► This duplicate menu module was only assigned to the left module position of the new template.

- ► The menu was assigned to a limited number of pages.

- ► The menu was assigned to a single link item (selected page) in the main menu.

- ► The new template only displays when the single menu link item is clicked.

The Default Home Page

As you may recall, you can assign any type of layout to the Home Menu Link Item and call it anything you want (Home is the preferred name), and the default template is automatically assigned to it.

In the Template Manager, templates can be assigned to just about anything, except there may be only one default template assignment. Absent the use or assignment of any other template, all the pages on the site assume the style, look, and feel of the default template. Figure 10-4 shows the Template Manager and the default template identification.

Figure 10-4
The gold star indicates the default template assigned to both the site front-end and the administrator back-end.

When using a single template, the only layout variations in the pages, are the assignments of the modules and their content to the menu link items, which will alter the content of the page, but not necessarily the visual appearance. Adding menu link items that display the content of components does the same thing—it changes the content but does not necessarily change how the site looks.

So, bottom line, when only using one template (the default), the site looks the same from page to page with the only variations being mechanical with respect to which components and modules are shown with which menu link items. The site's banner, footer, background, and other colorizations stay pretty much the same (absent the use of suffixes, as discussed in Chapter 8, "Module Basics").

Templates Assigned to Other Content Pages

In an earlier exercise, a different template was assigned to a menu link item, which resulted in a completely different look for the page that was called up by that link. With this feature, Websites can be designed with many different looks for different types of pages, for example, a really artistic opening page (sometimes called a splash page) for the site without a lot of side-positioned content. This would be the default template design and configuration.

From there, each menu link item can lead to a different page, with more relevant content and a different template. You don't have to use multiple templates on a site—most sites don't. However, multiple template use is becoming more and more popular and different company departments want different looks for their content. Joomla! 1.6 can do this, and it's a good idea to master the technique.

Modifying Templates

FIRST, UNLESS YOU ARE SKILLED in HTML and CSS coding and understand how it all works, modifying templates isn't something you should do beyond arranging and positioning the modules in different locations on the pages. Templates modified by unskilled coders can completely destroy a Website display.

Second, if you are going to modify the template, make sure you make a back-up copy of the entire Website. Backing up a Joomla! 1.6 Website is covered in Chapter 22, "Site Security and Backups."

So, let's assume you are somewhat skilled in HTML and CSS coding and you need to locate and edit the files. You can do this either via the Template Manager, which allows you to edit the template index page and the CSS page, or via an FTP connection to the site's files and using editing software to make the changes. The latter is a bit complicated, so we will only address the changes using the Template Manager.

Before we begin, just a brief reminder—you should not do this if you are not skilled in Website HTML and CSS coding. We are not going to work with the default template, so your site won't crash if you make any mistakes. Let's use the `jt005_j16-Default` template to make a few changes and give you a feel for how this works.

EXERCISE 5: ADDING A NEW MODULE POSITION

1. While in the Template Manager, select the Templates tab, as shown in Figure 10-5.

Figure 10-5
The Templates tab opens the area to access and modify the template file main page.

2. Before going any further, look at the template Preview and note the module positions. Note the `left` module position on the left side of the page. We are going to add a new module position directly under it called `myposition`.

3. With the Templates tab open, select the template by clicking on its name. This opens the detail screen shown in Figure 10-6.

Figure 10-6
The two links open the site index.php page and the style sheet for that page.

4. Go back to the previous screen and open the Edit Main Page Template link. A screen should open that is loaded with code.

5. Scroll down and find the lines of code shown in Figure 10-7. The image also shows the line of code you're going to add in the next few steps.

6. Copy the entire line starting with `<jdoc:include . . .>`.

7. Directly underneath that line, paste the copied line.

8. In the newly pasted line of code, change `left` to read `myposition`.

9. Click Save & Close.

10. Click Close in the top-right menu area.

11. If you preview the template for module positions, you should see them as displayed in Figure 10-8. If you see the same on your screen, you have added the new module position correctly.

12. If correct, click Save & Close.

Figure 10-7
This code is used to display modules in the left position of the template.

Figure 10-8
The template preview now shows the new module position.

Next, let's test the module position by assigning a module to it, which is done the same way as with other modules, except `myposition` is now going to be on the list.

EXERCISE 6: ASSIGNING MODULE TO THE MYPOSITION LOCATION

1. In a separate browser, open the site's front-end and click the My Category Blog menu link item you created previously. The new template should appear with the left side menu you configured earlier.

2. Go back to the Site Administrator screen.

3. Open the Module Manager.

4. Filter the module list by type = Search. A list of three search modules should appear, each with different module assignments.

5. Open the one assigned to position-0 by clicking on it.

6. In the blue Select Position field, type `myposition`.

7. Click Save.

8. Look at the front-end again after refreshing the page. The search module should appear at the bottom of the left column.

9. Click Save & Close. Note that the new module position for that module now displays where position-0 did before in the default installation template.

EXERCISE 7: CHANGING THE COLOR OF THE MENU LINK NAMES

In this exercise, let's modify the CSS style sheet so that the link items in the left menu are blue. This requires changing the hex value color of the CSS element. Hex codes are colors that are expressed in a value, such as #000000 for black. White is #FFFFFF, and other colors have other values. Search Google for hex codes and you will find all the information you need about them.

1. Go back to the Template Manager's Templates tab and open the orange template (`jt005_j16`) again.

2. Open `Edit css/styles.css` for the template in the Stylesheets area. This file is a collection of complex style sheet code, which is discussed further in Chapter 19, "CSS-PHP-HTML Basics." We know the links are gray. We also know the name of the CSS element that controls them. This is also explained in Chapter 19.

Use Caution with Code

As you may have noted in Figure 10-7, there is code in template files that, unless you are a Web developer or programmer, doesn't have any meaning to you. Therefore, be extremely careful when changing these codes unless you are skilled in doing so or have confidence that you can do it correctly.

3. Scroll down the list until you see this line:

```
#sidebar .module ul.menu li a
{display:block;margin:0; padding:5px
0 5px 20px;font-weight:bold;
line-height:20px;background:
url(../images/li.png) 0% 50%
no-repeat; text-decoration:none;
color:#999; font-size:13px;}
```

4. Look for color:#999, and change the 999 to 336699. Just change the numbers; do not change any other code.

5. Click Save.

6. Go to the front-end and refresh the browser. The link items in the left menu are now blue.

7. If correct, click Save & Close.

Hex Code Shorthand

If a hex code consists of all the same numbers (#FFFFFF, #000000, #999999), you can use shorthand with the first three numbers to make them #FFF, #000, and #999.

Make no mistake, editing template files and style sheet files should only be done if you have experience in doing so, or have some knowledge of what the code does. A site can completely bomb out if changes are not made correctly. Be careful and only do the things you know you can do. Later chapters in this book are helpful with more complex tasks, especially Chapter 17, "Advanced Topics," and Chapter 19.

Because templates are the main controlling part of Joomla! 1.6 that manage the Website display, learning how to modify their files and style sheets is helpful if you want to manage and help develop other Websites.

There are many, many Joomla! 1.6 templates available, and there are more to come, so looking at them, looking at their demo pages, and learning about templates is a good thing to do. Sometimes templates fit a client's Website; sometimes they are close and just need to be tweaked some. That's where knowing how to modify them comes in.

Of course, building your own templates from scratch or using a template builder is a whole world unto itself. Many sites are designed in Photoshop-type programs and then coded to work as a Joomla! 1.6 template. Doing that is almost a specialty area requiring advanced graphics skills, as well as experience building Joomla! 1.6 templates and their associated style sheets.

Template Overrides

OCCASIONALLY, AS YOU WORK with Joomla! 1.6 more and more, you will run into the term *template overrides*. What that refers to is making heavy-duty changes to the core files of the site and for a specific template.

Let's explain this further. For example, you want to change the physical layout of the login form, which is on the left side of the default page on your demo site. This is a module, so the change must be made in the modules folder of the site. This is not accessible via the Module Manager! It must be accessed via a file manager or FTP connection to the server location where the files are located.

What happens in creating template overrides is that the module is copied into an `html` folder called in the templates folder. It is copied there because, when the site loads, it will load the modules or whatever is in the `template/html` folder *before* it loads the core files. Any changes made in the duplicate content file will display, and the same files in the core location will be ignored, or one is overridden by the other.

Why copy the files to the `template/html` folder? This is done so that when you upgrade a site from Joomla! 1.6.2 to version 1.6.3, for example, the changes you made to the code will not be overwritten by the upgrade. Putting the files in the `template/html` folder keeps your changes intact, even if the files are replaced in the upgrade process, which they often are.

You can find an example of a template override in Chapter 17.

Summary

In this chapter, you learned the following:

▶ Templates control the visual aspects of CMS Websites.

▶ Templates consist of the module positions, colors, and other visual controls.

▶ Templates can be simple or complex with respect to module position layouts.

▶ If module positions exist and not used, the space allocated to them should not appear on the pages.

▶ There are many factors to consider when selecting Joomla! 1.6 templates.

▶ Templates may be obtained from any number of online resources, both free and commercial.

▶ Templates install just like any other extension.

▶ Templates are controlled via the Template Manager.

▶ Module positions in one template may not be named the same in another.

▶ Module positions can be identified by using the Preview feature in the template's manager.

▶ Duplicate content modules must be created to allow assignment to other template's module positions, which may be named differently.

▶ An individual module may not be assigned to multiple module positions without making duplicate modules.

▶ Template module layouts can be modified via the Template Manager and accessing the template's main page.

▶ Template visual features, such as font colors, may be modified by accessing the template's style sheet.

▶ Before modifying any template files, a backup copy of the original should be created.

▶ Great care should be taken when modifying the main page layout or the style sheet.

▶ Overrides of the core files (modules, components, plugins, and so on) can be done by creating a copy of the item in the `template/html` folder.

▶ When a site loads, it uses the template files for layout and content control before using the core files.

Image Basics

IMAGES ON WEBSITES ARE SIMPLY GRAPHIC ELEMENTS and not limited to photographs. Images on Websites can include backgrounds, banners, buttons, icons, and more. They are all lumped under the same heading in Joomla! 1.6, and the Media Manager organizes and manages them.

Typically, most of the images on a site are part of, and stored with, the site template, which explains why the entire look of a Website can change just by changing the template.

The images contained in content, such as articles, modules, and other areas, usually are not part of the template and are added as needed, such as a series of photographs in an article.

As with other general rules for Joomla! 1.6, there are always exceptions. This chapter covers some of the more glaring ones.

Also, if you are not familiar with using images on Websites, some types and their definitions are provided so you know what is being referenced in this and later chapters.

Static Versus Animated Images

STATIC IMAGES HAVE A FIXED SIZE and shape. They don't change—square is square, round is round. They don't turn, spin, or move around. However, a module or component can make an image move from one side of the screen to the other (one of those exceptions). The image isn't doing that, the module or component causes the movement. It's still a fixed, static image that is "being moved" rather than "moving" of its own accord.

Static images are files of themselves. A photo is a photo. It has a name, it's stored on the Website, and it uses certain codes to call it up for display. Static images come in many standardized formats, unlike animated images.

Animated images can be simple animated graphics, videos, or Flash files. These images contain motion—something on the image moves. Flash images are the ones you are likely to see on most Websites. These images have lots of moving parts and pieces and, to be honest, are often way too confusing, too busy, and just too darn big to load on the page.

All the images and moving parts of animated images, especially Flash images, are self-contained. A Flash file, no matter how complex, is a single file. This makes it difficult to change the content display. You need a Flash creation program and know how to use it. Flash tends to be popular among artsy types at ad agencies and less so with developers that build content with static images. I have nothing against Flash images per se, other than they are difficult to create, difficult to modify, inherently slow to load, and often overkill. Other than that, Flash files are fine.

Movies and videos are a form of animated image, but of a different class. This is discussed in Chapter 14, "Multimedia Basics."

What's in a Name

IMAGES HAVE MANY NAMES and formats, such as those described in this section. The important thing is that you know the differences between them, and know when one type is more appropriate than another. First, consider the types of images that you may find on a typical Website.

The images inserted in the previous exercises were JPGs (*jay pegs*), which is only one of a number of formats. The most common photo and image formats follow:

JPG. The format of choice for high-clarity photographs. JPGs can also be used for other images, such as buttons. They can contain millions of colors but have display issues if the file is compressed, or made smaller without special care. JPGs can generate large files, and large files take longer to download, which means the Webpage may take longer to load.

GIF. GIFs can be compressed without a loss of quality, but are typically used for buttons and other small, non-photographic images. If used for photos, there can be some clarity loss, but GIFs are widely used and display well in browsers. GIFs are typically limited in color range.

PNG. The most versatile image format that is most comfortable with new browsers. Older browsers do not display them well. It's safe to assume that there are few older browsers in use, so PNG file formats can be used confidently.

PNGs have high visual quality and can be compressed without loss, which makes them ideal for Websites.

ICO. Not so much a graphic format as it is a "thing." ICOs are those little images seen next to the Website name in the browser location bar, such as the small Joomla! logo seen on the Joomla.org Website. Some sites use them, some do not. No big deal either way! They can be added to any Website.

SWF. This is a resultant file format from Adobe Flash programs and other similar programs that product Flash output files. All the images and content are embedded within the file and cannot be edited or separated without using the source file that created the SWF.

SVG. This image format has been around for a while, but most browsers did not support it. However, the newer generation of browsers is doing so because the SVG format is now a standard that is supported worldwide.

TIF. Another type of image file (called tagged image format) that is rarely used on Websites because the files' sizes are incredibly huge, which affects download time for page loading. A TIF file has great clarity and color depth, but it is not a good choice for a page on a Website because of its size.

Templates Contain Most Images

FOR THE MOST PART, any site designed to use templates, as is the case with Joomla! 1.6, has the images contained within the template files. Each template has its own `images` directory and calls those images when the template loads onto a page.

Knowing this, it is safe to assume that site backgrounds, which can be textures, glares, and photos, are located within the template's file structure. So are the graphics and images to create buttons, fancy borders, and so on.

Some templates have multiple folders with different color options, each containing all of the image files for that particular template's color. Ten themes equal ten copies of everything to display the template.

Bottom line is that most site images that relate to look, feel, and noncontent display are managed via the site template.

Images in Articles

IMAGES IN CONTENT, however, are managed differently. Images that are not part of the site template are managed in the Media Manager, which is a special part of the site files that collects and stores the images. The Media Manager is accessible via the Admin control panel.

Let's take a look at it.

EXERCISE 1: EXPLORING THE MEDIA MANAGER

1. Go to the Admin control panel and open the Media Manager. The default installation should look like that shown in Figure 11-1.

2. Read the callouts that explain the various parts of the manager.

3. Browse the Options in the top-right menu. Don't change anything; just look.

The Filenames Change

When uploading an image file to the Media Manager, the format of the name changes automatically. This means that an image called The Big Brown Dog.jpg, which has capital letters and spaces, would become the_big_brown_dog.jpg, with lowercase letters and spaces changed to underlines.

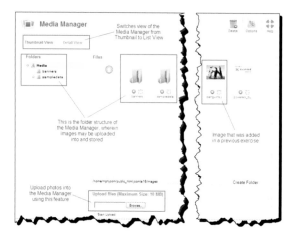

Figure 11-1
The Media Manager of the default Joomla! 1.6 installation.

4. Browse the Detail View tab content. This is the same as the Thumbnail View, but it is better suited for you have a lot of image files and folders and just want to look at names. If you want to see the images, use the Thumbnail View. The banners folder stores the images uploaded via the Banners component. The sample data folder contains the images used in other parts of the Website, such as the Parks and Fruit Shop content area, which have different templates. Note that you can create additional folders in the Media Manager. The bottom area is where images are uploaded from your computer to the site image folder. Images are deleted by clicking their check box and clicking the Delete icon in the top menu area. Image deletions are one-click permanent, so make sure you want to delete a photo before you do it.

How to Use the Media Manager

IF THERE ARE IMAGES YOU WANT to use in content, you can either load the image into the Media Manager and call it up via the Article Image Insertion function or upload it via the Article Image Insertion feature, which then copies the image to the Media Manager automatically. Let's do both in the following exercises.

EXERCISE 2: UPLOADING VIA THE MEDIA MANAGER

1. Open the Media Manager.

2. Go to the bottom and click the Browse button, which lets you access the images stored on your computer.

3. Browse to the My Pictures or Photographs folder on your computer and select one of the photos in the sample folder. Any one will do. The Koala Bear photo has been selected for this exercise. Use any photo you like for your site. The folder name may be slightly different, depending up which operating system your computer is using.

4. Click on the Koala Bear photo to select it.

5. Click the Start Upload button to start the process. The photo should upload and appear in the Thumbnail View of the photos in the /images/ folder. There is no need to save uploaded photos. Once uploaded, they are saved to the Website.

6. Exit the Media Manager and go to the Article Manager.

Now that an image is in place in the media storage area of the site, it needs to be inserted into an article, so let's do that.

EXERCISE 3: ADDING AN IMAGE TO AN ARTICLE

1. Go to the Article Manager and open the Professionals article, which is the leading article on the front page of the site with sample content. This article also has a Read More break, which means only the content above the break will appear when the article is in a category blog layout. The Koala photo will be added after the break.

2. Insert the cursor at the beginning of the line starting with Access control lists.

3. Scroll down the page and click the Image button under the content window. Do you remember doing this in a previous exercise? The Media Manager should open.

4. Click on the thumbnail of the image you want to insert and click the Insert button. If the image is way too large for the space, it's all right; that will be fixed.

5. Click Save.

6. Go back to the content window and select the image by clicking on it. Small boxes will appear on the corners and the middles of the top, bottom, and sides.

7. With the image selected, click on the Image Properties icon in the editor control bar. A control panel window opens, as shown in Figure 11-2.

Figure 11-2
The JoomlaCK Editor feature for modifying individual image parameters.

8. Enter 200 in the Width box. Note that the Height enters itself automatically. If you enter a Height, the Width adjusts the same way.

9. The photo should appear on the left side of the page, text to the right, so select Left in the Align drop-down.

10. Click OK (green button) to insert it into the article. Note that it is on the left side and the text is on the right, except the text is touching the photos, as shown in Figure 11-3.

11. Select the photo, and right-click on it to open the Image Properties box again. HSpace and VSpace refer to the space around the photo in the horizontal and vertical direction.

12. Enter 10 into each box, which "pads" the photo by 10 pixels and keeps the text away from it.

13. Click OK and view the results. The text should have moved away from the photo as in Figure 11-4.

14. Click Save.

15. View the page on the front-end by clicking the Read More link under the opening text of the Professionals article. The photo should appear in place and in an appropriate size.

Figure 11-3
Photo with text butted directly next to it on the right side because there is no "padding" space next to the photo.

Figure 11-4
Photo with the text pushed away ("padded") from the image area, which is a more pleasing and cleaner appearance, not to mention that it is the "proper" way to display images in text areas.

Padding Around Images

Padding is the space around images that keeps other objects "clear" or away at a fixed distance. Some editors allow different padding values for all four sides. The JoomlaCK Editor does not. Therefore, the image moves away from the left edge as far as it pushes text away from the right. The same goes for the top and bottom. This can be set manually in the Code view of the article, but only if you understand HTML code and how it applies to image positioning. The JCE Editor, when released, will have four-sided padding that may be set individually per photo.

EXERCISE 4: UPLOADING VIA THE CONTENT EDITOR IN THE ARTICLE MANAGER

In the previous exercise, the inserted image was uploaded to the Media Manager before insertion. You can also load images via the Article Manager without preloading them, which is the most common way photos are added to articles and modules.

1. Open the Article Manager and open the Professionals article again.

2. Place the cursor at the beginning of the line starting with New events thoughout.

3. Click the Image button under the editor window.

4. The Media Manager will appear in a pop-up window, but rather than selecting an image that is already in place, click the Browse button to find another photo on your computer.

5. When selected, click Start Upload to add the photo. The thumbnail appears in the Media Manager.

6. Select the photo and execute the Insert action.

7. Back in the editor window, select the photo, and then right-click to access Image Properties.

8. Enter these settings: Height = 150, HSpace and VSpace = 10, and Align = Right.

9. Click the green OK button.

10. View the image in the content editor. It should be on the right side.

11. Click Save.

12. View the article in the browser. The image should appear at the bottom-right area, adjacent to the link list.

13. Close the Article Manager.

The two preceding exercises demonstrated the two ways images can be added to articles, with both using the Article Manager to select the photo in the Media Manager and execute the Insert action.

Just a reminder: The Media Manager is used primarily to "manage" the images on a site that are inserted into content. It does not manage the images associated with the template as part of the design.

Images in Galleries

IF YOU HAVE A NUMBER OF IMAGES and want to organize them into something akin to a photo album, an image gallery is a good choice. These are components that are available in the JED and easily installed via the Extension Manager. The variables associated with image galleries are too numerous to detail here. Suffice it to say, almost anything you want to do with a collection of images can be done by using an image gallery.

Galleries create of catalogs or categories of content that can be displayed in a list view, where only the list of categories is displayed, or the image view where images are displayed. As stated, there are numerous ways to do this. Search the JED and look at the developer demo sites if you have interest in using one.

As far as applications go, aside from sorting family photos into albums, many businesses use galleries to display product photos to add captions to them. It is not unusual to see product catalogs with thumbnail images and a short title that, when clicked, opens a larger image with more information about the product.

Don't confuse galleries and how they function with the Banners component, which shows images, but in a different manner. If you have the choice, choose galleries over banners.

Images in Specialty Modules

IMAGES ARE ALSO USED in specialty modules that display images in sliders or rotational displays. These modules contain all of the code and functions to display the images and control how they're displayed. Also, they have parameter settings to further control the module display.

In most cases with these types of specialized modules, the images are called up from a folder in the Media Manager. The Media Manager would, in this case, upload the photos into a specific folder so the module can access them. For example, if you create a folder called topphotos, the modules may have a parameter that requires you to enter the path to the photos as /images/topphotos/. This is typically the way these types of modules work.

Optimize Images

Super large images take longer to load than images that are scaled close to the size of the final display size. Always optimize images by reducing their actual file size, which will display just as well but speed up page loading time, especially if you have several photos in the content.

Images and Screen Resolution

NOT LONG AGO, MOST computer monitors where big, old, clunky things that had limited screen resolution and a limited color display. Screen displays were typically 800×600 pixels and the color display range was limited to 256, which were called "browser safe" colors.

Back then, most Web developers, designed sites to an 800-pixel-wide screen format and everyone saw sites the same way. This is no longer the case.

Today, those types of monitors are few and far between, and modern, flat-screen monitors have resolutions that can often exceed 1600 pixels, or ultra-high resolutions. For example, if a site designed for 800-pixel display is viewed on a monitor set for 1600 pixels, the Website displays at one-half the size, or much smaller.

At present, many Websites are designed as either fixed-width or fluid-width, the latter becoming more and more popular, but with its own set of issues. Fixed-width sites range from about 950 to 1200 pixels wide, which allows good positioning of content elements, and the sites are well-viewed on most monitors. Granted, a 960-pixel site still displays smaller on a 1600-pixel monitor, but it's a compromise most sites can endure.

Fluid sites, on the other hand, display edge to edge, regardless of what monitor resolution is used. Fluid sites are more difficult to build because somewhere in the template there must be provisions for the content to expand without destroying the site's display. Images must be managed so that as the site grows, they grow as well. Everything must grow larger for high resolution, but the content gets smaller. There are workarounds, and good Website templates have them embedded.

In addition, there are templates that recognize browser types and monitor resolution and adjust themselves accordingly, though not completely.

Summary

In this chapter, you learned the following:

► Images on Websites are not limited to photographs, and all graphics are classified as images.

► Website images are either static or animated.

► There are many different types of image formats.

► Most images on Websites are part of the template.

► Images in content are controlled by the site administrator and are not part of the template.

► Images can be uploaded for future use via the Media Manager.

► Images may be inserted in articles via the Image plugin button, even though the image isn't in the Media Manager.

► Images inserted into articles are automatically saved in the Media Manager.

► Photos should not be butted up next to text, and padding controls are used to add space.

► Image collections are easier to display on Websites using image galleries.

► Website resolution affects the display size of both Webpages and images on the page.

Form Basics

I F YOU HAVE EVER LOGGED ONTO A WEBSITE, entered information, placed an order, and put in your shipping information, you did so through a form. That form took your information and used it. Maybe the form used your information to complete your transaction, or it simply stored your information, or it sent that data to be processed and e-mailed you a copy of what was entered.

The fundamental definition of a form is simply a place on a Webpage where you enter something and click a button to execute whatever the form was designed for or intended to do. For example, a username and password are entered on a login form, a submit button is clicked, the system searches to make sure you are authorized to view the content, and then it allows you to view.

Every time you log into the back-end of your Joomla! 1.6 Website, you are executing a form. When you enter data about yourself as a contact, you are filling out a form. When you submit a message via a Webpage, you are filling out a form. There are thousands of examples.

Let's take a look at the forms built into the default Joomla! install that are visible via the front-end. We won't address back-end forms because they rarely change. We will focus on the forms that are visible on the front-end, or user side of the site, often called the client-facing side.

Default Forms

THERE ARE SEVERAL FORMS that come as part of the default Joomla! 1.6 installation that are configured in the back-end and appear on the front-end, such as these:

▶ The User Login form

▶ The Login module User Registration form

▶ The "forgot" parts of the Login module

▶ The Contact User form from the Contacts component

▶ The Weblinks form from the Weblinks component

EXERCISE 1: CREATING CONTACTS

In order for a Contact Us form to show up on the front-end, the information must be entered on the back-end and connected to a menu link item to trigger the display. Some of the steps involved are a bit complex, so pay close attention to what you are doing (and just did), so you don't lose track.

Part 1: Creating the Contact Information

In this part of the exercise, we'll create a contact and enter some information. Normally, on a fresh Website install, there are no contact categories in place. But because the sample data was installed, there are several contact categories available for us to use. Let's use the Staff category in the Contacts component.

1. Open the Contact Manager via the Components menu in the back-end and select Contacts from the fly-out menu. The Contact Manager opens.

2. Select New from the top-right menu. The Contact Manager: Contact screen will display, as shown in Figure 12-1. We'll work with the left side of the screen first.

3. Enter Website Manager into the Name field.

4. Select Staff in the Category drop-down menu.

5. Click Save.

Figure 12-1
The left side of the New Contact Manager with the name and category fields highlighted.

Once the individual contact is created, information about that contact can be entered (using a form, of course!), and displayed on the front-end of the site.

6. Go to the right side of the screen and open the Contact Details drop-down.

7. Enter your own information. Enter `Website Manager` as your position.

8. Fill in the rest of the fields. You can ignore the three sort fields for this exercise.

9. Click Save & Close. We'll deal with the Display Options shortly.

Part 2: Creating the Menu Link Item

Next, let's create a menu link item so that site visitors can click on it and get contact information.

1. Open the Main Menu in the Menus drop-down.

2. Click on New in the top-right menu to open the individual link item editor.

3. For Menu Item Type, select Single Contact from the list in the pop-up box under Contacts.

4. For Menu Title, enter `My Contact Info` into the form field. On the right side of the page, you need to select which contact associates with this item.

5. Select the Website Manager contact we just created.

6. Click Save & Close.

7. Go to the site's front-end and look at the bottom of the This Site menu. The My Contact Info Menu Link Item should appear.

8. Click on it. A page with the information you entered previously in the Contact component should appear.

9. Note that there is a title—which is the name of the contact—and Website Manager below it, appearing twice. The latter is the Position field you filled in earlier. Let's remove that.

We do not go into the Contacts listing to delete the information and remove the field from the display; instead, we go into another area of the Contact Manager and disable the field from showing. Here's how we do it:

Part 3: Altering the Contact Information Displayed

1. Go back into the Contact Manager and open the Website Manager contact entry.

2. When it opens, go to the right and open the Display Options drop-down area. You should see the screen shown in Figure 12-2.

3. For the Contact's Position, change Use Global to Hide in the drop-down.

4. Click Save.

5. Go back to the front-end, refresh the page, and view the listing again. The second reference to Website Manager is now gone.

The preceding exercise illustrates how populated form fields can be set to display or not through global parameter setting, and how to control them using a toggled override. This example is pretty much how it is with Joomla! 1.6, where form information is used to display information, and that some of the information can be selectively off or on as needed.

Figure 12-2
The Contact's Position will be hidden so that it doesn't show on the page.

So, how does all that relate to forms on the front-end?

If you have the My Contact Info page open, underneath the Contact Info section is another slide-open section called Contact Form. Open it. This is the form that was created along with the actual contact entry, and when it's filled out, it will send that contact an e-mail with the message entered. This is the default contact-the-contact form that comes with Joomla! 1.6.

Obtaining Forms

A SEARCH FOR JOOMLA! 1.6–compatible extensions in the JED will yield a good number of available forms and form programs, which are used to create forms of any type for use on a Website. Most of the canned forms are login and contact types, each of which offers a slightly different take on the same form and its display.

Basically, canned forms are usually extensions in the form of modules. The build-a-form types are usually extensions in the form of a component, which should give you a clue about the sophistication of such extensions. Components have much more in them than modules, which are fixed page parts (modules) that can be placed into module positions.

While surfing the JED for Joomla! 1.6 forms, make note that most of the extensions are commercial, which means you have to pay for them. Noncommercial extensions usually require you to register on the download site, which usually means that you need a subscription to download.

It is strongly suggested that you thoroughly review any form extension you plan to use before purchasing it. Forms are not that complicated, but not all that easy either. Every component that generates a form has its own unique complexities in building the form.

Installing Forms

As in the past, installing and using an extension is the best way to learn how it works. Let's do that with a form that installs a new Contact form on your site, one that is separate from the contact-the-contact built-in form earlier.

Exercise 2: Installing the Fox.ra.it Contact Form

In this exercise, we will download and install a free Contact form. If you recall, it was mentioned previously that extensions sometimes come as both components and modules. This is one of those.

1. Go to http://fox.ra.it and review the site and form information.

2. Download the component.

3. Download the module.

4. Install the component.

5. Install the module.

Before we get into the component's configuration and using the module of the downloaded form, some information about form elements may be helpful.

An excellent form tutorial can be found at http://reference.sitepoint.com/html/elements-form, along with other tutorials on coding used on Webpages. You can find other tutorials by searching Google for form elements or a similar topic.

The following are some typical form elements and what they are used for:

Label. This is the label associated with form input elements, e.g., Your Name and the like.

Text Input. This form field is one line of text, such as entering your name, address, and so on.

Text Area Input. A form area to enter a paragraph of text, such as comments.

Select. A drop-down that has a list of choices to select, such as Your State, which lists all of the states in the U.S. so you can choose one.

Radio Button. A round button, usually found in pairs, where one or the other is selected and they toggle back if the other is selected. Only one may be selected. An example is a Yes or No option.

Check box. This is for checking more than one item, for example, "Which flavors of ice cream do you like, check all that apply." It can also be used like a radio box, but with more choices than just yes or no.

Submit Button. This button "submits" form information to an e-mail or a database, or to trigger another action or bring up a new page.

Reset Button. This clears all of the form field entries and deselects buttons and boxes.

Captcha/ReCaptcha. Asks the form submitter to enter a code or value before submitting to verify the form submitter is a human and not a robot that sends spam. An example of this security element is shown in Figure 12-3.

Please input the code above | AURUFM

Figure 12-3
A type of form security that generates an image of characters that must be typed into the box to allow the form to be submitted, or to complete the transaction of the form.

Using the New Contact Form

NOW THAT YOU'RE MORE familiar with form elements of forms and what they do, let's activate the form component and module we down-loaded previously. If you open the Fox Contact component, it tells you to create a menu link item. Do you recall our previous discussion about some components not having configuration settings in the component? This is one of those.

EXERCISE 3: DISPLAYING THE FORM

1. Go to Menus > Main Menu.

2. Click the New icon in the top-right menu. The Menu Manager: New Menu Item screen opens.

3. Click the Select button in the Menu Item Type area.

4. The Fox Contact component appears on the list in the pop-up, so click the Fox Contact link.

5. For the menu link item title, enter My New Contact Form.

6. Click Save.

7. Go to the front-end and click the New Menu Link Item at the bottom of the This Site menu. You should see the form shown in Figure 12-4.

Figure 12-4
The Contact Us form with the field to be removed highlighted.

8. Go back to the admin area and the right side of the Manager screen.

9. To make the form send properly, enter your e-mail address in the Email To field in the Basic Options drop-down.

10. Click Save.

11. Open the Form Fields drop-down; you will see a lot of configurable options for this form.

12. Let's remove the How did you hear about us? drop-down question from the form.

13. Open the Form Fields section on the right, and scroll down to the drop-down list fields section. Note the way the choice fields were established, where the items that become the "choices" in the drop-down are typed in and separated by a comma. That is typical for drop-downs. Alternatively, you can enter them on a separate line.

14. Select Disabled in the State drop-down.

15. Click Save.

16. View the front-end and refresh the browser window. You should no longer see the form field. All of the other form fields can be modified the same way.

17. Additional fields can be entered into the form under Text fields. You can add some if you like, but we are not going to do it in this exercise.

18. Look at the spam filter, located in the Security drop-down. Here you can add spam prevention "bad words." Unfortunately, to eliminate really bad words, you need to specify them here by entering them. The system needs to know that you do not want e-mails with that content sent. Some systems have these bad words built into the form control.

19. Take a look around the other form options. Most form extensions have similar option controls.

20. Click Save & Close when done.

Modifying Forms

EVER NOTICE THAT SOME WEBSITES have plain, vanilla-looking forms and other Websites have colorful, good-looking forms? Form appearance is controlled via the template's Cascading Style Sheet (CSS). However, in many cases where a form component is installed in Joomla! 1.6, it comes with its own style sheet and CSS attributes separate from the template.

If the controls are in the component, that's great! It means that somewhere in the component's manager, there are setting parameters for width, color, text color, input box color, borders, and more. These parameters change the look of the form and fancy it up some.

Chapter 19, "CSS-PHP-HTML Basics," covers some of the CSS code adjustments that can improve the look and appearance of form fields for components that do not have those features.

Form Security

TO PREVENT SPAMMERS, robots, and other evil-doers from using your forms to send malicious e-mail, or e-mail that you do not want, a security feature can be added that requires users to type characters displayed by an image generator. Some examples are shown in Figure 12-5.

If a form is added to your site, make sure that the component has some type of security feature. This is important for forms that send information. A Login form isn't in that category, so no concerns there. It is only the forms that send the information via e-mail, and write the information to a database or storage system. These form submissions should be protected from malicious attacks.

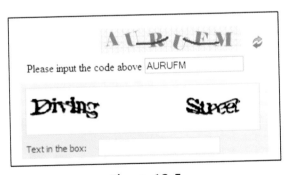

Figure 12-5
Two different types of captcha-like form elements that are actually graphic images that robots can't read.

Another way to prevent bad e-mails via forms is to have e-mail addresses submitted two times in two different form fields. How many times have you done that yourself and wondered, why? It's a protection to ensure that a real, live, human is entering the data because the robots can't. So, don't get mad next time you have to enter your e-mail twice. It's just a security precaution the Website is using. Who knows, you may be using the same feature on your Website one day.

If a form does not have any captcha-like security, there are extensions in the JED to add that element to a form. Search the Joomla! 1.6–compatible extensions for captcha and to find many available extensions, most of them commercial.

Selecting Form Extensions

IF YOU WANT TO HAVE COMPLEX forms on your site, some due diligence is needed to make sure you select the correct component, because you are going to pay for it. Good form components are not free, and rightly so. A lot of work goes into those extensions, and developers want to be paid for their work.

You should take a close look at all form packages and demo forms on the developer's Website.

Also, make sure that there is a demo of the admin back-end for the component via the administrator. A good developer's Website will have access to the back-end of the component so you see it, play with it, and learn how it works.

Go to the JED, search for forms, investigate several of them, and make your choice based on what you see on the developer's Website.

Forms That Auto-Fill

EVER GONE TO A WEBSITE that requires a login, and when you open it, the information in the login fields is already filled in? Or have you ordered a book from Amazon.com and the shipping information was already populated in the form? That's done with cookies, which is code the visited site writes back to your machine's browser for the next time you visit the site. That's the basics of it.

Joomla! 1.6 does not generate cookies with user browsers, although some browsers may locally allow username/password storage for a particular site. This is sort of a reverse cookie, where the browser stores the information for the site.

Either way, cookies are not an evil, but they do require some concern in some situations. All major Websites have them and use them. You can disable cookies in your browser controls, but then you may run into sites that you can't access with cookies disabled, so you may as well just leave them turned on, or selectively clear them out as desired.

Summary

In this chapter, you learned the following:

▶ Joomla! 1.6 has some built-in forms used for login, contacts, and Weblinks.

▶ The default forms cannot be easily modified.

▶ Additional extensions can be installed to modify forms.

▶ Extensions that have control and configuration parameters included can replace the default forms.

▶ Form extensions install just like any other extension added to a Joomla! 1.6 Website.

▶ Forms typically are added to the site as modules.

▶ Form components help create complex forms, which are added by linking the form to a menu link item that connects to the component.

▶ Some form extensions can create and display any type of complex form.

▶ Forms consist of configurable elements.

▶ Added security features prevent spam and robots from using the form to mail malicious materials.

User Management and

Access Control

ONE OF THE NEWEST ADDITIONS TO JOOMLA! 1.6 is the ability to manage users and control access to the Website, or parts of the site. It is now possible to configure access and action settings down to individual content items. And while this may not seem like a significant change for a small, personal Website, it is a major improvement and highly desired feature for Websites that have a lot of content contributors.

A good example of where the Access Control Levels ("ACL") feature can be put to good use is a newspaper Website, where there are many, many content contributors and editors. With ACL, the sports department would only be able to access and add/edit content in their section. Other departments would likewise be limited to what content they could add, edit, or delete. Also, editor levels can be created that have limited or expanded privileges.

ACL can create what are known as user groups and assign users into one or more groups at the same time. By controlling users in a "grouped" hierarchy, it gives Website managers control of access and editing permissions. Back to the newspaper example, the sports department could be a group, with individual editors responsible for only their articles. ACL can establish access, privileges, and actions as needed.

While ACL may seem a bit confusing at first, especially if your site is small and you are the only content contributor, it's good to know in case you ever become a Website manager.

If you are operating your site as the only content contributor, you can just glance over this chapter and return to it later if you want to study ACL in greater detail. There is no need to do the exercises if you are the only manager, editor, or contributor.

Access Defaults

In the default installation, all users are set to the Inherit mode. This means that all users inherit the same access as the Public, or Guest User, unless set otherwise by a user group on an individual user basis or content item level.

What Does ACL Actually Do?

ACL DOES SEVERAL THINGS both collectively and individually, depending on how it is applied on a site. Here are the two main elements of ACL:

▶ **Action Permissions.** Sets what users of the site can do with content.

▶ **Viewing Access Levels.** Controls what users can see in both the front-end and back-end.

While there are only two main parts of ACL, implementing the controls on large Websites can really get complex. In most cases, the default installation ACL settings work just fine; in other cases, a lot of fine-tuning is needed to get the groups configured and the users within them set up properly.

As shown in Figure 13-1, the three groups of users under Public are Manager, Registered, and Super User. You can access this information via Admin control panel > User Manager. The groups' roles are explained in the following:

▶ **Public.** These are the users who can access the site. Everyone starts out as Public, and then the ACL is used to modify their permissions and access.

▶ **Manager.** These users have some ACLs set to "allow," but they can't access everything.

▶ **Registered.** These users can log into the site to view content that is restricted to "registered" users, and they have limited permissions by default, unless modified.

▶ **Super User.** This is the user that has full control over everything on the site, including managing user groups and individual users. As far as ACL is concerned, Super Users pretty much have the run of everything, including ACL settings for groups and users of all types.

Figure 13-1
User groups created by the default installation with sample content installation selected.

Who Can Access What by Default?

LET'S LOOK AT EACH OF THE DEFAULT users and what their permissions and access levels are set to. We'll use screenshots to help you understand the controls.

The Default Public ACL

By default, ACL for the Public user group does not allow any actions on the site, other than to view the content that is set Public. Another way of thinking about the Public group is that they are Website guests and may only view content that you let them view, nothing more. This is the lowest level, for lack of a better designation, of user groups.

To view the default for ACL, go to the Global Configuration and open the Permissions tab, as shown in Figure 13-2. Spend a few minutes viewing the various permission settings to become familiar with them.

Figure 13-2
The items in the left column are the action permissions. Those in the right are the settings that apply to each of the individual permissions. The Public user group is not allowed to perform any actions with regard to content.

The Default Manager ACL

The default Manager can "do things" to the content of the site except for acting as a Super User or accessing any of the component extensions. Figure 13-3 shows the permission settings for a Manager. Managers, Administrators, and Super Users are the only groups that can log into the back-end of the Website to manage content, subject to the limitation of their individual ACL. There is one other group that can log into the back-end, called Special. This group is discussed later in the chapter.

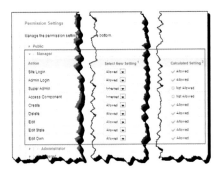

Figure 13-3
The calculated settings on the right are a visual representation of the settings for each. Note that the permissions are more selective for a Manager, granting more than that for Public ACL.

The Default Registered ACL

As shown in Figure 13-4, users who have login privileges on the front-end are called Registered users and can only log in to view items designated by the Registered group. They are the same as any other site visitor, except they can log into the site on the front-end. Registered users cannot contribute content, unless specifically allowed to via ACL settings.

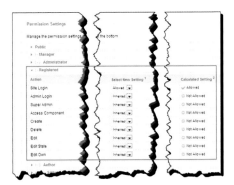

Figure 13-4
In this instance, Registered users are only allowed to log into the site. Their content access is based on the settings in the content item.

In the "user food chain," Super Users are at the top, followed by Administrators, Managers, and Publishers. Publishers cannot access the back-end. They can only access their content items via the site's front-end, so they need a login module to log in.

Administrators and Managers may access the back-end. Managers can create, delete, and edit categories and articles—they "manage" content. Administrators have all of the Manager privileges and can add, edit, delete, and change the status of other users, articles, categories, and more—they "administer" content.

The Default Super User ACL

As shown in Figure 13-5, the Super User has access and permission to do anything and everything on the site, which includes managing the ACL for existing groups and users and creating new ones.

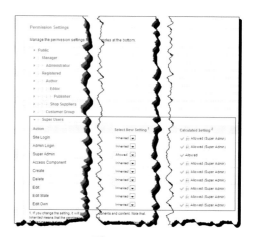

Figure 13-5
The term "wide open" is a good way to describe the ACL the Super User is granted by default.

What Are Actions?

ACTIONS ARE SIMPLY THINGS that users can do. All users, of any level or group, can be granted (or denied) the same actions, which are:

Site Login. User can log into the site via a front-end Login module.

Admin Login. User can log into the site as an Administrator.

Super Admin. User has the status of a Super User.

Access Component. User can access and make changes in a content component.

Create. User can create content items after logging in.

Delete. User can delete the content item.

Edit. User has editing privileges to change the content of the item.

Edit State. User can change the state of the item, e.g., published, unpublished, and so on.

Edit Own. User can edit any content the same user created.

The Site Login, Create, Delete, and Edit actions can be found in many other places in the admin back-end, because these may also apply to the components, categories, and other individual content items.

ACL Has Levels of Access

To HELP VISUALIZE THE LEVELS of access, look at Figure 13-6. This is where the Level part of ACL comes into play. The following are four levels of controllable access and actions, which start globally and end at the individual item level, with respective permissions.

LEVEL I. Sets global configurations, such as Site Login, Admin Login, Access component, Create, Delete, and Super User.

LEVEL II. Sets permissions for components, such as the Access component, Configure, Create, Delete, Edit, Edit State, and Edit Own.

LEVEL III. Category-level permissions, such as Create, Delete, Edit, Edit State (publish, unpublish, and so on), and Edit Own.

LEVEL IV. Item-level permissions are Delete, Edit, and Edit State (publish, unpublish, and so on).

LEVEL I — **GLOBAL CONFIGURATION:** *Site-Wide ACL Permissions*
Sets the permissions for each group and their allowed actions.

LEVEL II — **COMPONENT CONFIGURATION:** *Component ACL Permissions*
Sets the permissions at the component level.

LEVEL III — **CATEGORY MANAGER:** *Category ACL Permissions*
Sets the permissions at the category content level.

LEVEL IV — **ARTICLE MANAGER:** *Article ACL Permissions*
Sets the permissions at the individual article content level.

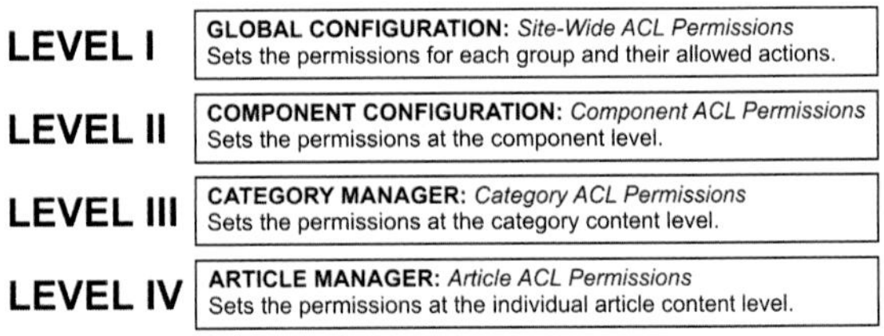

Figure 13-6
Levels of access in Joomla! 1.6. The category and article are used for example purposes.
Level III and IV extend to components, categories within components, and individual items in the categories.

Controlling Viewing Access

THIS IS ANOTHER IMPORTANT part of the Joomla! 1.6 ACL, because it controls how site visitors access and see content. They cannot edit anything, of course, so this is strictly to control what they can view.

Going back, Public access was defined as the way visitors or guests are allowed to see what is on the Website. Registered is similar to Public, except these are visitors that are "registered" on the site and there is content that only they may view after logging in. At the content item level, the drop-down shown in Figure 13-7 defines the viewing level.

There is also Special, which is simply a class of content that only Managers, Administrators, and the Super Users can see. It is only visible to those that can log into the back-end of the site.

For content access control purposes, Special is actually the most important classification of user. This class, combined with the ACL settings, controls what the user sees after they log into the site's back-end, not as a Super User, but simply as a user with limited access, permissions, and privileges.

In addition to articles, the Access configuration parameter can be applied to modules, components, and menu link items (entire menus as well, but via the module for it), which will allow a menu, for example, to only appear when a registered user has logged in and is not visible under any other view conditions. Remember, Registered users can only log into the front-end of the site and view designated content items.

What this amounts to is splitting the site content into Public and Registered viewing. Content with Public access can be viewed by everyone, while Registered content can only be viewed by users logged into the front-end.

Figure 13-7
The typical Access configuration parameter of a content item, in this case, an article opened in the Article Manager. This same parameter can be found in most content items of any type.

How ACL Is Accomplished

Understanding ACL is important on sites with multiple Content Managers. The larger the organization, the more complex the ACL can be for controlling who can do what. Two people in the same office may not necessarily have the same action permission based on their role, e.g., a manager versus a secretary.

Understanding Parent > Child Relationships

WITHIN THE JOOMLA! 1.6 HIERARCHY is a system that relies on a parent-child relationship. In categories, the parent is the highest or top level. The child would be a subcategory that is "under" the parent. If there is a sub-subcategory in the subcategory, the parent for the sub-sub becomes the sub, which is a child of the main category. The following rules apply to ACL in this regard:

▶ Global settings are inherited by all top-level parent items.

▶ A parent is a top-level item, an item that is "above" another, or another item is contained within ("below") it.

▶ A child is any level that has a controlling parent, such as a subcategory, which is a child of a category, and so on.

▶ Settings for the parent control the settings for the child.

▶ The child inherits settings from the parent.

▶ Child settings cannot override those of the parent.

▶ Anything that is denied or not allowed by a parent cannot be allowed in the child permissions.

The ACL Configuration Process

AT FIRST, THE ACL CONFIGURATION process might be a bit confusing. But, if you follow a systematic approach to setting up groups, users, access levels, and permissions, it isn't that difficult.

There are five parts to setting up ACL:

▶ Create a group.

▶ Set the access levels for the group.

▶ Set the actions for the group member-users.

▶ Set the permissions at the Content Item or Component level.

▶ Create a user in the group.

Multiple Steps at the Same Time

In most exercises, we show Save and Save & Close as separate steps. This is done so you can see the results of the Save action.

If you go through an exercise and feel confident, complete the exercise without the Save step and just click Save & Close when complete.

Let's do a few exercises that will illustrate how to create a user group, set access levels, set actions, set permissions, and create a user within the group.

EXERCISE 1: CREATING A USER GROUP

In this exercise, we will create a new user group and assign parent permissions to it, which will be inherited by all of the Child-Level Groups. The process of creating a new group is simple and straightforward, as explained in the following:

1. Go to the Admin control panel and open the User Manager, as shown in Figure 13-8.

2. Open the User Groups tab, as shown in Figure 13-9.

3. Click on the New icon in the top-right menu.

4. When the User Manager: Add New User Group window opens, enter My ACL Group in the box and set Public as the parent, as shown in Figure 13-10.

5. Click Save & Close. The My ACL Group should now appear on the list as a child-item to the Public group parent.

6. View the list of groups to verify the group was added properly.

Figure 13-8
Access the User Manager via the Admin control panel as shown, or via the Users menu in the top-left menu bar when the Administration back-end is open.

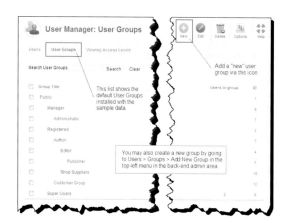

Figure 13-9
When the User Manager is opened, the existing groups may be displayed under the User Groups tab. The New button may also be used to create a new user group.

User Manager: Add New Action Permission Group

User Group Details

| Group Title | My ACL Group |
| Group Parent | Public |

Figure 13-10
In the User Manager: Add New Action Permission
Group, the user group name should be entered
with the Group Parent set as Public.

EXERCISE 2: SETTING THE ACCESS LEVELS FOR THE GROUP

Now that a group has been created, let's set the access level for it.

1. Go to the Users menu and open the Viewing Access Levels tab.

2. Open the Special level. You should be on the User Manager: Edit Viewing Access Level screen, as shown in Figure 13-11. A list will appear showing which user groups will have Viewing Access under Special. Special is a class of users that permits logins on the back-end for content administration. Click on the Special group name or select the check box and select Edit in the top-right menu.

3. Check the check box next to My ACL Group, also shown in Figure 13-11.

4. Click Save & Close.

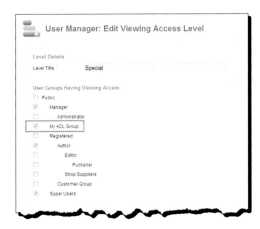

Figure 13-11
Manager screen for access levels showing the Special
groups allowed to log into the back-end.

EXERCISE 3: SETTING THE ACTIONS FOR THE GROUP

Now that a group has been created, let's set the actions. This is done in the Website's global configuration area, as follows:

1. Go to Site > Global Configuration either via the Admin control panel or the top-left menu.

2. Open the Permissions tab.

3. Click on My ACL Group to see the actions allowed.

4. Change the drop-down selectors to configure the settings, as shown in Figure 13-12.

5. Click Save & Close.

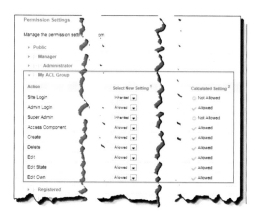

Figure 13-12
Configure the global Permission Settings for
My ACL Group as shown.

Figure 13-13
The permission settings for the Article categories
should be set as shown.

EXERCISE 4: SETTING PERMISSIONS ON A CONTENT ITEM

In this step, we will set the permissions on a content item to allow this user group to alter its content, settings, and display. This exercise sets permissions for the article categories.

1. From the Admin control panel or the Content menu, open the Category Manager.

2. In the top-right menu, click the Options icon to open the Article Manager Options.

3. Click on the Permissions tab in the pop-up window.

4. Configure the drop-down selectors to the settings shown in Figure 13-13.

5. Click Save.

6. Check the settings to make sure they are correct.

7. If they are, click Save & Close.

Users Cannot Self-Register into ACL Groups

Within the Joomla! 1.6 ACL, there is no provision for users to register themselves directly into ACL user groups. Users may register on the site, if that option has been selected. If not, users must be created in the site's back-end, and group assignments must be made manually on a user-by-user basis. This prevents unauthorized individuals from adding themselves to user groups. Special ACL group assignments for registered users must be performed manually by the Super User.

At this point, all of the configurations for ACL have been set. The only thing missing is a user to assign to the group. Exercise 5 takes you through that process.

EXERCISE 5: ASSIGNING A USER TO THE NEW GROUP

Let's assign a user to the My ACL Group created in Exercise 1.

1. Open the User Manager in the Users top-left menu, or access it via the Admin control panel.

2. Select Add New User or click the New icon to create a new user.

3. Enter My ACL User for the name, and myacluser for the login name.

4. Enter a password for this user, your choice.

5. Under the Account Details section, complete the requested information. Note—you cannot use the same e-mail address as the Super User. Just put info@yourdomainname.com in the space for an e-mail address. The e-mail won't be used, so any nonexistent e-mail address is fine. However, you may use the same password. You can use info@yourdomainname.com if you like.

6. Click Save. You should see the User successfully saved message appear on the screen.

7. Scroll down to Assigned User Groups and check My ACL Group, as shown in Figure 13-14.

8. Uncheck the Registered user group if it is checked. Only the My ACL Group should be checked.

9. Click Save & Close.

Figure 13-14
When creating a user in a group, the group assignment connects that user to a specific group. Users can be assigned to more than one user group if needed.

Now that we are done with that, how does it apply to the site? What is the function of this particular ACL group and user?

What we configured in this ACL exercise is the creation of a user in a group that has viewing access and permission to modify content in the categories and articles, and nothing else. This is a configuration that you might find in a company with a lot of content contributors who can only access their own content and no one else's.

Let's see what the results of the My ACL Group and My ACL User configuration produces.

EXERCISE 6: THE ACL FOR CATEGORIES/ARTICLES

1. First, log out of the back-end as a Super User. The Administrator Login screen should appear.

2. Log in as myacluser with the password you gave this user. Figure 13-15 shows the next screen that should appear after login, which is a version of the Admin control panel with only the buttons/icons allowed under the permissions visible.

Figure 13-15
This screen shows the areas of the back-end that this group may access. The group cannot access any other content in the back-end. The Component menu is visible because this screenshot is also used in the next exercise.

EXERCISE 7: THE ACL NEWSFEEDS

1. Log out of the back-end as the ACL user and log back in as the Super User.

2. Open Components > Newsfeeds > Categories manager.

3. Open the options for the newsfeeds (top-right menu).

4. Under the Permissions tab, open the My ACL Group and configure all the settings to Allowed and click Save. Check to make sure that all items have the Allowed status after the Save action.

5. Click Save & Close.

6. Log out of the back-end.

7. Log back in as myacluser and view the screen.

8. Note that the Components menu is now visible. Open it, and the Newsfeeds component is accessible. This particular user now has access and permissions to modify the site's newsfeeds.

The preceding exercises will help if you need to set up sites with a lot of users who edit content in many areas. Let's do one more exercise that demonstrates how to set a content article category so that this user *cannot* access it or make changes to it when logged in.

1. You should be logged in as the Super User.

2. Open Content > Category Manager. The list of categories will appear.

3. Open the Sample Data – Articles category.

4. Click the Set Permissions button, which opens the ACL for this category.

5. With My ACL Group open, change all of the settings to Denied, as shown in Figure 13-16.

6. Click Save.

7. Check the settings. All should show the Not Allowed setting.

8. Click Save & Close.

9. Log out of the back-end as the Super User.

10. Log back in as myacluser.

11. Open the Category Manager.

12. Note that the Sample Data –Articles are now grayed-out and not accessible, but the Uncategorised and My First Category items are live links.

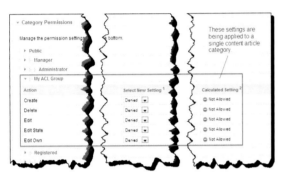

Figure 13-16
Changing the settings to Denied, which is equivalent to Not Allowed, limits this category for the user group.

In the preceding exercises, the user group was created, configured, and allowed to view content controls in the back-end and edit and modify the content on a limited basis. Then content was further modified to *prevent* the user group from accessing it at all. This placed limitations on access by setting different permissions on the item level. In this case, the item was a Content Article category. In a category, individual articles can have permissions set to deny access. This is the lowest level of ACL that can be applied—the item at the lowest level of its respective hierarchy, the article in a category.

You can create and apply more complex settings and configurations of the ACL, but again, these kinds of controls are only needed on sites with a lot of content and many contributors. For smaller sites, without making any of the changes demonstrated in this chapter, the ACL is virtually transparent, even to the Super User.

To Deny to One Is to Deny to All in a Hierarchy

In the parent-child scheme of things, where all permissions are inherited, there is one thing that you simply cannot do. Permissions can be set at the parent level, which sets permissions at the child level. And individual permissions can be set at the child level.

What you cannot do is grant permissions at the child level for something that is denied or not allowed within the parent level for the child. If a content item is set as Denied or Not Allowed within the parent, it *cannot* be allowed in the child, because it is an override of a parent permission. Parent settings may be applied to the child, but the child setting cannot be a higher permission level of access than what the parent has set in the inheritance system.

Summary

In this chapter, you learned the following:

- ▶ ACL is used to control access to the site's content.

- ▶ ACL is more likely to be used on larger Websites than on smaller, personal sites.

- ▶ The default ACL settings are inherited from the Public or Guest user, which only has viewing privileges and no content-editing access.

- ▶ ACL controls action permissions and viewing access levels, which work in conjunction with each other.

- ▶ By default, there are three user groups and a Super User.

- ▶ Public, Manager, and Registered are the default user groups.

- ▶ Public users can view the site content on the front-end.

- ▶ Manager users may access the back-end and edit content, but they cannot alter the site configuration or access certain parts of the administration area.

- ▶ Registered users can view content on the front-end that is restricted from Public users or guests.

- ▶ The Super User, by default, controls everything on the Website and can override any of the settings.

- ▶ Users are allowed to perform actions regarding content items.

- ▶ The four levels of ACL are global, component, category, and item.

- ▶ Viewing access is granted to Public and Registered users.

- ▶ The Special class of users includes those that may log into the Website's back-end.

- ▶ The Joomla! 1.6 system relies on a parent-child hierarchy of both content and users.

- ▶ The parent-child system has rules, and settings are inherited from parent to child.

- ▶ Child settings can only be modified to the same level as the parent, and cannot be set to override.

- ▶ ACL is established by creating groups, setting access levels, setting allowed action, setting permissions, and creating a user.

- ▶ Content categories and content items may have their own ACL settings and can be used in combination to grant or deny access to them.

Multimedia Basics

THE TYPES OF IMAGES USED ON WEBSITES were discussed in Chapter 11, "Image Basics." All of those images were static, except the ones that may have some limited animation or movements to them, such as Flash files. This chapter covers multimedia imagery.

The most popular form of multimedia is video. Entire Websites owe their popularity to their video content. Other types of multimedia include audio presentations, images with motion and sound, and several others.

Multimedia and Extensions in Joomla! 1.6

IN A NUTSHELL, multimedia is nothing more than multiple forms of media tied together. A slide show with a music background is multimedia. A Website that discusses a rock band and plays their music in the background, or upon clicking a link, is a form of multimedia. The site may also include a video, which is a third form added to the other two.

There is also an interactive multimedia class, best illustrated by video games and similar items distributed on discs. However, that type of multimedia is rarely found on Websites, even if a Website is described as interactive. It's a different kind of interactivity.

An Internet search can provide more general information on multimedia. In this chapter, multimedia video displays are the primary focus of discussion and the exercises.

Joomla! 1.6, in and of itself, has no multimedia functionality. Multimedia is displayed by using extensions designed to play music, show a video, or show an animation that may include sound.

For the purposes of this chapter, we will not consider animated banners or images with motion as multimedia. Only multimedia that contains sound or video or slide shows with sound will be discussed. Just because something slides, jumps, and moves, such as collapsible menus, does not make those items multimedia, even if a sound is associated with them. They are simply images with animation.

The Joomla.org Joomla! Extensions Directory (JED) has a category reserved for multimedia extensions. To find out which ones work with Joomla! 1.6, open the Joomla! 1.6 Compatible directory and enter `multimedia` in the search field. As you look through the search results, you will see that most of the extensions that are true multimedia deal with video and audio capabilities.

There are extensions that are pop-ups or modal boxes that can display video and play audio, so they too can be considered multimedia extensions, but more on the fringe. They are actually more like multimedia containers, not unlike the multimedia specialty modules.

Displaying Videos

THIS FORM OF MULTIMEDIA is something that many now consider a must-have on a Website. YouTube has thousands of videos that can be embedded into the site. However, YouTube isn't the only source for videos. There are videos available from many, many other sources.

One thing to keep in mind when embedding videos into a Website is they can disappear as fast as they appeared. Embedded videos are just links to the hosting site, so if that site disables or removes them, your site ends up with a big hole in it where the video used to display. So, *choose reliable sources.*

Videos can be embedded into Websites via a video player that has a link to the video hosted at another location, or via an object, which is nothing more than code that does the same thing. Videos cannot be embedded directly into articles, which are essentially just simple code, nor can they be dropped into a standard Joomla! module. It requires more than that.

To play multimedia, you need a multimedia extension. So let's go get a free one, download it, install it, and set it's configuration to play multimedia on your Website. Let's downloaded a noncommercial (free) extension plugin that, once activated, will let you embed code into articles to play videos and audio files.

EXERCISE 1: CREATING A FOLDER FOR MULTIMEDIA FILES

For the following exercises, create a folder via the Media Manager to hold any uploaded multimedia files. Complete the following steps to add the folder.

1. Open the Media Manager via the Admin control panel.

2. Enter `mymultimedia` into the box at the bottom-right and click the Create Folder button. A new folder should appear in the left column between `banners` and `sampledata`.

3. When you upload media, make sure you open the `mymultimedia` folder by clicking on its name in the main list, or the list to the left.

4. When you upload the media files to that location, use the Browse and Start Upload features at the bottom on the screen.

Now you have a location for uploaded media files. For most extensions that display videos and play audio files, there is an input box in their parameters or option settings to specify the location for the files. Simply enter `mymultimedia` when required, or `images/mymultimedia`, depending on what the extension requires.

Exercise 2: Using the JPlayer Extension

The JPlayer is a plugin extension that inserts certain code into articles or custom HTML modules that play video or audio files. To get the JPlayer, a noncommercial extension, do the following:

1. Go to the JED, filter the list for Joomla! 1.6 Compatible, and search for JPlayer. Note in the results that this extension works for Joomla! 1.5 and 1.6.

2. Click on the extension title.

3. Spend some time reading the information about JPlayer to get an idea of all the things you can do with it.

4. Click Download and select the 1.6 version, as shown in Figure 14-1, and click on the Download button.

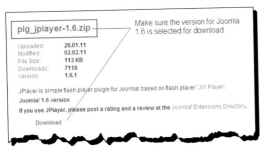

Figure 14-1
Download the plugin for the JPlayer, version 1.6, by clicking the Download button.

5. Install the extension per the usual procedures. The filename is `plg_jplayer-1.6.zip` and should install easily.

6. After installation, open Extensions > Plug-In Manager.

7. Scroll down to Content-JPlayer and click on the title to open it.

8. Enable the plugin.

9. For the purposes of this exercise, Basic Options may be left as the defaults, except for the locations boxes, which should be `images/mymultimedia`.

10. Make note of the location of both the video and audio folders, as shown in Figure 14-2, which is the location in the Media Manager to upload the files.

11. Click Save & Close.

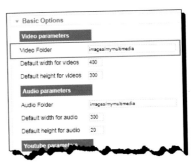

Figure 14-2
Note the location in the Media Manager to upload the files, which is the mymultimedia folder created in Exercise 1 under the /images/ folder.

The extension itself does not display on the front-end because it is a plugin. Plugins only do something when triggered (remember that from Chapter 9, "Plugin Basics"?) and allow content to display. For this extension, codes must be embedded into either an article or a custom HTML module to display the video or play the audio. The code is activated or triggered by the plugin when the content item is opened. The format for the code is shown in Figure 14-3. In Exercise 2, we'll embed an FLV-format (Flash) video into an article.

Figure 14-3
Codes to insert into articles or modules to display video or audio content.

Limited Video File Upload Size

JOOMLA! 1.6 HAS A FILE SIZE limit of 10MB for uploaded images. If the video you want to display is larger than 10MB, you can embed the file or create a link to the video's remote Website location. Even if the file is under 10MB, it may take some time to upload depending on your Internet connection speed and other factors.

As an alternative, you can upload the file via FTP into the /images/mymultimedia folder on the site.

Remember, what goes up, must come down! Large files take a long time to download, so don't post huge videos. While they will stream somewhat, you don't want them to be large files under any circumstances.

In the next exercise, there may be an issue with file types when attempting to upload an FLV file. Complete this exercise to add the FLV filename extension as a legal file for Joomla 1.6 to handle.

EXERCISE 3: ADDING ALL FLV FILE TYPES

1. Open the Media Manager.

2. Select Options in the top-right menu.

3. The pop-up screen should open to the Components tab.

4. As indicated in Figure 14-4, add the flv and FLV filename extensions. You need to enter it one time as all lowercase letters and another in all capital letters.

5. Select Yes for the Enable Flash Uploader permission.

6. Click Save & Close.

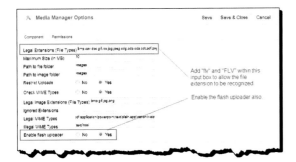

Figure 14-4
Add the flv and FLV file types as shown, and
toggle Enable Flash Upload to Yes.

In the next exercise, now that FLV is a legal filename extension, a video will be loaded into a
module, which may then be positioned anywhere
on the site.

EXERCISE 4: EMBEDDING AN FLV VIDEO INTO A MODULE

Before we begin this exercise, locate an FLV video
file on your computer. It needs to be uploaded
to the Media Manager location, which is the
/images/mymultimedia folder.

If you have a mobile device that can record
video and connect to your computer, you can
make a short video of your cat, your dog, or your
child—any video will do. Upload the video to the
images/mymultimedia folder on your Website via
the Media Manager, as shown in Figure 14-5.
Figure 14-6 shows the Media Manager with the
uploaded file in the mymultimedia folder.

If you already have an FLV file on your computer,
you can use it. Any FLV file will work. It just needs
to get into the images/mymultimedia folder on
the Website server.

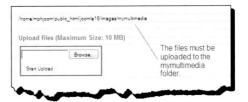

Figure 14-5
Upload multimedia files in the Media Manager
using the upload utility.

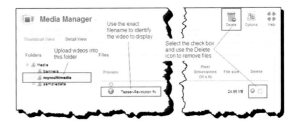

Figure 14-6
After uploading, your video should appear at
this location in the Media Manager.

The following exercise illustrates how a video can
be inserted into a module using the plugin code.
The same procedure applies for inserting the code
into an article. Simply open an article and insert
the code either above or below any content.

The video viewer will appear when a menu link item is clicked to open the article.

1. Open Extensions > Module Manager.

2. Create a New Custom HTML module.

3. Name the module `My First Video Module` and assign it to position-12.

4. Click Save.

5. Enter `{flv}Teaser-Revolution{/flv}` in the Content Editor exactly as shown. Refer to Figure 14-3 for code variations that must be used in combination with the plugin and the content item (article or module). Enter the filename between `{flv}` and `{/flv}`, but do not include the `.flv` extension. It is automatically recognized as that type of file extension.

6. Click Save.

7. Make a Menu Assignment for this module on the Home page.

8. Select Only on the Pages Selected in the Menu Assignment area.

9. Open the Main Menu tab.

10. Toggle the selection to clear the check boxes.

11. Check the Home box.

12. Click Save. The module is now configured to display video in position-12 only on the home page.

13. Go to the front-end and check it. You may need to refresh the browser screen. Test the video player and see if it plays.

14. Click Save & Close.

EXERCISE 5: USING THE FLEXI CUSTOM CODE EXTENSION

Another way to display videos or play audio files is to *embed* the code into a module. There is just one problem—Joomla! 1.6 standard modules do not accommodate the code properly. Therefore, a special module extension must be installed so special codes can be inserted.

In this exercise, we'll download a module called Flexi Custom Code via the JED and install it. Let's begin.

1. Go to the JED, open the Joomla! 1.6 Compatible extensions, and enter `custom code` in the search box.

2. The Flexi Custom Code extension should appear at the top of the list. Click on the title and select Download, which takes you to the developer's Website. Click the download link and save the file to your computer.

3. After it's downloaded, unzip or extract the file. The downloaded file contains the extension for both Joomla! 1.5 and 1.6, so you have to unzip it to access the correct one to install.

4. Go to the admin back-end > Extension Installer and browse to the unzipped folder for the module.

5. Select the Joomla! 1.6 version and install it.

6. After installation, go to Extensions > Module Manager and click the New icon.

7. Select Flexi Custom Code from the list of available modules.

8. Name the module `My Second Video Module`.

9. Assign the template to position-12 via the Select Position button.

10. In the Menu Assignment area, select Module Assignment: Only on the Pages Selected in the drop-down.

11. Click on the Main Menu tab, and then click Toggle Selection to clear the check boxes.

12. Select the Home check box.

13. Click Save.

The module is now configured to only show on the site home page on the front-end and no others. Postion-12 is at the top of the page, above the main content area where articles are normally displayed.

The next thing to do is to get the code to embed a video on the site using the module. We selected a video from the National Geographic Website to use. Their site has a Video button in the menu bar that allows access to their library. We selected a video about Antarctica for this exercise.

14. Open the My Second Video Module Flexi Custom Code module if it is not still open.

15. From the National Geographic Website, copy the code in the Embed box under the video. Make sure you copy all of the code.

16. Place your cursor in the Code box of the module's Basic Options. See Figure 14-7.

17. The code should begin with <embed> and end with </embed>.

18. Click Save & Close. The video should now appear on the front page, similar to that shown in Figure 14-8.

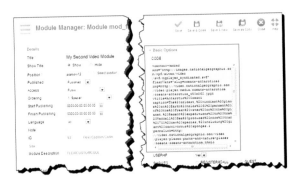

Figure 14-7
Paste the copied code into the Code box as shown, and then click Save & Close.

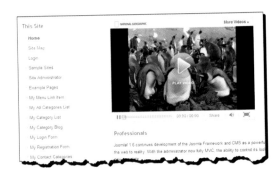

Figure 14-8
The Website front page with the embedded video visible.

Those are two ways to include video on your Website, but they are not the only ways of doing so. There are other methods, but they are somewhat code-intensive tasks and not that easy to implement.

Video files can be huge. Most modern video players start downloading the file and begin playing it while the remainder of the file continues to download. For small files, this works pretty quickly. But, for larger files, the downloading in the background can be near-continuous as the video plays.

Observe Copyright Laws

Just because a video or music file exists on a Website doesn't mean you can use it on your site. Some sites grant linking permissions (YouTube), but many absolutely forbid it. You can get into serious trouble embedding music files on your Website, so use extreme care and caution when doing so. Make sure there are permissions associated with the file.

Summary

In this chapter, you learned the following:

▶ Multimedia is a combination of content used in conjunction.

▶ Website multimedia usually consists of video or audio files.

▶ Joomla!, by itself, cannot display multimedia content.

▶ Specialized extensions are required to display videos and play music files on a Joomla! Website.

▶ The extensions can be either modules or plugins.

▶ Plugins typically facilitate multimedia displays by adding code to other content items.

▶ Modules display multimedia directly and in module positions.

▶ Multimedia files can reside on the Website's server and display from there.

▶ Multimedia files may be hosted on other servers and linked through plugins or modules to display them.

▶ Avoid large multimedia files if possible.

▶ Copyrights and permissions should be observed when displaying multimedia content that is owned by others.

Media Icon Set
01

The Joomla!
Menu System

BY NOW YOU'VE BEEN EXPOSED TO THE PROCESSES involved in creating menu link items to Joomla! 1.6 content items. The process is simple: you go to a menu, create a menu link item, select the type of link, and then connect it to an article or some other content item. That's easy enough, but how did that menu get there to begin with? This chapter is devoted to creating and managing menus.

A menu is nothing more than a specialized module created in the Menu Manager, then controlled by the Module Manager. The individual menu link items are established back in the Menu Manager. There are several steps involved in menu creation and management.

► A menu is created in the Menu Manager.

► A menu module is created in the Module Manager.

► The menu module is associated with a specific menu to display.

► The menu module is positioned in the Module Manager.

► The menu link items are created in the Menu Manager by opening the respective menu.

The Default Top Menu

IN THE DEFAULT INSTALLATION, there is a horizontal top menu. This menu is located in template position-1 and has attributes for style and appearance inherited from the templates style sheet. Most templates have a horizontal menu that, when placed in a specific module position, displays the style and attributes of the template style sheet.

If the menu is moved from position-1 to position-7, it loses the visual attributes of position-1 and implements those applied to modules in position-7. What does this mean? It means that visual appearance is totally dependent upon the Cascading Style Sheet (CSS) code. For example, if the Top menu module was relocated to position-10 (center, bottom of the page), its visual appearance would be completely different. It would still be a menu per se, with links, but it would appear as a vertical bulleted list, which is the default style for the template.

The bottom line about all this is if you want to change the appearance of a menu, or locate a menu in another module position with a different look, the CSS must be changed to accommodate the new location and appearance. This can be a hopeless task for anyone who isn't a programmer or CSS coder.

Fortunately, nonprogrammers are not resigned to CSS purgatory in Joomla! 1.6. There are third-party extensions that can create a menu using the extensions and built-in attribute controls and place that menu in any module position on the page. If you want to add a menu that looks different or performs differently than the one assigned to the template module positions, a third-party menu extension is the way to do it. These extensions are a perfect workaround to the coding skills problem and let you install an extension with an easy-to-use admin interface. An extension of this type will be added in Exercise 5.

Before we get into third-party menu extensions, let's look at creating a new menu, creating a new menu module, connecting the two to display on the page, and creating menu link items to content.

EXERCISE 1: CREATING A NEW MENU

The steps for creating a new menu are simple. You just create it by giving it a name and saving it. That's it.

1. Open the Menu Manager in the Admin control panel and select New in the top-right control bar. You can also use the drop-down Menus > Menu Manager > Add New Menu. Either way will open the Add Menu screen.

2. Enter My First Menu into the first two fields.

3. Enter This is my first menu. in the description box. Refer to Figure 15-1 to see these entries.

4. Click Save & Close.

5. Go to the Menu Manager, open it, and look for the new menu by name (see Figure 15-2).

Figure 15-1
Add Menu screen with entries for the exercise.

Figure 15-2
The menu name should appear in the Menus list.

EXERCISE 2: CREATING A NEW MENU MODULE

With the menu created, now we need to create a menu module to connect to it. This is necessary because menus by themselves cannot be assigned to template positions. Only modules can be assigned to specific locations, so a module must be connected to a menu to place it on a page. Let's place the menu at position-6, which is the right column of this template.

1. Open the Module Manager in the Admin control panel and select New in the top-right control bar. You can also use the drop-down Extensions > Module Manager > and select New. Either way will open the selection pop-up screen.

2. Select Menu for the type to create. This will open a blank module menu that needs to be configured in the Details, Menu Assignment, Basic Options, and Advanced Options parameter sections.

3. In the Details section, name the menu My Menu Module and assign it to position-6, as shown in Figure 15-3.

4. Click Save.

5. In the Menu Assignment section, make the Menu Assignment Only on the Pages Selected.

6. Open the Main Menu tab and uncheck the check boxes.

7. Select the Home Menu Link Item to associate with this module.

8. Click Save.

9. Do not exit the module.

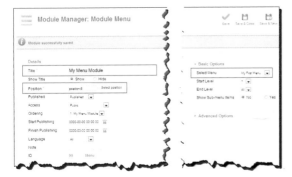

Figure 15-3
The Menu Module with Details added. The menu will appear in the bottom center of the page after menu link items are added.

No Menu Link Items, No Display

Even if a menu is created, a module is attached to it, and a module position is identified, the menu will not appear unless there is at least one menu link item in the menu that is linked to content. When building a menu, add at least one menu link item to force the module to display. It must also be in the Published state to display.

EXERCISE 3: CONNECTING THE MODULE TO THE MENU

The last configuration in the Menu Module is to actually connect the named menu with the positioning module so that menu link items will appear in the module position.

1. In the Basic Options section, the module is assigned to a menu.

2. In the Select Menu drop-down, select My First Menu from the list. This is why the menu needed to be created to begin with. It would not appear on the list if that first step were not completed.

3. Leave the other settings as is.

4. Click Save & Close.

The preceding exercise completes the mechanics of creating a menu and an associated module, and connecting the two together. Now the menu needs to be populated with link items.

EXERCISE 4: CREATING MENU LINK ITEMS

In this exercise, we'll link articles to a menu link item in the new menu. We'll look at one example step-by-step, and then do two more with just simple instructions.

1. Go to Menu Manager > My First Menu and open it. No menu link items should appear. You can also do this via Menus > My First Menu > Add New Menu Item.

2. Click on the New icon in the top-right control bar.

3. For the menu item type, select Single Article.

4. Enter Link One as the link title.

5. Select the Getting Started article via the Required Settings | Select Article function. See Figure 15-4 to view the screen with the entries.

6. Click Save.

7. Repeat the steps and link Link Two to the Using Joomla! article, and link Link Three to the The Joomla! Project article. Save after adding each link.

8. There should now be three link items in the menu, as seen in Figure 15-5.

9. Click Save & Close.

Figure 15-4
Enter the information and make selections as shown in the New Menu Item Manager.

Figure 15-5
The list of links for My First Menu after adding the menu link items.

If all the steps were completed properly, the front page of the Website should show the menu in the right column, as seen in Figure 15-6. The main menu is on the left and the new My Menu Module should be on the right. The menu should only appear when the site is in the home page display.

Figure 15-6
After the menu and menu module have been created and assigned to position-6, it should appear on the front page of the Website as shown.

If you recall the discussion about how modules in different module positions can be coded in the CSS to appear differently, this is a perfect example. Run the mouse up and down the menus in the left column and the mouseover mode will show a gray background. In the right column, the mouseover shows a blue background with white text. Also note the variation in the module title. All of these parameters are controlled by CSS, relative to the module.

The Module Class Suffix (CSS for the entire module) and the Menu Class Suffix (CSS for the individual menu items) are discussed in Chapter 19, "CSS-PHP-HTML Basics," if you feel brave enough to modify the CSS style sheets for the template.

Using Menu Extensions

AS MENTIONED EARLIER, the default menus are subject to how the designer coded the template being used. The default Joomla! 1.6, admittedly, doesn't have an impressive menu design. It works for demonstrating the software, but not so much for a Website. In addition, other installed templates (commercial or noncommercial) will have the same issues regarding giving the menus different looks. So how is this done? Simple; we'll use an extension.

Let's download a menu extension and configure it. We'll use a noncommercial extension called SWMenuFree, which is actually a component that creates menu modules.

Before you go through the download steps, it is recommended that you go to www.swmenupro.com and view the live demos. Use the Preview button to look at each menu style to get an idea of what kind of menus can be created with the extension.

This extension was chosen because it is free, is a combination component and module creator, and produces many different types of menus that allow an exceptional amount of customization without the need to know CSS coding. Be prepared to learn a lot in these exercises.

Here is what we will do in the following exercises:

- ▶ Download and install the SWMenuFree extension.
- ▶ Create a menu module within the SWMF component.
- ▶ Connect the module to My First Menu.
- ▶ Configure individual menu link items with coloring and other parameters, again, within the component.

EXERCISE 5: DOWNLOADING AND INSTALLING THE EXTENSION

By now you should have a pretty good grasp on the extension downloading and installing process but, if not, let's go through it one more time for the SWMF extension.

1. Go to the www.swmenupro.com Website.

2. Spend some time investigating the extension and looking at the demo of menu types.

3. Download SWMF Version 6.3 for Joomla! 1.6. Make sure you download the correct version. There may be more than one screen before you get to the actual download link.

4. After it downloads, install it as you would any other extension.

Exercise 6: Creating the Menu Module in the Component

The last exercise installed the SWMF extension to the Component Manager. Everything that is done with the extension starts by opening the component. After the menu module is created and configured, nothing else is done with the module and everything is accomplished in the component.

1. Open the SWMF component via the Component Manager. You can access it via the Admin control panel or via the Admin menu.

2. Name the module `My Menu Module 2`.

3. Under Menu Source Settings, select Trans Menu from the drop-down list as the Menu System option.

4. Under Menu Source Settings, select Use Content Only from the drop-down list as the Menu Source in the system. We'll change this in the next exercise.

5. Click Save. The same screen will remain in the browser window.

6. In General Module Settings, select Yes for the Show Module Name option.

7. In General Module Settings, select Yes for the Published option.

8. In the Position & Access area, select position-6 for the module.

9. Click Save.

Limited Menus in Demo Version

You can only create four kinds of menus in the demo version of SWMenuFree. If you want more menu types, consider purchasing the extension's pro version.

Exercise 7: Configuring the Module as a Menu

If you recall from the earlier exercises, after a menu is created, a corresponding module must also be created and linked to it. Even though we're using SWMF, this still needs to be done.

With the SWMF component open, do the following:

1. In Menu Source Settings, change the Use Content Only selection in the Menu Source drop-down to my-first-menu.

2. In Style Sheet Settings, change the Load Style Sheet option, which is a good idea because it separates the module style sheet completely from the template.

3. This is important! Every time you save a change made to the menu module, you *must* also export the style sheet. They are two separate files, and unless you actually overwrite the external style sheet, the changes will not take effect. So Save and Export must be done each time.

4. Go to the site's front-end, refresh the browser window, and you should see the menu on the right side of the page, as in Figure 15-7.

5. Because the module heading is controlled by the template style sheet, it is the proper width. The menu link items, however, are controlled by the SWMF style sheet, which is why they appear different.

Figure 15-7
After activating the module, it should appear as shown on the front page.

The status of the menu modules is now this:

- ▶ The module has been created and named.

- ▶ It has been assigned to a module position on the template. Remember, different templates may have different module position names, so if the template is changed, the module may need to be reassigned.

- ▶ It has been connected to a previously created menu. Menus are separate from the modules that display them, and they must be connected, or associated, with each other.

- ▶ The module has been published, so it's viewable on the front page.

- ▶ The module, via the SWMF component, may now be "dressed up" and given its look and appearance by setting parameters, which are then written into an external style sheet, which is completely separate from the one(s) for the template.

Viewing the Settings

In the SWMF component, the round green circles with the "i" inside them display hint text that basically tells you what the options do. These are only accessible on the menu module settings and not on any of the tabs at the top.

Exercise 8: Configuring the CSS for the Menu Link Items

The menu module and menu are connected and appear on the front page of the site. Right now, the menu is pretty generic looking, so let's make some minor changes.

1. Open the Size, Position & Offsets tab near the top of the component window.

2. In Menu Item Sizes, enter 200 into the Top Menu Item Width field.

3. Click Save and then you can Export.

4. View the front page. The menu link items should be the entire width of the module space.

5. Open the Colors & Backgrounds tab near the top of the component window.

6. In the Background Colors section, change #135CAE to #000000, which is the hex color value for black.

7. Click Save, and then you can Export.

8. View the front page. The menu link item background should now be black. When black is used as a background, the type (font) tends to blur at the edges. A bold font makes it look better.

9. Open the Fonts & Padding tab near the top of the component window.

10. In the Font Weight section, change the drop-down for Top Menu Font Weight to bolder.

11. Go back to the Colors & Backgrounds tab and open it.

12. In the Background Colors section, change Top Menu Over Color to #E1E1E1, which is the hex color value for a light gray.

13. Click Save, and then you can Export.

14. If you run the mouse over the items, the background color will now be a light gray. The type is still the default yellow color and needs to be changed.

15. Open the Colors & Backgrounds tab near the top of the component window.

16. In the Font Colors section, Top Menu Over Font Color parameter, change #FFFF85 to #000000, which is the hex color value for black.

17. Click Save and then you can Export.

18. Now, when you mouse over the menu link items, the background color is a light gray and the text is black.

There are dozens of additional parameters that can be configured for the module via the SWMF component. Take some time and experiment with the settings. An easy way to see what's going on after entering a change to any parameter is by executing the preview, which opens the menu, by itself, into a separate pop-up window. If you like what you see, you can click Save and then Export; if not, just cancel and continue, which brings you to the last saved configuration for both the module and the external style sheet.

Hide the Module When...

WHEN THE MODULE WAS CREATED, by default, it was assigned to show itself with every menu link item in every menu. That means, no matter which link is clicked, the menu will continue to appear for the default template. Let's change that so the menu only appears on the Website's home page. Here's how to do that:

1. Open My Menu Module 2 in Extensions > Module Manager.

2. Go to the Menu Assignment section of the manager.

3. Change the Module Assignment selection in the drop-down to Only on the Pages Selected.

4. Open the Main Menu tab. None of the menu link items should be checked. Click Toggle Selection if needed to uncheck all items.

5. Check the check box for the Home Menu Link Item.

6. Click Save & Close.

7. Check some of the menu link items on the front page. Only the Home item should allow the module to show. And while the rest don't actually hide it, they are simply not assigned to the module to even let it display, in effect, hiding it from view.

Summary

In this chapter, you learned the following:

▶ Menus are first created in the Menu Manager.

▶ To display a menu, a module must be created and assigned to a template module position.

▶ The menu must then be connected to the module, or the other way around. Either way, they must be connected by assignment correlation.

▶ Menu link items must be created in the menu for the module to appear.

▶ Menu look, style, and appearance are controlled by the CSS for the template.

▶ Nonprogrammers and those not familiar with editing CSS style sheets limit how much a menu's appearance can change, unless a provision in the module extensions contains modification controls.

▶ There are extensions that will create a menu module and allow all of the parameters and variables to be configured independent of the template stylesheet.

▶ The extensions for creating menu modules are installed in the same manner as all extensions.

▶ Some menu module extensions consist of a component that creates modules.

▶ The module that is created is managed like any other module via the admin back-end.

▶ The component controls all of the visual and menu element configurations.

your site

☆ ⌂ ✉

About Us

- ▶ **News**
- ▶ **Lorum**
- ▶ **Sample**
- ▶ **Sample**
- ▶ **Sample**

Lorem ipsum dolor sit amet, consectetur adipisicing elit, sed do eiusmod tempor incididunt ut labore et dolore magna aliqua. Ut enim ad minim veniam, quis nostrud exercitation ullamco laboris nisi ut aliquip ex ea commodo consequat.

Lorem ipsum dolor sit amet, consectetur adipisicing elit, sed do eiusmod tempor incididunt ut labore et dolore magna aliqua. Ut enim ad minim veniam, quis nostrud exercitation ullamco laboris nisi ut aliquip ex ea commodo consequat.

Lorem ipsum dolor sit amet, consectetur adipisicing elit, sed do eiusmod tempor incididunt ut labore et dolore magna aliqua. Ut enim ad minim veniam, quis nostrud exercitation ullamco laboris nisi ut aliquip ex ea commodo consequat.

Lorem ipsum dolor sit amet, consectetur adipisicing elit, sed do eiusmod tempor incididunt ut labore et dolore magna aliqua. Ut enim ad minim veniam, quis nostrud exercitation ullamco laboris nisi ut aliquip ex ea commodo consequat.

Additional

Content Topics

I N PREVIOUS CHAPTERS, the topics were designed to keep you focused on the task at hand and without adding too much extraneous information about "stuff" that was taking place, or could take place under various conditions. In this chapter, we'll cover some of those "intentional omissions."

Fast Access to the Control Panel

"Why didn't you tell me earlier" is going to be your reaction to this information about navigating around the back-end. Remember every time you were asked to open the Admin control panel and you had to go to the Site Menu to do that? Well, you could have just clicked Administration at the top of the screen (see Figure 16-1) and it would have opened it for you immediately. You had to take the long way for a while to get used to navigating the back-end, so forgive the omission. But, from now on, when you need to access the control panel, just click on Administration at the top left of the screen. Of course, after that you need to open a manager of some type and, in the same number of clicks, you could have used the menu itself. However you want to do it from now on is your choice.

Figure 16-1
Fast access to the Admin control panel via the Administration page title.

The Joomla! Core Versus Extensions

EVEN THOUGH WE ADDED a lot of extensions in previous chapters to give you an idea how things work, you can put together a pretty decent Joomla! 1.6 Website using nothing but the Joomla! core. This term refers to the default installation and the components and modules that come with it.

Without adding any extensions, other than different templates, a Joomla! 1.6 Website can take on a different look and appearance without much work. The core works with every template that is Joomla! 1.6 Native. Because all of the visual is controlled by the template, and all of the content is controlled by the core, we have a perfect Content Management System (CMS) environment.

The core is pretty good; extensions just make it that much better.

The Extension Manager

AND WHILE ON THE TOPIC of extensions, let's look at the Extension Manager a little closer. Thus far, we've only used the Install part of the manager. It has other important functions as well.

The Extension Manager serves five major tasks, accessible via their named tabs:

Install. This is the pivot point for all extensions. They need to be installed, and this part of the Extension Manager is where it happens. You installed extensions in previous chapters, so you should know how this works.

Update. Joomla! 1.6 extensions are supposed to have a feature that shows if the extension has been updated by developers. It is not an automatic notification. This item needs to be executed. If there are any updates, a message will appear, and you can decide to update or not.

Manage. This tab opens a complete list of installed extensions. It also enables, disables, and uninstalls extensions. Note that even though the core extensions cannot be uninstalled, they can be disabled. But, disable them with care! You can sort and narrow the extension list using the drop-down filters.

Discover. This task helps you upload extensions that cannot go through the normal Install procedure and may need to be uploaded via other methods. This feature helps identify those extensions. It also allows you to install multiple extensions at the same time.

Warnings. This task is helpful in determining if you have any issues with an extension and why it did, or would not, install successfully. When you click on the Warnings tab, if there are any warnings, drop-down sliders will appear for each issue.

Setting Publishing Dates for Content

IN PREVIOUS VERSIONS OF JOOMLA!, the publishing start/stop dates could only be set for articles. Joomla! 1.6 extends those options into modules, which are nothing more than self-contained content items.

In the following exercise, we'll set the publishing dates for a module, but keep in mind the same method applies to articles as well. In articles, the settings are in the Publishing Options area. In modules, the settings are in the Details area. That's the only difference.

By default, all publishing settings are either published immediately or never stop publishing (open-ended). When an article or module is created and saved, it is immediately viewable and never changes.

Also by default, the time to set the starting and finishing times on designated content publishing dates is 12:00 midnight, or 00:00:00 a.m.

There is no setting selection within the calendar date picker to set this time value. However, times may be set by placing the cursor at the end of the resulting date field, backspacing, and changing the HH:MM:SS (Hours:Minutes:Seconds) values to the desired time on that date.

EXERCISE 1: SETTING PUBLISHING DATES FOR A MODULE

1. Open My Menu Module 2, which is the module we created in conjunction with the SWMenuFree extension.

2. The starting and finishing settings should be set with no values. If you change Start Publishing to a future date, the module will stop appearing on the page and not show up again until that date has been reached. The time to Start/Finish Publishing can be manually entered after the date, as shown in Figure 16-2.

3. Change the Start Publishing date to tomorrow (from whatever date you are doing this exercise).

4. Click Save & Close.

5. If you check the front page of the site, the module should no longer appear.

6. Leave the module in that state and come back tomorrow, after midnight, and it should be back into view again. Make a note to do that to verify the module published itself.

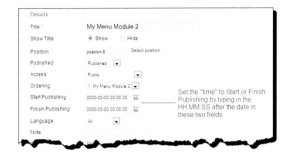

Figure 16-2
The actual time to Start or Finish Publishing must be set manually in the date fields.

Nonactive Content

NONACTIVE CONTENT ISN'T A BIG DEAL on smaller sites because you can just change it by updating the articles or module content. On larger sites, like the newspaper Website from an earlier chapter, you may want to save and store the content for reference. This is called archiving content, which can then be restored or trashed. Let's discuss archiving first.

By definition, archiving is simply a method of storing content so that it may be retrieved and/or restored to its original state/location on the Website.

In fact, there is a module in the core installation that will display a list of archived articles, going back any number of months, using the created date as a reference point. The module can show a list of the calendar months and the articles that are archived from that time period.

If an article was authored, for example, in April 2011, a link to April 2011 would automatically display and when opened, would show any articles that were published in that time period and archived. Let's do an exercise to give you some experience archiving a content item and displaying the archive list.

EXERCISE 2: SETTING ARTICLES/MODULES TO ARCHIVED STATE

To store an article or module for retrieval, it must be set to Archived status, as follows:

1. Open My First Article, which you created previously.

2. Change the Status of the article to Archived, as shown in Figure 16-3.

Figure 16-3

Change the Status of the content item to Archived to place it into the archive library.

3. Click Save & Close.

4. Go to Article Manager > Article List view.

5. Filter the list for archived content. My First Article should appear on the list.

At this point, the only way you know that an article is in the archive is by viewing the article list via the Article Manager and filtering it by selecting Archived in the first drop-down. What if you wanted site visitors to see what articles have been moved from published to archived, such as a monthly newsletter?

This is done by adding an Archived Articles module to the site and placing it into a module position. Exercise 3 takes you through the process.

EXERCISE 3: ADDING THE ARCHIVED ARTICLE MODULE

In essence, the Archived Article module is nothing more than a self-generated category list that only sources its content from the archived location. The only access to the archive is via the Article Manager in the back-end. Adding the module allows you to place it on the front-end of the site.

1. Open the Module Manager and select the New option.

2. For Module Type, select Archived Articles from the list. Figure 16-4 shows the setting we'll set in the next few steps.

3. When the Module Manager opens, enter `My Article Archive` for the title, as shown in Figure 16-4.

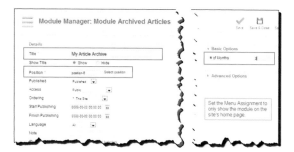

Figure 16-4

Setting to configure the Archived Articles module to display archived content.

4. Assign the module to position-6.

5. Set the menu assignment so the module only appears on the front page by designating it to appear Only on the Pages Selected, and then only on the home page of the main menu.

6. In the Basic Options area of the module, set the period to three months.

7. Click Save & Close.

8. Go to the site's front-end, select Home, and view the right side of the screen. You should see the module displaying, as shown in Figure 16-5. February, 2011 was when the archived article was created. Your date will likely be different. There also may be other archived articles visible.

9. Open the link. My First Article should appear.

Figure 16-5
The Archived Article module displaying a dated category list of archived articles by their date of publishing.

Using Trash to Delete Content

SOMETIMES JUST DELETING content is the way to go, especially if you have created something incorrectly and just want to get rid of it. For articles and modules, this process is called trashing.

EXERCISE 4: TRASHING AN ARTICLE

To permanently get rid of content, you must designate it as trash in the system.

1. Open the Article Manager.

2. Create an article called `Article to be Trashed`. You will need to add something to the content editor in order to save it.

3. Click Save & Close.

4. Go back to the Article Manager, Article List view.

5. Articles cannot be trashed when open, so select the check box next to the article name.

6. Click on the Trash icon in the top control menu. This is a one-click step. When the Trash icon has been clicked, the article is trashed.

Oops! That was a mistake! How do we get it back?

EXERCISE 5: RESTORING TRASHED CONTENT

Even though there was no confirming action required to trash the article, it can be restored. This is how you can restore an article (or module) in Joomla! 1.6.

1. Open the Article Manager and filter the list by selecting Trashed in the drop-down for Status of articles. This is the first drop-down on the left.

2. The list displays all of the articles in Trashed, and they will remain in the trash archive until the trash is emptied, which permanently deletes them.

3. Select the article to be trashed by checking the box next to its title.

4. Click on the Publish icon in the top control bar. This republishes the article back into its assigned category. This can be done two ways, as shown in Figure 16-6.

5. Refilter the article list as Published and the article should show up on the list, indicating that it has been restored.

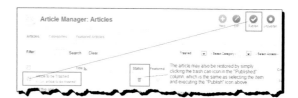

Figure 16-6
Two ways to restoring a trashed article.

Permanently Deleting Content

TRASHED ARTICLES AND MODULES can be permanently deleted from the database, which clears up space. There is no need to keep trashed content because it was incorrectly created to begin with. To permanently delete content, you must purge the trash archive as follows.

EXERCISE 6: PERMANENTLY DELETING CONTENT

This process involves emptying the trash, which has the net result of permanently deleting the items selected.

There is no recovery after this step.

1. In the Article Manager, filter the list using Trashed in the first drop-down.

2. Select any items that should be removed permanently. Please note, there will be no confirmation of the Empty Trash action in the next step.

3. Click the Empty Trash icon in the top control menu. The trash archive has now been emptied of the selected content. There is no way to get the content back at this point.

Summary

In this chapter, you learned the following:

▶ The Admin control panel can be accessed via the Administration link at the top of the page.

▶ The Joomla! core is powerful and can configure a wide range of content.

▶ Extensions enhance the core but are not necessary.

▶ Any number of Websites can be created with templates and the core features.

▶ The Extension Manager has additional features to install and upgrade extensions, and to give notifications on extension status settings.

▶ Articles and modules can have specific starting and finishing dates and times.

▶ Dates can be selected via a date picker feature to set publishing dates.

▶ Publishing times must be set manually by entering the information into the data field.

▶ Articles and modules can be assigned to an archive for storage.

▶ The archive can be displayed as a category list in a module to view the historical content.

▶ Content can also be trashed, which reassigns it to a "trashed" category and allows it to be restored.

▶ Trashed content can be restored to its original location.

▶ Items in Trash can be permanently deleted from the system.

▶ There is no way to recover content from the Empty Trash action once it has been initiated.

Advanced Topics

I N PREVIOUS CHAPTERS, MANY OF THE TOPICS and exercises dealt with learning how to manage content, make it visible, and otherwise configure the Website for viewing. Those topics focused primarily on the "basics" of getting things done and how to do it. This chapter covers some special topics that are important to know, but not necessary to use. It is good to know this information should you want to add a module position, create different looks for different modules and article pages, change some of the terms used to display content and, if needed, create a template override to modify how a module or component displays.

Warning!

Do not attempt any of the exercises in this chapter unless you are familiar with general HTML or CSS coding. Doing so incorrectly could corrupt and destroy the Website layout. All the exercises require access to files that you would not normally change or edit. Therefore, all of the files on your Website should be copied to another location before attempting to make any changes.

What You Need

To PERFORM THE EXERCISES in this chapter, which involve editing certain files and making changes, you will need the following:

▶ An FTP program to access the server and download/upload files.

▶ An editing program, such as notepad or other plain-text editor, or an HTML editor. There are free ones available and commercial ones that don't cost much. A "visual"-type editor is not required as you will not be able to see the results of the changes because these are coded files and not actual Webpages.

▶ To search the Internet and spend some time reading up on Cascading Style Sheets (CSS), HTML, and the coding and requirements for editing them.

While an editing feature has been built into the Joomla! 1.6 back-end to open template pages and CSS style sheets, it's a bit cumbersome and clumsy to use. If you have an FTP program and an advanced HTML/CSS editor program, accessing and modifying the files is much easier to accomplish.

Chances are, you have been inundated with Web 2.0 something or other. But what the heck is Web 2.0 exactly? First, Web 2.0 isn't a "thing" or something tangible like that. You can't say: "I want a Web 2.0 Website," because it isn't something that specific. The more accurate phrase would be: "I want a Website that has Web 2.0 features."

The general accepted definitions for Web 2.0 follow:

> Web 2.0 technology refers to Websites or applications accessible via the Internet that allow users to participate or alter content. Some examples would be social networking, wikis, and blogs. Twitter and Facebook are two prime and more notable examples of a Web 2.0 environment.

> The term Web 2.0 is associated with Web applications that facilitate participatory information sharing, interoperability, user-centered design, and collaboration on the Web.

> Web 2.0 is the generalized term for Internet-based tools and how to use them. The technologies encompassed by Web 2.0 generally include, but are not limited to, blogging, tags, RSS, social bookmarking and networking, along with others that are emerging almost on a daily basis.

> The philosophy of Web 2.0 focuses on the idea that all who access the Internet and are active contributors help customize the media they access for their own purposes, as well as those of their communities. Facebook, again, is a prime example.

So, in summary, Web 2.0 is more of a way of presenting content that allows users to interact with it. There are no Web 2.0 templates in the real sense, because it isn't a "thing." There are templates that contain Web 2.0 features—which can be as simple as including a link to the site owner's Facebook page, or social networking locations. Web 2.0 is the content interactivity level.

Tableless Layouts

IF YOU WANT TO COMMIT A SIN that will put you in Internet Purgatory, create a Website using tables. Back when the Web was just emerging, tables where used to create columns across the screen to add content. That was pretty cool back then. But using tables nowadays will almost get you tarred, feathered, beaten to a pulp, jailed, ostracized, banned from society, and eaten by aliens. However, tables may still be used "in content" for presenting tabular data, but they *should not* be used for template page layout purposes.

With the advent of Websites using templates with advanced HTML and CSS coding, tables have become the dinosaurs of Website layouts. The preferable way to do things, such as create column layouts, is to use what is known as layers or, in code terms, <div>s. A layer is a <div> and is controlled by CSS, as shown in the generalized example in Figure 17-1. That is by no means the only way to do it. CSS coding can get really crazy with <div>s, so do some searching and read up on <div>s and how they can be coded. Layers are also referred to as *divisions*, so if you see both or either, they are the same thing code-wise.

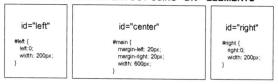

TYPICAL 3-COLUMN LAYOUT USING <DIV> ELEMENTS

Figure 17-1
Example of using <div>s to create a
three-column layout on a page.

In the example, each <div> is given a name (ID). This ID then has an associated set of CSS parameters that only apply to that page element, the <div> with that particular ID. Almost all <div>s have an ID or a class, which are topics you should study extensively if you plan on getting deeper into modifying Joomla! 1.6 templates, and their design, layout, and colors.

Chapter 18, "Specialty Applications for Joomla! Websites," covers the use of the coding, as seen in Figure 17-1, along with other topics relative to CSS, HTML, and PHP, which together form the infrastructure of all Joomla! 1.6 templates.

Using Class Suffixes

THE TWO FORMS OF CSS CODE for any element on a page are classes and IDs. Classes are used for most coding, but that's not a steadfast rule. Classes are CSS code elements that can be used multiple times on a page, whereas an ID name may only be applied to one element, one time.

Let's look at an actual example using the sample content and default template for the Website. Let's use the My Menu module as the example for the following exercises. Here is what we need to apply a class suffix to that module:

EXERCISE 1: MODIFYING THE CSS FOR MODULES IN THE TEMPLATE STYLE SHEET

1. Identify the CSS that applies to that module container.

2. Assign a class suffix to the module to identify it as a unique element.

3. Change the CSS in the template to make the module look different.

4. Go to Extensions > Template Manager and identify the default template. It should be beez_20 and is named Beez2-Default in the back-end.

5. Switch the view in the Template Manager from Styles to Templates.

6. Open the beez_20 Details template file by clicking on its name. The screen in Figure 17-2 should open.

Figure 17-2
The beez_20 template details showing the Template Master Files and the style sheets associated with it.

7. Click on Edit css/layout.css in the style sheets list.

8. Scroll down the window that opens until you find the CSS code, as shown in Figure 17-3, item A. Note on the front page that no border surrounds the module.

9. Add border: 2px solid green; to the original code exactly as shown in item B. Make sure there is a semicolon (;) at the end of the line. If the file does not save properly, the "permissions" for the css/layout.css file may need to be set to 0777 via FTP.

10. Click Save.

11. View the front-end. All the modules on the right side should have a green box around them. This means that the correct CSS code is being altered. The Login and My Latest News modules also have a green border because the CSS applies to all those modules generally at this point.

12. Go back to the CSS in the style sheet.

13. Copy the code for the .moduletable declaration and paste it immediately below and modify the code.

14. Remove the CSS code for the border in the original section of code so that it looks exactly as shown in item A. You should now have code that looks like items A and B.

15. Modify item B so that it has the code changes as indicated in item C. This includes changing the name of the element by adding _mysuffix and changing the padding parameters. The border can remain the same. The padding was added to clear the module content from the green border box.

    Use the underline character as the first character in a suffix name.

16. If your code looks like items A and C, you have entered the code correctly. There should be no code that looks like item B; only the code as appears in A and C.

17. Save & Close.

In this next exercise, we'll add some module suffix code to the My Menu module, which will alter how that module appears. The earlier code changes placed a green box around all of the modules. This second block of code will display the green border around only one module: the suffixed one.

```
.moduletable
{
        margin:0px 0 20px 0;
        padding:0px 0;
}
```
A

```
.moduletable
{
        margin:0px 0 20px 0;
        padding:0px 0
        border: 2px solid green;
}
```
B

```
.moduletable_mysuffix
{
        margin:0px 0 20px 0;
        padding:0px 10px 0 10px;
        border: 2px solid green;
}
```
C

Figure 17-3
Change the CSS code as shown in items B and C. First find A. Then modify item A to appear as item B. Then copy item B and make modifications per item C. Restore item B to its original state: item A.

EXERCISE 2: ASSIGNING A CLASS SUFFIX TO THE MODULE

1. Go to Extensions > Module Manager.

2. Open the My menu module in the Module Manager.

3. Open the Advanced Options drop-down on the right side of the screen.

4. Enter _mysuffix in the Module Class Suffix box, as shown in Figure 17-4. Note the underline is the first character of the suffix name.

5. Click Save & Close.

6. View the front-end. A green box should appear around only that module, no others.

By default, the module was coded as a module-table and by adding the suffix, the coding applied is the code for moduletable_mysuffix, which changed it, but only for that module. All other modules using the moduletable code remain the same. In more complex CSS coding, adding a suffix allows for more subtle or dramatic changes to the individual element that has been class suffixed using this procedure. In menu link items, something similar can be employed via the Page Display Options configuration.

Figure 17-4
The Module Class Suffix is added to the field shown and relates to modified code in the template style sheet.

Multiple Modules with the Same Suffix

Suffixes can be applied individually or selectively to several modules. The same class suffix can be applied to more than one module. Several modules can have the same class suffix assigned, which makes them appear identical. This allows, for example, a certain look and appearance for the modules on the left, and another set of styles for those on the right side. There are several ways of doing this, but the suffix method is the easiest to implement via the back-end.

Other Display Options

WHEN A MENU LINK item is created, there are two areas a CSS class can be added to change the appearance of the page content displayed from a menu link item and the menu link item itself. Each of these options is described in the following sections.

Page Display Options

A page is displayed by clicking a menu link item, and that item has parameters that can be set to configure a page display that is different than the default for the Website. This feature is called the Page Class and is found in the Page Display Options drop-down menu of Menu Manager: New Menu Item.

Page Class is applied in a manner similar to the module class suffix, except you are not suffixing anything. An entirely new CSS class is created with all of the parameters defined for this particular content item. This allows the use of full CSS coding to create a page that has a well-defined and distinctive look.

What this feature essentially allows is the creation of a CSS class that might, for example, call for a green border to appear around the outside of the page. A class called green could be created with the border parameters in the CSS code (see Figure 17-5).

You would enter green in the Page Class box. The result would be that page, and that page only, appears with a green border. The Page Class can be applied to any other pages that should be similarly displayed.

A Link CSS Style menu link item is created in the CSS for the template, and the class name entered in the box to implement it. Should you want that menu link item to appear in red, a CSS class called menuitemred could be created and that name entered in the box. The result is the menu link item would appear as red.

However, if you wanted all menu items in the menu module to be red, suffixing the module would be easier than doing each individual one as a Link CSS Style. This feature is designed for selected menu link items, not globally or for all link items in a menu. This is a prime example of the creative opportunities for template designers and Website managers to create unique designs based on content variables implemented through suffixes and classes, and controlled via CSS— keeping design separate from content and invoked under preset conditions.

Figure 17-5
The Page Class is entered in the box shown after the creation of the CSS that controls the page display via this assignment.

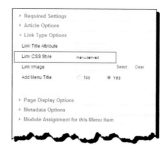

Figure 17-6
The Link CSS Style is entered in the box shown after the creation of the CSS that controls how the menu link item displays.

Link Type Options

In the Link Type Options drop-down, in the same manager as before, a feature similar to Page Display Options is available, except that it applies to the menu link item. When configured and implemented, the parameters only apply to this particular menu link item and no others.

Creating a CSS class for use with Page Classes and Link CSS Styles is covered in Chapter 20, "Search Engine Optimization."

Changing Terms

EVER SEE A WORD OR SOMETHING on a Website that you just don't like? What if one of those words was on your site? Well, if it is, you can change it. The Joomla! 1.6 platform has language files, which are not the same as language extensions. Language files contain all the words you see on the site.

In this next exercise, we'll modify a term in the Login module. Look at Figure 17-7, where it says Create an Account. Let's change it to Create a User Account.

Figure 17-7
The default Login module with standard terminology.

EXERCISE 3: CHANGING A TERM IN THE LOGIN MODULE

1. FTP to your Website location and open the root directory, which may be `htpdocs` or `public_html` or something along those lines, depending upon which type of server is hosting the Website.

2. Open the `language` folder.

3. Open the `en-GB` folder (English, Great Britain), the default language folder.

4. Find the `en-GB.mod_login.ini` file.

5. Right-click on the filename and set the Properties value to 0777.

6. Right-click on the filename and select Edit as the action to take. Scroll down until you see `Create an account`.

7. Change the term to Create a User Account.

8. Save the file.

9. Check the front-end, refresh the browser, and see if the change applied.

10. If so, change the file permissions back to 0644 and exit.

Any system-generated term used in the front-end display, or in the admin back-end, can be changed via an individual language INI file in the `languages` folder. When editing the default text items, make sure you open the proper language INI file for the content. There are plenty of them, so make sure that you know what you are doing and open the correct file to edit.

What If You Screw Up a Language INI File

Not a problem. Open your FTP program and copy a clean file (from the Joomla! 1.6 zipped file on your computer) into the language folder. You don't need to copy the entire folder, just the INI file that was messed up. Now you can start again.

Using Template Overrides/Alternative Layouts

OVERRIDES ARE CHANGES to the core files that are incorporated with the Website template. In Joomla! 1.6, you may find them referred to as alternative layouts, which is an appropriate term. Overrides are good. If you make a change to the core files for any reason, and you update, for example, version 1.61 to version 1.65, the core files will likely be overwritten. What happens to your changes? Well, they get overwritten also.

Joomla! 1.6 has a function that reads the template files first, including anything in the template HTML folder, and then reads the core files. If there is an override or alternative layout in the template, the core file is ignored. Great! This means that an upgrade won't wipe out your previous changes.

You can implement an override and/or alternative layouts for the following four content types:

- ▶ **Components.** All extensions installed as components
- ▶ **Modules.** All module types installed as extensions
- ▶ **Categories.** Any content that has categories, such as articles, contacts, Weblinks, and so on
- ▶ **Menu link items.** Any link item in any menu

Because of the level of coding knowledge needed, there is no exercise on creating overrides or alternative layouts. Creating overrides should only be performed by skilled and experienced coders familiar with HTML, CSS, and PHP coding. Everyone else should *stay away!* You can bomb your entire Website with a click of the mouse.

If you have the skill set, the new template overrides in Joomla! 1.6 put a ton of visual and layout horsepower at your control. Joomla! 1.6 gives you much more control than version 1.5. The Joomla! 1.6 wiki page at http://docs.joomla.org/Layout_Overrides_in_Joomla_1.6 discusses overrides and explains their implementation.

Using Fonts

USING FONTS ON WEBSITES has been problematic for some time. There have been many approaches to the problem by the "big boys," but none were implemented because they don't want to share their technology, which means fonts can't be used across the board in all Web browsers.

Several methods have been made available in recent years such as converting words to images created from the desired font. This method works pretty well for headings and short pieces of text, but can you imagine every letter on a Website being loaded as a separate image? Well, you get the idea.

The problem with fonts is that browsers "look" at the resident computer, into the font folder, and if a font is present there that is called for on the page, it renders the font properly. If Wedding Script is called for, and Wedding Script is resident on the system, it displays. If not, the default font is used.

Also, the problem with fonts has been the need to download them from a server to the browser, which takes a long time to display a page if there are several fonts, and if the fonts have licensing restrictions, you can't do it anyway. However, given that the Internet is now operating at higher speeds (bandwidth), the download time is no longer an issue. The licensing, yes; the download speeds, no!

With the advent of TrueType and Open Type font formats, the licensing issue is starting to be less and less of a problem. There are hundreds of thousands of TTF and OTF fonts available and, surely, one of those could be found to use on a site that is similar to a proprietary license-restricted version. Bottom line: use any font you want, as long as it can be legally uploaded to a server and downloaded by others without risking your house, car, spouse, kids, or pets to the license enforcers that seem to show up now and then.

Font implementation is done via a CSS attribute called Font-Family, which is discussed in Chapter 19, "CSS-PHP-HTML Basics."

Adding Languages

JOOMLA! 1.6, AS DID PREVIOUS VERSIONS, has the ability to add multiple languages to a site. If you recall, the language you installed initially was English-UK. Additional languages may be added, and then managed via the Language Manager.

Adding additional languages to a Joomla! Website isn't an easy thing to do. Sure, at first glance you'd think that all you do is add a language and it's done. It's not. Just a quick reading of the wiki on Joomla! 1.6 languages should be enough to deter even the bravest Website Manager. The wiki can be found at http://docs.joomla.org/Language_Switcher_Tutorial_for_Joomla_1.6. Spend some time there and read things over. It explains the complexity of it pretty well.

Because of the complexities involved, the Language Manager and Switcher are not covered in this book, as they require experience, language knowledge, and some knowledge of coding and other skill sets. But, along those lines, here are just a few things you should know about the subject:

- ▶ The Language Manager and Switcher manage the language display on both the front-end and the back-end.

- ▶ When a language is switched, the only items that display in the language are the default language items from the Joomla! 1.6 core language files, such as admin menus and column titles, as well as system-generated text.

- ▶ What are not automatically displayed in the switched language are things that are named during their creation, such as categories, articles, menus, menu link items, and others.

- ▶ In order to display categories, articles, menus, menu link items, and other content in a different language, they must be entered as such, i.e., Spanish must be entered in Spanish, and so on.

- ▶ The feature does not translate content. It cannot, for example, change English to Spanish throughout the entire site.

- ▶ The Language Switcher will only change the site display language from English to Spanish if you installed the language and created a parallel site content in the language. In other words, everything that you have on the site, must be duplicated in the selected language.

- ▶ For each language used, each content element must exist in that language, so if you want English, French, Spanish, and German, you need four of every content item.

- ▶ Also, every content item, be it a category, article, content module, or all the rest of it, must also be present in each language version and be designated as assigned to that language in the Language Manager.

You can see that adding languages to a Joomla! 1.6 Website is complicated and somewhat difficult to implement.

Language Packs are extensions that install in the `site language` folder and contain the translation of the standard English core language in the specified language. When another language is selected, it is the translation in those files that displays instead of English. The Language Packs do not translate site content.

Summary

In this chapter, you learned the following:

- ▶ To edit certain Joomla! 1.6 files, an FTP program is required along with a program to edit coded files.
- ▶ Web 2.0 isn't a "thing"; it refers to Websites that have user interactivity with the content, such as Facebook, Twitter, and similar Websites.
- ▶ Tableless layouts are the preferred format for modern Websites, and a <div> is a page element that can be positioned using CSS parameters.
- ▶ Module class suffixes can be used to alter how individual modules appear.
- ▶ Module class suffixes can be applied to one or more modules at the same time.
- ▶ Page Display Options can be used to change the look of individual pages.
- ▶ Page Display Options are modified by adding a Page Class to the menu link item associated with the content item.
- ▶ The menu link item display can be changed by using a Link CSS Style.
- ▶ The Link CSS Style is usually applied to individual menu link items to change their appearance but not globally to large numbers of items.
- ▶ Default terms and words on the site can be changed to other, more preferred terms.
- ▶ Fonts used on Websites generally depend upon which fonts site visitors have installed on their computer.
- ▶ Font displays have limitations, but there are ways of displaying other fonts on a Website.
- ▶ Languages can be added to Joomla! 1.6 sites, and they can modify the default terms and text displays.
- ▶ Language Packs are extensions used to add other languages to the site.
- ▶ Language Packs do not translate actual content. They only change static site and admin text.
- ▶ Languages are controlled via the Language Manager.

Specialty Extensions for
Joomla! Websites

ONE OF THE GREAT THINGS ABOUT JOOMLA!, and Joomla! 1.6 in particular, is that specialty applications can be added to perform specific roles in creating and managing content. This chapter discusses some of these applications along with some tips on implementing and using them.

As with all other extensions, the Joomla! Extensions Directory (JED) is the primary source for Joomla! 1.6 extensions. There are a lot of extensions that can be classified as specialty applications, which present content in a specific way. In this chapter, we'll cover some of the major and more popular specialty extensions.

Social Networking

EVERYBODY KNOWS WHAT SOCIAL networking is and the many ways it is being used. Facebook, Twitter, LinkedIn, and hundreds more exist. Joomla! has its own extension for creating a social network on your Website.

The following are are some of the better and more popular social networking extensions that can be added to a Joomla! site as components. This list is not inclusive, so do your own research on the JED and find the appropriate extensions for your site.

Community Builder ("CB"). This extension as been around for a long time and is a well-developed and supported component with a large community of Websites that use it. It is a free extension with plenty of add-ons that "extend" the extensions. Extensions for CB run into the hundreds, but make sure they are Joomla! 1.6 Native before using them with a component. There is a free, advanced, and professional version and, depending on what you want to do, it may be worth investing to get the full flexibility and customization.

JomSocial. This is a powerful and robust extension. It is also a good social networking extension, but it isn't free, and depending on how you want to use it, the price may be a little stiff. Still, if you want a good, solid, well-formed extension, JomSocial would be a pretty good choice. There are also lots of add-ons for this extension.

Ecommerce Components

ECOMMERCE IS THE GENERALIZED term for shopping carts that appear on Websites. They are comprised of catalogs of items for sale and have a method of ordering and paying for the products. There are so many ecommerce sites today that it's almost impossible to list and classify them. If someone is selling anything, chances are the products can be purchased online.

You can add ecommerce component extensions to Joomla! 1.6. The JED has over 25 shopping cart extensions that range from very good to absolutely awful, so some diligence is needed before you choose one to use on your site.

By doing a little research, especially if you are only going to sell a few products, you may find a nice, tidy little cart extension that will do the job.

VirtueMart ("VM"). This is the "biggee" of Joomla! ecommerce extensions. It has a long history of use and implementation across thousands of Websites worldwide. It is a free, noncommercial extension with add-ons galore. The features of the shopping cart and its administration are as long as your arm, which makes VM a good selection. It manages catalogs and products, along with built-in payment processors for most of the world's most-used services. At the time of this book's printing, VirtueMart was testing version 2.0 that installs on Joomla 1.6 Websites.

However, VM is not the only available option in the JED for shopping cart extensions. View the available demos for all of the carts, especially those that are commercial, pay-for products.

Let Someone Else Process and Store Credit Cards!

Do not attempt to process credit cards on your Website and store the information. There are strict laws that deal with how credit card information must be stored and protected from invasion by hackers. To set up a PCI-compliant Website costs tens of thousands of dollars. However, having credit cards processed by a company like PayPal puts the burden on them to be compliant, which they are. So, when adding ecommerce, use another company to process payments. It's well worth the small amounts they charge per transaction.

Membership Management

IN THE CONTEXT OF THIS SUBJECT, we are not referring to the Joomla! ACL. Membership management in this section deals with extensions that allow you to create a Website where people join as free or paid members.

This category of extensions is similar to those for social networking, except they don't have all the user interactions. These extensions are strictly the type that allows users to join and access the content on your Website. Users can join for free, be charged a one-time fee, or charged a recurring fee.

Combine this kind of extension with the ACL, and you have connected some serious horsepower for control of what and how users access site content and information. Members can even have levels of access with different fees, such as bronze, silver, and gold.

Quite honestly, digging out pay-to-access extensions in the JED isn't easy. Their classification system for extensions does not have them categorized that way. But, if you do a general search for membership, the results will give you a pretty good list of extensions.

You could just let users register on your site for restricted content, but the ACL system does not include any method for charging users a fee to join the site. That is a function of the specialized membership extensions.

Combination Extensions for Membership

There is another extension with a Joomla! version that can be used for membership management, but it isn't limited to only that kind of application. CiviCRM is a free-standing program that has been also written as a Joomla! extension. Unfortunately, at the time of this book's writing, it was not yet available for Joomla! 1.6. It likely will be released for version 1.6, so a brief discussion of its features and use is appropriate.

CiviCRM is a combination of several parts, the most important of which are:

CiviMember. Online membership registration and management, which includes various levels/types of membership along with multiple levels of dues structures that can be applied.

CiviEvent. Allows members to register for events that have been posted to the system, which could be free or pay to attend. Any kind of event can be entered and displayed.

CiviMail. In conjunction with CiviMember, sends e-mails and newsletters to members that opt-in to receive them. Multiple newsletters can be sent to group categories.

CiviContribute. Can be used for accepting donations. Can be used by nonprofits to accept funds on a year-around basis. Can be configured in several different ways.

CiviCase. Used primarily for social worker application, whereby each client-case can be managed, activities can be recorded, and more.

CiviReport. Allows reports to be created, such as types of members and their activities, donations received, and so on. A great utility for analyzing related activities.

CiviCRM is an open-source and free product. CiviCRM is hosted on a Webserver, can be internationalized, and designed to meet the needs of advocacy, nonprofits, and nongovernmental groups. Using it for simple membership management is also possible, but there are other extensions that can do that without all of the other features CiviCRM offers.

The Joomla! 1.6 Wrapper

No, THIS ISN'T ANYTHING TO DO with music. A wrapper is a feature in Joomla! 1.6 whereby another Webpage or Website can be "wrapped" into the content area of the site. The wrapper is also known as an iframe in coding parlance. This is activated via a wrapper menu link item, created the same way as any other content link. While this feature will display other Website content, there are some negative considerations as well, such as:

► The wrapper displays another Website exactly as you see it in a browser window when viewing the site by itself.

► The width of the wrapper can be controlled, but not the content that displays in it, if that content is another Website. If your content area is narrow, the other site will appear with horizontal scroll bars; vertical scrolling may also be required.

► The Website displayed cannot be altered. The header, menus, content, and footers all display.

How can the wrapper feature be used to display content? Here are a few examples.

Example 1: Displaying Another Website

Displaying another Website is sometimes used to show visitors something and keep them on your site all the while. However, the links and destinations on the wrapped site can take visitors anywhere, beyond your control, even knocking them off of your site.

In practical terms, while another Website can be displayed, it really isn't a good practice. It's easier to just send visitors to the site with the menu link item set to open in another browser window.

Example 2: Displaying a Single Webpage

If, for example, you are an affiliate of another Website that sells products, you may want to display your affiliate page on your site. The wrapper can be used to create a menu link item in one of the menus that will open your affiliate page into the content area of your site. Another example would be a special topic page on another site. Also, you could create a Webpage in HTML format, upload it to a directory on your server, and then use a wrapper to display it. The HTML page may even come from another site, such as one from a group that you are a member of.

Example 3: Displaying an External Application

An excellent use of the wrapper is to embed a separate, stand-alone Web application into your site. This could be a forum, shopping cart, blogging content, or something similar. Let's say you don't like any of the Joomla! ecommerce extensions and want to use another that is free-standing and could be a Website by itself, but you want it wrapped into your site instead. You can do that. You put the ecommerce site together in a subdirectory on your site, remove the header display, and then link a wrapper connection to it.

Exercise 1: Adding Content into a Wrapper

To understand how the wrapper works, this exercise will create a wrapper link in the My menu module that will display an external Website (amazon.com) in the content area.

1. Open Menu Manager > My First Menu, which was created in a previous exercise.

2. Create a new menu link item called My First Wrapper.

3. Refer to Figure 18-1 to add the link item, link name, and the wrapper URL (amazon.com).

4. Select Iframe Wrapper in the pop-up window.

5. In the Basic Options area, enter `http://www.amazon.com` for the URL.

6. Click Save.

7. Go to the front-end, refresh the browser, and view the menu to ensure that the new menu link item has been added.

8. Click on My First Wrapper. Amazon.com should now appear in the content area window.

9. Click Save & Close.

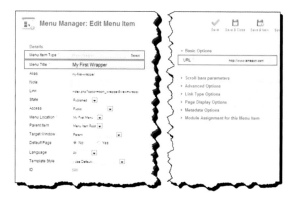

Figure 18-1
Select Iframe Wrapper as the link type, name the menu link item My First Wrapper, and connect it to www.amazon.com as the Website to display in the content area.

As with all other menu link items, additional parameters may be set to configure display conditions and relationships with other content on the site. Explore the other drop-down parameters and check the settings.

One of the biggest problems with using wrappers is their height in the content area. The content area does not automatically grow to the full height of the embedded Website's height. Here is how the settings work in two parameter option areas: scroll bar parameters and advanced options.

Scroll Bar Parameters

Scroll Bars. Yes, no, or auto are the choices, and should be selected based on how the wrapper displays in the content area.

Width. Can be set to any width, but is controlled by the width of the content area. Horizontal scroll bars are added if width exceeds the content area.

Height. For pages on your own domain, height is automatic. For external pages, height needs to be set to accommodate external page heights; otherwise, scroll bars will appear.

Advanced Options

Auto Height. Will automatically set the height to the same height as the URL page, but *only* if that page is on your own domain. For external sites, the height must be set manually in the Scroll Bars parameters.

Auto Add. Adds *http://* to the domain name entered in the URL box in Basic Options.

Forums, Discussion Boards, and Blogs

FORUMS, DISCUSSION BOARDS, and blogs all belong to the same class of extensions. They can be considered Web 2.0 extensions because they allow users to interact with the content. With a forum and discussion board, the users add comments to a posted topic. With blogs, it's a never-ending series of comments on the content.

Forums and discussion boards tend to be free-standing components with a content structure. Blogs, when added to a Joomla! content item, simply accumulate user interaction and comments with that particular piece of content.

If you have technical subjects and need to archive user input, then a forum or discussion board is probably a better extension choice. If you have more of a free-form need for user commenting, a blog works better, especially if the blogs are for article content, which then archives with it.

Again, as with all extensions, search for the one that will work best for your site.

WordPress Blog for Joomla!. This is a Joomla! 1.6 Native extension that adds the Wordpress blog platform to Joomla!. Wordpress is the most-used blogging platform in the world. This extension installs easily and works great.

Galleries

IF YOU WANT TO PUT A PHOTO gallery on display on a Joomla! 1.6 Website, you don't need to look too far or too long to find plenty of them. Search the Joomla! 1.6 JED for "galleries" and see the results. You can spend a day searching through nearly 100 of them. There are commercial and noncommercial types of every configuration and display format.

It makes no difference if you want a simple photo grid or a slideshow; they are all there and they are all Joomla! 1.6 Native. Some are easy to configure, some a bit more complicated. Most of them collect their images from a folder in the Media Manager. Remember that from previous chapters?

All you need to do to select a gallery is:

▶ Decide what kind of gallery you want to display.

▶ Decide if it will be static images or videos.

▶ Decide how you want the display to look.

▶ Decide on the kind of animation.

▶ Decide on a lightbox (pop-up view) that you want, if any.

▶ Decide if you want to pay for the extension or want to use a free one.

The extension categories in the following sections have come into their own in a short period of time. As Joomla! 1.5 gained traction in the world of Website CMSs, extensions were created to fill niche areas. The following extensions give Joomla! just that much more horsepower among other CMS platforms. Joomla! 1.6 extensions are catching up in these areas as developers convert their 1.5 versions to 1.6. Monitor the JED regularly for updates to extensions.

Classified Listings

IN THE U.S., THESE EXTENSIONS are called classifieds; in European jargon, they are called ads. Classifieds usually consist of products that are listed in categories. There is a category view and then a product detail view. Most classifieds allow the buyer to purchase the product and make payment. Some do not process payment but, rather, put the buyer in touch with the seller and they make their own arrangements.

Sometimes it is difficult to separate classifieds from regular ecommerce shopping carts, because both operate essentially in the same manner. If you want to add this kind of content to your Website, make a decision between the options based on what you are selling, how you want to sell the products, how you want the displays to appear, and if payment processing will be used.

Most classifieds and ecommerce extensions connect to fully secured payment processing services.

Link Directories

THE NUMBER OF JOOMLA! Websites that display links has dwindled as search engines have taken over the way we find information. In the past, a link site was visited to find things. Now, search engines have taken over that roll by offering a million instant results for a single search term.

But that does not eliminate the need for onsite links, which can serve to expand the content of a Website by offering users links to relevant resources related to the main site content.

Using the Wrapper for Classifieds and Links

Actually, there are not that many extensions in the JED that display classifieds or link directories. This is where the Joomla! 1.6 wrapper can play a role by using free-standing classifieds software hosted on your domain, then wrapping it into the content area. There are open source and commercial programs available for both that can be installed on a server and then displayed via the wrapper feature on Joomla! 1.6.

Calendars

CALENDAR EXTENSIONS ARE APLENTY in the JED. If you want to display anything via a calendar, there is an extension in that category to do so. Search the Joomla! 1.6 extensions in the JED for calendars, and the results will keep you busy for hours.

Calendars can be added to a site that connects to the Google calendar, operates all by itself, or displays dates that are fed information from another Joomla! extension. Also, there are calendars that can allow bookings or reservations, as described in the next section.

Many calendar extensions have a mini-calendar that displays in a module, which can then be positioned anywhere on a page, with display conditions. The actual calendar is administered as a component; therefore, any menu link item created to display it results in the calendar appearing in the main content area of the site.

If you are involved in groups or organizations that have scheduled events and you include that information on your Website, then a calendar extension is a great way to do it.

Reservation and Appointment Systems

GETTING JUST A BIT MORE sophisticated with a calendar-type extension, reservation and appointment systems can be added to your site as an extension. These allow you to set blocks of open time that people can sign up for.

If you operate a beauty salon, you can use it to book appointments; a restaurant can book reservations; basically any kind of service that books appointments on a daily basis, which can be broken down to small time increments, can use a reservation and appointment system. Local music concerts, church and social events, and any activities that require ticketing can accept ticket requests through these extensions.

Real Estate Listings

WHILE MOST REAL ESTATE OFFICES have Websites that are a part of their parent franchise company, many small real estate offices don't have that kind of Web presence. To fill that need, there are several good real estate–themed extensions that can be added.

In fact, some of these extensions also have inclusions that work for Canada and the U.K., with their postal codes, along with the U.S. zip codes. They have search features and filtering systems to narrow searches for real estate property.

Many also have ways to contact the seller, which could be one or more agents in the same office, and other information about the property, pricing, and features.

There are also excellent extensions that manage vacation rentals and allow you to post availability dates and allow users to book days or weeks of time. There are also calendar updates for dates that are booked. Some even have prepayment features for the bookings.

Document Repositories

MORE AND MORE, WEBSITES are beginning to store documents and make them accessible online. Documents such as product technical and safety sheets, production information, catalogs, and instructions are not unusual to find on a Website. To facilitate the organization and management of document collections, a library or repository is used.

Joomla! has several such repository extensions, although not all of them are Joomla! 1.6 Native. Extensions in this category have not been updated to 1.6 but, as time goes by, and driven by the need, extension developers will provide both commercial and noncommercial versions that will manage document libraries.

A classifieds or links directory could also be used as a document management system with some minor adaptation and repurposing of their use from ad and link displays, to links to categorized documents.

Summary

In this chapter, you learned the following:

▶ A group of Joomla! 1.6 extensions exist that are special applications for many different uses.

▶ Joomla! 1.6 Websites can have social networking content using a specialized extension.

▶ Ecommerce components add shopping cart features to sell products.

▶ Memberships can be managed using specialized extensions.

▶ The Joomla! 1.6 wrapper can be used to add content to your site that comes from other sites, or from special pages created on your domain.

▶ The wrapper has limitations in its configuration and how it is implemented.

▶ Forums, discussion boards, and blogs can be added via a specialized extension.

▶ Galleries are used to display photos in many different ways.

▶ Classifieds and links directories are used to display ads and links in an organized manner.

▶ Calendars can be used to display events and activities for clubs, organizations, and other scheduled activities or milestones.

▶ An extension can be installed that will allow a Joomla! 1.6 site to host a reservation, booking, and appointment system.

▶ Real estate listings can be included on a site using a specialized extension.

▶ Documents of all types can be made available on a site using a document repository extension.

▶ Classifieds and links directories can alternatively be used as document repositories.

CSS-PHP-HTML Basics

I N PREVIOUS CHAPTERS, THERE HAVE been discussions regarding Cascading Style Sheet (CSS) code in template style sheets, and you have made some minor changes to them in some of the exercises. In this chapter, we'll take a closer look at using (X)HTML, PHP, and CSS to modify the look and appearance of your Website.

Figure 19-1 shows the relationship between layouts and content using the Joomla! 1.6 platform. The Joomla! core is the foundation that extensions build upon. The main extensions are components and modules, which contain content. The difference between the two is that components display in the main content area, while modules can be placed anywhere on the Webpage using module positions. The style sheets control the look and appearance of pages.

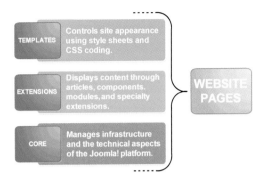

Figure 19-1
Relationship between the parts of Joomla! 1.6 that
control operation, content, and appearance.

In this chapter, the topics mostly center on the templates of a Joomla! 1.6 Website, along with some coding aspects of style sheets and the CSS parameters.

Although the template style sheet CSS file can be accessed via the Template Manager in the admin back-end, it is much easier to edit these files by accessing them via FTP and using an editor program. Our instructions and exercises are based on that assumption.

HTML, XHTML, PHP, and CSS

HTML IS SHORT FOR HYPERTEXT markup language, and XHTML stands for extensible hypertext markup language. Technically, XHTML is a family of markup languages that extends versions of the widely used HTML. We use the term (X)HTML in this chapter when referring to both.

As far as CSS references go, there are numerous books about CSS and style sheets. No attempt is going to be made to replicate that content here. We chose topics that you will run into often if you modify index.php pages and the accompanying CSS files. The index.php pages are the template "home" pages for the Website. Each template has its own index.php page that controls the physical layout of content on the site.

To get up to speed on editing these types of files, it is recommended that you pick up some reference books on the subject to gain some proficiency and have a look-up resource readily available to check coding. Searching the Internet is also an excellent way to find out more about CSS and style sheets.

Also, opening the index.php and CSS files for Joomla! 1.6 templates and studying them will give you some insight on what it will take to modify the file.

Using FTP and an Editor

Editing CSS files correctly is important. Therefore, it is recommended that you acquire a suitable editor commercially, or via open-source, to edit (X)HTML, PHP, and CSS documents.

Templates and Style Sheets

PREVIOUSLY, WE IDENTIFIED templates as the extensions that control the look, feel, and appearance of the pages on a Website. The templates consist of the index page and the style sheet, and work together as follows:

Index Page. This page controls the page display and has module positions and other code (PHP) that manages how the pages display. It uses a combination of (X)HTML and PHP code to set up the physical structure of the pages, which then interact with the linked style sheet.

Style Sheet. All of the code that controls the look, feel, style, and appearance is contained in this file as CSS code. CSS elements control the display, as was illustrated in the module suffix exercise you completed in a previous chapter.

Templates are accessed via the site root director in the `templates` folder, then by the individual template. Regardless of whether a template is assigned to different menus and modules, all templates are located in the `templates` folder and are automatically added there during the extension installation procedure.

See Figure 19-2 to see the templates installed and the drill-down path that takes you to the `index.php` page and, eventually, to the CSS. When using FTP to access template files, make sure that the drill-down follows the correct path to the destination files. Each template has its own folder and, within that folder, files and additional folders. Within the CSS folder, you may find one or more CSS files that will probably be designated by their use.

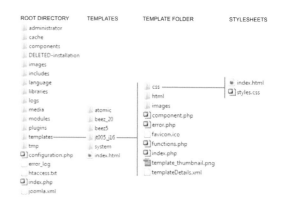

Figure 19-2
Location of the Joomla! 1.6 templates showing a path to CSS files using FTP access.

Basics of CSS

BEFORE WE BEGIN TO LOOK at the CSS code for the templates, it is recommended that you first spend some time on the Internet, searching for CSS basics via Google or any other search engine.

There is a great tutorial at www.cssbasics.com that can be downloaded as a PDF document. Go to the site, look at the tutorials, and download the document for future reference. In fact, this is actually required reading for the discussion that follows, so be sure you brush up on the principles of CSS before proceeding. Pay attention to the use and coding for an external style sheet, which is what is being used in Joomla! 1.6 templates. Otherwise, the code is added to the <head> section of the index page, in which case, it is called an internal style sheet. The reference is only a 35-page document if you download the PDF version, so print it out and spend time, a lot of time, studying it and referring back to it. If you need more info on any single CSS attribute, conduct a Web search and find what you want to know that way.

Tableless Layouts

Tableless layouts are Webpages that do not use tables to establish the mechanical layout of the page to create columns. In tableless layouts, this is done with divisions (<div>s), which are positioned by code. Today's Websites, as compared to those of not long ago, are constructed without using tables. It is okay to use tables in actual content for displaying information, but not for actual template structure.

The PHP coding system, in combination with (X)HTML, is used to actually rearrange the content via the template index page. The CSS is used to give each part of the page a certain look, feel, or colorization. Tableless layouts use a combination of these to create a layout.

About the < and > Codes

Every piece of inline code needs an opening and closing arrow, such as . Not only that, but when applying the code, it must always terminate, such as , with the slash indicating that this ends the previously implemented code. In some cases, there is no separate closing code, so it appears as <jdoc:include type="modules" name="position-14" />, which inserts a module position into a template. Note that the slash is included at the end of the string. This satisfies the requirement to close the code. As you work with CSS and inline coding more, you will learn when and how this is used.

How to Enter CSS Code in Style Sheets

CSS code consists of the selector, which identifies the element, and the property, which assigns parameters to the element. This code is entered in the style sheet either inline or stacked, as shown in Figures 19-3 and 19-4. It has an applied example of the code, which is how body text is specified. This means that all of the text on the site would assume those attributes and all other text inherits from it, unless otherwise modified by additional CSS.

As you study the CSS Basics document, you will find more complex versions of sample CSS code.

Comment the Code Please!

When adding or modifying a style sheet of CSS code, it's a good idea to add comments into the files so that you can remember what it was for, or someone coming behind you can know the purpose of the code. A comment is added like this: /* This is a comment */. Anything with /* ... */ will not affect the CSS code above or below it. See the /* black */ comment in Figure 19-4. The comment can be on a line by itself.

```
selector { property: value; }
```

Applied Example:

```
body {font: arial;}
```

Figure 19-3
A sample of a simple line of CSS code for the body style, which is the default text on a site.

```
selector {
property1: value;
property2: value;
property3: value;
}
```

Applied Example:

```
body {
font: arial;
color: #000000; /*black*/
font-weight: bold;
}
```

Figure 19-4
A sample of more-complex CSS code. The code can be typed inline or stacked, so long as the overall properties for the selector are enclosed in { } and each property terminates with a semicolon (;). The CSS will fail if the code is not enclosed or terminated properly.

Basics of Template Pages

TEMPLATE PAGES START as (X)HTML or PHP pages, and build the infrastructure of the page layout, assigning this part here and that part there. Module positions, which were explained previously, precisely locate content on the page. Figure 19-5 shows a typical section of combined (X)HTML and PHP code, which is the footer for the default beez_20 template page.

In the example code shown in Figure 19-5, there are <div>s with ID names along with class names. This helps separate the CSS code into IDs and classes, and each is applied in a different manner, which we'll discuss shortly. Note there is nothing in the code that mentions fonts, colors, sizes, height, width, or other physical attributes. This is all defined in the code and relates to the item IDs and classes by name.

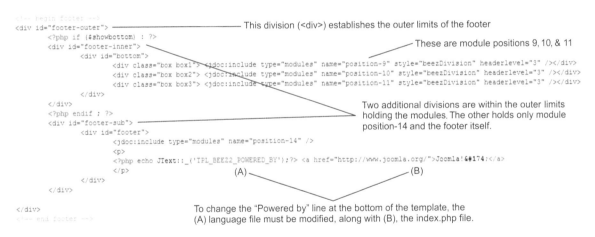

Figure 19-5
PHP and (X)HTML code is combined to create an area on the index.php page that will display three module positions horizontally, an additional module position below it, and a promotional line for Joomla! within the footer area of the pages.

IDs and Classes

Within coded pages, you will find terms like id=name and class=name, each of which relates to CSS code and each with two sets of rules on how they are applied. These may be confusing, so let's clear up the differences between them. Here are the general rules:

The Class Designation:

▶ Classes are CSS codes that can be used multiple times in a file.

▶ Classes, when used, appear as .name in CSS files, with the preceding period.

▶ In PHP/(X)HTML, classes are implemented as <p class="yellowtext">.

▶ In the CSS file, the class selector would be .yellowtext (with the preceding period).

▶ All other CSS properties can be applied to classes.

▶ The class="yellowtext" can be used many times in the index.php file to display text as yellow.

Back It Up or Suffer the Consequences!

Before opening and editing any template file, make sure you have a duplicate copy of the unmodified file stored on your system in case your code doesn't work and the site explodes into nothingness. Simply copy the template file backup to the appropriate location on the server via FTP to restore the site.

The ID Designation:

▶ IDs are CSS codes that can only be used one time in a file. Once specified, the ID with the same name cannot be applied to any other page division element.

▶ IDs appear as #name in CSS files, with the preceding pound sign.

▶ In PHP/(X)HTML, division IDs are implemented as <div id="abstract">.

▶ In the CSS file, the <div> selector would be #abstract (with the preceding pound sign).

▶ All other CSS properties can be applied to divisions.

▶ The <div id="abstract">, as an example, may only be used one time in an index.php file.

Style Sheets/CSS

There are many CSS code and Selector properties variations. The world authority for CSS code is the World Wide Web Consortium (W3C). They can be found at www.w3c.org. If you want to know "everything" about coding for Websites, this is the place to go. However, because it has highly technical instructions, the information presentation may not be too user friendly for you at this point.

On the other hand, there are plenty of independent Websites that have an abundance of good tutorials on HTML, CSS, and much more. Search for CSS tutorials, pick a site, and dig in. If you don't like the way the information on one site is presented, try another. After a few tries, you'll find one that presents the information to your level of understanding and go from there. Bookmark all of the CSS reference sites that you like.

CSS isn't mysterious or cryptic. It is simply code that can be applied in many ways, either by itself or in combination with other coding methods. Also, CSS within a style sheet can be combined with different CSS selectors to give individual page elements unique and different looks, or it can be used to force visual standardization, should many individuals be involved in contributing content. CSS takes the "look" out of the hands of the content contributors so a visual standard can be applied across Websites with massive amounts of content.

Summary

In this chapter, you learned the following:

▶ Joomla! Website pages are controlled by core files, extensions, and templates working together.

▶ Templates control the look, feel, and appearance of Webpages.

▶ CSS style sheets contain the code that controls all of the elements on a page and how it looks.

▶ The template index page controls the physical structure of the page.

▶ The style sheet contains the code that applies to the physical structure.

▶ Tableless layouts are the standard for today's Webpages.

▶ CSS must be entered in style sheets in a certain format.

▶ Comments can be added to style sheets to notate the actual code.

▶ IDs and classes are used to designate elements on a Webpage.

▶ Divisions may only have one ID per page apply to content elements.

▶ Classes may be used numerous times per page to apply content elements.

▶ Certain rules apply to both divisions and classes.

▶ CSS and coding resources are easily obtained on the Internet.

Search Engine

Optimization

Having an Internet presence is one thing; getting found is something else altogether. There are millions of Websites that do not show up any search engine results. And then there are those that show up at the top of the results list every time. What's the difference?

In the first case, the sites were created and placed online and that was that. They may have great and interesting content, but no one knows about it. In the second case, effort was made on the sites with regard to Search Engine Optimization, or SEO. By using a combination of techniques, these sites were able to increase their visibility because of their Search Engine Friendliness (SEF). This chapter discusses steps you can take to make Joomla! 1.6 friendly to search engines, increasing your likelihood of being seen in search results.

SEF simply means you can use URL references that are shorter and more meaningful when referencing pages on a Website. Instead of long strings of URL code, especially those generated by database-driven Websites, the URLs are concise with the name of the actual page displayed. Joomla! 1.6 has a built-in feature to manage this.

Joomla! 1.6 SEF Configuration

To FACILITATE THE CREATION of human-friendly URLs, Joomla! 1.6 has setting controls in the Global Configuration manager, as shown in Figure 20-1. There are two settings relevant to SEF in the SEO Settings panel. There is also another setting in some content items called Alias, which is explained in the following:

▶ **Search Engine Friendly URLs.** Selecting this option changes system-generated URLs to more common names that are human friendly.

▶ **Adds Suffix to URL.** This will add the `.html` suffix to the article name, which makes the URL even friendlier to both humans and search engines.

▶ **Edit Article > Alias.** Using an article as an example, the URL name for the article derives from this field, which automatically uses the article name if left blank when saving. A name may be entered as an alias, and the URL will display it, even if the actual article title is different, as in Figure 20-2. Not all content items have the Alias option. However, for most content, the alias displayed will be the name of the menu link item used to open the page.

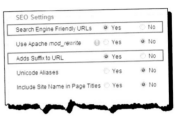

Figure 20-1
Two options must be set to Yes in the SEO Settings area to display human-friendly URLs.

Figure 20-2
The actual page name for the SEF URL can be derived from an alias or its associated menu link item.

Confused About SEF and SEO?

To keep terminology in perspective, anything that is done to a site to enhance its ability to be found by search engines is called SEO. SEF is but a small part of SEO and, while it is a separate function in Joomla! 1.6, it works in harmony with SEO techniques in making a site optimized for search engines. A human-friendly URL increases the ability of search engines to enter that URL into their databases.

Human-Friendly SEF

The term human-friendly will pop up now and then. It simply means that the URL of the Website can be read by humans. A nonfriendly URL might look like this: www.SITENAME.com/2011/directory/04/28/index.html?hpt=Sbin-652438KRTWjsenyh.

On the other hand, a human-friendly URL would look like this: www.joomla.org/announcements/release-news/5370-joomla-163-released.html. Note the difference. The second one is easier to understand than the first, and this helps when creating links or sending the link to others.

What Is SEO?

SEO IS A METHOD OF IMPROVING a Website's visibility in search engines. Search engines are services like Google, Yahoo, and others that will display links to Websites as a result of a query or search request. The method by which the search engines gather Website information is a highly guarded secret set of algorithmic parameters. However, there are some basic things that can be added to a Website that will make it friendly to search engines, which pull information from the site in an organized manner. In other words, they "look for stuff" on the site that meets their searching criteria.

Joomla! 1.6, by itself, is not SEO, or optimized, for search engines. It does, however, have the means and mechanisms as part of the platform that will allow Website Administrators to make a site SEO.

This facilitation can be applied to the following parts of a Website:

▶ The Website itself, via the Global Configuration, may have SEF/SEO information that applies to the site as a whole.

▶ Components can be included, although not necessarily all of them.

▶ Menu link items may include SEO information.

▶ Categories may include SEO information.

▶ Articles may include SEO information.

▶ Modules usually do not have SEO options, but some may have the feature.

▶ Templates, themselves, do not have SEO features.

▶ Extensions, depending on the developer, may have SEO options included.

SEO Information

LET'S FACE IT, GOOGLE IS PROBABLY the most used and most popular search engine company. Knowing that, what better location to get SEO information. In fact, Google has an SEO Starter Guide available online. It's a 32-page document that is easy to read, and the contents are easy to understand, with examples of how SEO is applied.

Just like Cascading Style Sheets (CSS), there are many books written on SEO. There is no need to duplicate their content here, so we will focus on a more practical side—how to implement SEO on a Joomla! 1.6 Website.

The remainder of this chapter is devoted to applying SEO techniques within the Joomla! 1.6 content structure, but first, there are a few additional SEO topics to cover.

SEO is possible because of a standardized method of presenting Website information to search engines. This method involves the use of meta-information, which contains tag words and a description of content relative to the Website. This information is added to a Website without making it available to site visitors. It is information hidden from public view, but readily available to search engines and their "crawlers," also known as "spiders." Crawlers are automated processes that constantly search the Internet and millions of Websites each day for metadata and store it in a huge database to generate search results.

Let's look at each:

▶ **Meta-Description.** This is a meta-tag that describes the Website with a short statement that search engines "see" when a Website shows up in their search. This statement should be kept to a maximum of 400 characters.

▶ **Meta-Tags.** These are keywords that describe the content of the site and words that the search engines relate to site content for recall when search requests are made using those terms.

Best SEO Practice

The impact of meta information for search engine rankings on Google is negligible because many other factors come into play to rank high on search results. However, it is important for the other search engines for cataloging a Website. The best practice is to build a Website that has content with key-words that a person would use as a search term on Google.

Joomla! Metadata Options

Most content items have Metadata Options that can be configured to provide information about content to search engines. Articles, menu link items, some modules (depending on what they do), and some components have metadata information that can be included on the content page, which is not seen by site visitors. Search engines know exactly where to look for this information, and Joomla! provides the path for that type of search.

Figure 20-3 shows the typical metadata information for an article. In this case, it is the article on Joomla.org that announced the release of Joomla! 1.6.x. Note the concise statement for the Meta Description and how the Meta Keywords are entered, separated by commas. This is the information the search engines are looking for when they crawl a site.

What's important in using the Metadata Options is that the information entered should not be repeated on each page, or each location on the site. Make the information unique to the individual content item that is being tagged with metadata. The more unique, the more likely the search engines will yield the information when users search the Internet.

In Metadata Options is a setting relative to robots, which are the crawlers constantly looking for meta-information and meta-content on sites to place in the search engine databases. After entering a meta-description and keywords, you can instruct the robots on what they can, or cannot, do relative to searching the Website, beyond the primary pages.

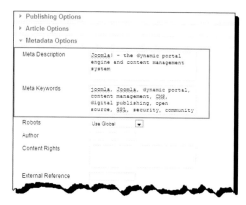

Figure 20-3
A brief description should be entered accompanied by keywords that are relevant to the content of the item.

These options follow:

► **Index, Follow.** This is the default setting, even though it may appear otherwise. The spiders will index the entire site and all of the other pages that have links in menus or in content.

► **No Index, Follow.** In this case, the site is not indexed, but the content pages are.

► **Index, No Follow.** Allows the spider to index the site, but go no further than the index page of the site. It does not attempt to access any other pages for metadata.

► **No Index, No Follow.** This one is obvious. It does not allow indexing of anything.

Check the Help Pages

If you are stuck on something in the admin back-end, and open a Help page, make sure that it is specific to Joomla! 1.6. The Joomla.org Documentation area for Joomla! 1.6 may not have accurate or proper pages in place. Look at the screenshots and compare them to your site. If they are different, chances are the information is not accurate either.

The Sitemap and Extensions

A SITEMAP IS A PAGE that has links to all other pages on the site and can be self-generated by Joomla!, or manually created by the administrator or Super User. Sitemaps help search engines catalog a site's content. By creating a sitemap, an administrator is informing the search engines about the URLs on the site that are available to search. Because the spiders typically do not look at rich content, which is Flash-based and other similar content, the sitemap tells the search engines to "Look at these pages, too!" However, a sitemap is not a substitute for good meta-descriptions and keywords. A sitemap is an addition to the meta-information, not a replacement. In fact, a sitemap has a greater impact on SEO than does meta-information, as was explained previously.

Joomla! 1.6 does not have a preconfigured feature for generating a sitemap. Therefore, an appropriate sitemap extension must be installed and configured. In the following exercises, we'll apply some SEO techniques using noncommercial SEO extensions, which we'll download and install. You may notice a Site Map link at the top of the This Site menu, which you worked with previously. Well, it may look like a sitemap, and it may act like a sitemap, but it isn't a sitemap. The link is simply a List All Categories type. This isn't a sitemap in the Google-ese sense, so let's install a real sitemap.

A search for sitemap in the Joomla! Extensions Directory (JED) under Joomla! 1.6 extensions will give you three results for extensions that enhance SEO and build a sitemap. A search for SEO returns over 60 extensions that are related to SEO in one form or another.

In the SEO extensions, many of them are commercial, meaning you have to pay for them. Take care in doing so! Make sure you can see an admin demo for these extensions to see if they will actually do what you think they will.

EXERCISE 1: CREATING A SITEMAP USING XMAP

1. Search the JED for Xmap and download. The extension installs as a component.

2. Before beginning, go to the Main Menu Manager and unpublish the Site Map menu link item. When the menu is open, click on the green checked circle in the Status column for that item. A red circle should appear when it is off.

3. Open the Xmap component via the Components Manager.

4. Select New in the top-right menu.

5. Name the item My Site Map.

6. Enter This is a generated Site Map using the XMap Extension. in the editor area.

7. Select Published for the State of the item.

8. Click Save.

9. Look at the right area of the manager and note that each menu on the site is listed with check box selectors.

10. Select Main Menu and My First Menu from those available. You may notice that the My Menu Module and My Menu Module 2 are not listed. This is because the menus were created via SWMenuFree rather than the standard Joomla! 1.6 menu system.

11. If you have a small site, you may want to set the menus Change Frequency to Monthly. If you have a site where content is added daily, the appropriate setting may be Daily or Hourly.

12. Click Save & Close.

13. Go to the main menu in the Menu Manager.

14. Create a new menu link item called My Site Map.

15. For the type, select Xmap > HTML Site Map.

16. At the right, under the Required Settings tab, Change the My Site Map content item.

17. Click Save & Close.

18. Go to the front-end and refresh the browser window. The menu link item should now appear on the front page at the bottom of the This Site menu.

19. Clicking it should show a page with all of the link items from the two menus selected in the Xmap component admin.

20. Note that My Menu Module links are on the list, near the bottom of the page. My Menu Module 2 isn't listed. Why? Because it is a duplicate of the My Menu Module using the same source menu module.

What happens now is that the crawlers or spiders will search your site, find the sitemap, follow the links, and glean information from the content. If you have No Follow selected, the sitemap will be useless to the search engines, but helpful for site visitors. The site must be set to Index, Follow for the sitemap to have search engine relevance.

The Very, Very Important \<h1\> Tag

SEARCH ENGINES ARE OBSESSED with looking for the \<h1\> tag on Webpages. This is in addition to the meta-tagging information which, together, determines the relevance of your pages. The primary head for all content articles and so on can be styled with CSS, but \<h1\> is actually an HTML specification for browsers.

Here are some tips about \<h1\> use:

▶ A unique \<h1\> tag should exist for each content item.

▶ \<h1\> text should be short and only occupy one line.

▶ Use \<h1\> only as intended; overuse works against SEO. Having several \<h1\> tags per page isn't a good practice, and the search engines may reject your site if you overuse this tagging feature.

▶ If you duplicate \<h1\>, don't make it exactly like any other title. Change the words around.

There is a huge furor among Website-types whether \<h1\> has any value for SEO. Everybody has the right to their opinion about the subject. Typically, Webpages have a heading hierarchy that begins with \<h1\> and ends with \<h6\>, each having their own CSS properties associated with them. And, until Google, Yahoo, Bing, and other search engines tell the world, "We are not going to consider \<h1\> tagged content," the use of the tag is a good practice to maintain. They may not be necessary for search engines, but you do no harm by using the CSS tag as it was intended—the highest order of content heading in CSS styling.

Major search engines place a lot of emphasis on page titles, so when creating your site and naming your articles, try to use terms and heading verbiage that relates to the content in a relevant way.

The Reality of SEO and SEO Services

LET'S FACE SOME REALITY HERE. Just because you have a Website and have followed all of the rules of SEO and optimized your site to the hilt, nothing guarantees that it will appear above page 50 in the search results. Your site would have to be incredibly unique, with keywords never used anywhere before by any other Website, to pop up on the top. It takes a lot of work and effort to achieve a high page ranking.

Or, you could always "pay your way" into a search ranking position. The search engine companies would be thrilled to have you shovel money their way to appear in the "paid" section of search results. The other results, below paid ads, are called organic search results.

If you have crates of money you want to throw away to pay an SEO Service to improve your search engine ranks, go for it! If not, you may want to keep your wallet closed. There are hundreds upon hundreds of companies, large and small, that will do SEO for a fee.

There are highly reputable companies that provide this service, and they are not cheap. You need to think long and hard and compare dollars and potential earnings (if you sell stuff on your site) to make sure that several thousand dollars per month will give you sufficient return.

Buyer Beware!

SEO scams are abundant. Small two-person providers are sometimes more reliable than huge companies that have hundreds of people behind computers who just sit there and click on bookmarks all day as their computer's IP address changes constantly. These are the same outfits that keep hitting pay-per-click links to drive up revenue. Website owners must pay for the clicks, which are worthless.

Black Hat Techniques

IN SEO PARLANCE, "black hat techniques" are things done by the bad guys, not the good guys. In fact, if you are a good guy, and start using that "black hat" stuff, you could be classified among the bad guys, and your site could be banned from appearing on search engines.

Go to a search engine and search for black hat SEO and view some of the results. You'll learn all about what will get you on a "black list" faster than a speeding bullet.

Just don't use black hat techniques, and you'll be on the safe side of the fence with the search engine companies.

Summary

In this chapter, you learned the following:

▶ SEF techniques create human-friendly URLs.

▶ SEF settings in Joomla! 1.6 are in the Global Configuration manager.

▶ The alias can have a different name than the content title, and it is the alias that shows up as a human-friendly URL page name as well as the name of the menu link item, depending on the type of content.

▶ Joomla! 1.6 also has built-in features for SEO.

▶ SEO can be applied to components, articles, menus, and some modules, depending on their content fuction/display.

▶ Meta-information contains tags and descriptions of content.

▶ The meta-description is a short, concise statement about the content of the Website or Webpage.

▶ The meta-keywords and single words, or short terms, define the content.

▶ Joomla! 1.6 has Metadata Options for almost all content types, but the use of content and page titles offers better results with search engines.

▶ Website content can be configured to allow crawlers or robots to index and record keywords beyond the site's front page.

▶ A sitemap is valuable to both site visitors and the search engines for indexing information about the content of a Joomla! 1.6 Website.

▶ There are extensions available for both SEF and SEO enhancement.

▶ The <h1> tag should be used for primary content headings.

▶ SEO meta-descriptions and meta-keywords should not be duplicated throughout a site.

▶ Each page of content should have unique information for SEO.

▶ Black hat SEO techniques and practices should never be used at the risk of being ignored by search engines.

Web 2.0

Considerations

THE TERM WEB 2.0 IS BEING USED EVERYWHERE as short-hand for Websites that have user interaction with the content. In Chapter 17, "Advanced Topics," Web 2.0 was defined as Websites that allow users to participate or alter content, which includes blogs, wikis, and social networking sites such as Facebook, Twitter, and others. When site visitors add comments or reviews to posted content, they are in a Web 2.0 environment.

To view it another way, Web 2.0 Websites have come about through improvements in technology that allow the interaction activity by site visitors. Up to a point, not too many years ago, Websites were simply static pages of information. With Web 2.0, these pages now have user interaction though polls, comments on content, Real Simple Syndication (RSS) feeds, wikis with user input, and more. None of this functionality was available in the Web 1.0 era, thus the evolution to Web 2.0, which changed the Internet.

Because Web 2.0 Websites are based on user interaction, new programming languages are being used on Websites that were not used before. Websites such as YouTube, MySpace, Facebook, Wikipedia, LinkedIn, Digg, Technorati, and StumbleUpon are part of the new Internet world that is commonly referred to as Web 2.0.

These Web 2.0 applications are being written in every possible coding language that can be parsed to a Web browser, and the more interactivity and the more content-sharing, the more complex the programming.

The Look of Web 2.0

Even though Web 2.0 refers to the type of content and user interaction, the look of Websites changed about the same time Web 2.0 was gaining traction via the social networking communities. The layouts of pages changed, the look of the graphics changed, and the little round pudgy people figures started to show up everywhere. Buttons began to have a "glassy" look and that little bit of shading between the top and bottom of the button. These kind of graphic techniques have been mistakenly associated as Web 2.0 styles. They are not. Those kinds of graphics can be used on any Website, which reinforces the true definition of the term.

Don't be surprised to see terms like Sales 2.0 or Learning 2.0 and other similar phrases being applied to Websites, online applications, and those ever-growing Apps that technology-oriented human beings can't live without.

Web 2.0 Templates

Some templates for Joomla! 1.5 and 1.6 have been mistakenly touted as a Web 2.0 template. That isn't a correct use of the term. A template, by itself, a Web 2.0 Website does not make! It may have the look of popular Web 2.0 graphics—which is a liberal use of the term in any case. Just because a template claims something about Web 2.0, unless it includes all of the interactivity for users, it simply does not make the grade. Just having the look of Web 2.0 doesn't necessarily make it a Web 2.0 site Without the user interactivity, it's probably just a pretty template with view-only pages.

Building a Joomla! 1.6 Web 2.0–Featured Website

If you build a site that is Web 1.0-ish, you are building a site that has view-only pages. If you build a Website that is based on Web 2.0 features, you bring a wealth of interactivity to the screen through which users can interact with the content. Within the Joomla! 1.6 realm, here are some 2.0 "things" that can be included on a site:

▶ Social networking connections and interaction between them

▶ Wikis

▶ Web logs, commonly called blogs

▶ RSS

▶ Comments on content, such as viewer reviews, ratings, polls

▶ Photo galleries, such as Flickr and similar photo-sharing platforms

▶ Video streaming or casting, like YouTube and others

▶ Audio streaming or casting, also called podcasts

▶ Forums and discussion boards

▶ Google apps, such as GoogleCalendar, GoogleDocs, GoogleGroups, and other apps

▶ SMS text messaging and content posting from mobile devices

Facebook, Twitter, and Joomla! 1.6

AT LAST COUNT, THERE WERE over 100 extensions in the Joomla! Extension Directory (JED) that allow some sort of interaction directly between Joomla! 1.6 and Facebook and Twitter, and there is no indication that the end is near. More and more extensions are being added to take advantage of all of the connections that can be created ("exploited!") between social networking platforms.

An example is an extension that makes the Facebook Like and Share This buttons as part of the content of any Joomla! 1.6 (and 1.5) Website. When a user executes the Like or Share connection, the content of the Website has just been extended to their personal pages and that of all of their friends, and their friends, and their friends, and so on.

Get an Account!

To take advantage of social networking, you should have accounts on those sites, which can then be connected on a two-way connectivity system through extensions. You can establish personal and business accounts on most social networking sites.

Server Overload

When building an online community, consideration should be given to the capacity of the server hosting the site. If you are using a low-cost, minimal hosting service, chances are that you will overload the server or easily exceed your permitted bandwidth if you have a community with many members. If you plan to host a large community, upgrading to a server with greater capacity and bandwidth should be considered.

The extensions, which are easily installed (as you know from previous exercises), can be added as page content via modules, although some are components of sorts. This means the content can be assigned to menu link items for display on selected pages on the site.

There are at least a dozen social networking sites that now are accessible via extensions added to Joomla! 1.6, which connects a single Website to the entire net-sphere of social networking sites. Through these connections, a small, simple Website can become a part of the greater Internet community through integration of social networking. In fact, there are extensions that will publish content directly to a Facebook page from content originated on a Joomla!-based site. It also works the other way around: Facebook content published to the Joomla! site.

Joomla!'s Social Networking Extensions

TWO EXTENSIONS in the JED allow the addition of a mini–social networking platform to a Joomla! 1.6 site: Community Builder and JomSocial. The first is free, the second is not. Both essentially set up a community of users on your Website.

For an informational site, social networking extensions are not needed. But, if you are running a Website for a group or organization, and you want interactivity, adding social networking can be a positive addition. Within each component extension, groups can be created, and individual members may have profiles.

In addition to the basic components, other developers have created add-ons to them. If you search the JED for CB, you will find over 250 results for extensions that can be added to Community Builder. These extensions to the extensions can connect your community to Facebook, Twitter, and others. There are many, many useful extensions that work with Community Builder. JomSocial has its equal share of extensions that may be added to its base functionality. Both Community Builder and JomSocial are well-supported with useful add-ons from excellent developers.

Summary

In this chapter, you learned the following:

▶ Web 2.0 is not a "thing" by itself.

▶ Web 2.0 Websites have a high degree of user interactivity built into them.

▶ Joomla! 1.6 Websites can include many different Web 2.0 interactivity features.

▶ Extensions are readily available that will add Web 2.0 to a Joomla! 1.6 site.

▶ There are add-ons to the extensions that increase functionality for users.

▶ Joomla! 1.6 can be integrated with Facebook, Twitter, and others.

▶ Joomla! 1.6 sites with social networking should have sufficient server capacity and bandwidth.

Site Security

and Backups

AFTER A JOOMLA! 1.6 WEBSITE HAS BEEN CREATED, deployed, and made available for public viewing, site security and backups should be the next phase of consideration. Unless the proper steps are taken to secure the site, it can remain vulnerable to hacking attacks by those who have nothing better to do with their lives.

Also, and this goes along with security, the Website should have some sort of backup program so that, in the event of a malicious hacking attack or server corruptions, the site's files and databases can be restored and the site can go back online.

Secure the Site

IF YOU RECALL, DURING INSTALLATION a username for the Super User was required. In previous versions of Joomla!, the username was automatically created as admin, and most people just left that name in place, assuming that their password kept the site secure. By keeping admin as the username, 50 percent of a hacker's effort was eliminated because he already knew what the username was and now only needed to crack the password.

Joomla! 1.6 fixed this problem by asking for a username that was unique and not admin. Along those lines, there are other steps that can be taken to secure your site beyond just the Super User name and password. Another security hole was that the admin user was always numbered one in all installs. Joomla! 1.6 does not create that obvious user ID number, thus eliminating that vulnerability.

The Joomla! 1.6 Joomla! Extensions Directory (JED) has a number of extensions that deal with site security, which should give you a clue as to the importance of making sure your site is secure from hackers.

Change It Now!

If you created your Website with admin as the Super User, change it right now! Go into the User Manager, open the Super User profile, and change the Login Name to something more secure or more unique. This may prevent a hacker from doing damage to the site.

During installation, there were two actions needed to install the Joomla! 1.6 platform on your server or hosting location. First, the actual core files needed to be uploaded to the server. Second, a database needed to be created and the site connected to it. Both parts are vulnerable to hacker attacks, which can consist of rewriting files, such as the `index.php` page, to show malicious content. The database can be subject to what are called SQL injections, which enter information into the database that should not be there, resulting in undesired content showing up on site pages.

Within the Joomla! core, the only action that can be taken to secure the site is using a unique Super User name and associated password. Anything beyond that requires an extension to make the site more secure and to guard against hacker attacks.

As for the Joomla! 1.6 MySQL database, direct access to it is usually protected by the security controls on the server hosting the site. Sometimes site files and the database are located on separate servers. Access to the database is made by logging into the server. However, hackers can use the Joomla! 1.6 site to inject SQL commands into the database, creating havoc all over the place. The more protection applied to both site files and the database, the less likely the site will be subject to penetration attacks. SQL is a structured query database language that includes data insert, query, update and delete, schema creation and modification, and data access control, which can be harmful if done maliciously.

Security Is More Than ACL

THE JOOMLA! 1.6 ACL WAS discussed in Chapter 13, "User Management and Access Control." ACL is actually a form of security for the site in that it limits who can access what and the actions that can be performed. This is all well and good for a defined list of users and content access. What about security that does not involve known users?

When you access your site via FTP, you should notice a file called htaccess.txt or .htaccess, depending on which type of server is hosting your site. This file is actually the "front line" of site security, because it will either contain code that prevents intrusions, or you can add codes to prevent them.

There are many ways to secure a site via the htaccess file, and an Internet search will show results with instructions and inexpensive software that will configure the file in any number of ways to add access restrictions. It is worth the time, and the few dollars, to learn more about htaccess.

Actually, understanding how htaccess works will help for almost any type of Website you may administer. There are inexpensive software programs to manage the htaccess file and configure it, so that part is easy enough to do.

Back Up the Site

THE BEST INSURANCE POLICY against hackers and malicious attacks is to have the ability to restore the site should such an event occur. This means having an up-to-date backup of all of the site files, including those that have been added post-installation as extensions. Also, the MySQL database should be backed up, because that is where the actual content of the site resides.

There are two excellent, free extensions in the JED that perform comprehensive backups of all the files on a Joomla! 1.6 site and its associated database. These two extensions are Akeeba and XCloner. Both of these programs create one-click backups and can be set on timers to do automatic backups. Most importantly, they back up both the file and the database, which allows full restoration of the Website, if needed.

Akeeba Summary

▶ Works in Joomla! 1.6 Native mode

▶ One-click manual backup

▶ Direct transfer

▶ Multiple archive formats

▶ Easy automation

▶ Granular control

▶ Back up everywhere

For a small fee, a Professional version of Akeeba is available, which includes the following:

▶ Cloud backup

▶ Powerful filters

▶ Integrated restoration

▶ Encrypted archives

▶ Extensions exclusion

▶ Import archives

▶ Include all for multiple databases

▶ Native CRON script

▶ Save space

Akeeba Has More

In addition to Akeeba, the same developers also offer an eXtract Wizard that will back up archives to your PC, admin tools that perform common admin tasks and enhance site security, and other useful products. Spend some time looking at their other extensions to see if they will help protect your site files.

XCloner Summary

▶ Works in Joomla! 1.6 Native mode

▶ Backup and restore

▶ Customized backups

▶ Automatic backup/CRON scheduled

▶ Share backups

▶ Remote backup storage

▶ Incremental backup for large databases

▶ Incremental backup for large file content

Pay Attention to Security Releases

When needed, the Joomla! 1.6 developers issue a security release. When you get one, do not hesitate to upgrade the files on your site. The process usually involves only copying new files onto your server via an FTP connection. These types of releases are made when a security issue has been discovered and the code modified to prevent such vulnerabilities from affecting the site. Do not treat security upgrades lightly. They are important in protecting your site's installation.

Because both Akeeba and XCloner are free, you can install and test both to see which one you prefer. Some users find Akeeba easier to use, while others prefer XCloner because of some of the features. Both give you the ability to restore a Joomla! 1.6 Website after a disaster, be it malicious hacking or simply server failure. If the backups are stored off the server, the entire server could crash and the site files and databases are still secure and ready to restore to a new server, because they are located off-server in a safe location.

It is possible to only back up the MySQL database associated with the site. All of the categories, articles, and menus, along with component content are stored in tables in the database. No actual content information is stored as hard files in a Joomla! 1.6 installation. Only the core files and the extensions you installed along the way are stored as files on the server.

It is possible that a good number of extensions may have been installed on your site, especially if it is large with lots of users and content. Backing up the files also backs up the installed extensions, so simply backing up the database only keeps the content, which can be restored, while the extensions would all need to be reinstalled.

This is why Akeeba and XCloner have the advantage over a database-only backup plan. They back up everything into one restorable package.

For small sites with no more extensions than a template, a database-only backup would suffice, but for anything larger, with additional plugins, modules, and components installed, the comprehensive backup solution is the better practice to employ.

Summary

In this chapter, you learned the following:

▶ The Super User login name should be anything other than `admin` during installation.

▶ Joomla! 1.6 Websites have two parts: files and the database.

▶ Files consist of the core installation and any extensions added afterward.

▶ The database contains all of the content that has been added to the site.

▶ The `htaccess` file is the first line of defense against malicious hacker attacks.

▶ ACL limits access and actions by authorized users and content providers.

▶ A regular method of backing up a Joomla! 1.6 site should be implemented.

▶ Extensions are available that will perform complete backups of a site.

▶ Backups can be secured and stored in safe locations for restoration, if needed.

Index